American Smuggling as White Collar Crime

When Edwin Sutherland introduced the concept of white-collar crime, he referred to the respectable businessmen of his day who had, in the course of their occupations, violated the law whenever it was advantageous to do so. Yet since the founding of the American Republic, numerous otherwise respectable individuals had been involved in white-collar criminality. Using organized smuggling as an exemplar, this narrative history of American smuggling establishes that white-collar crime has always been an integral part of American history when conditions were favorable to violating the law.

This dark side of the American Dream originally exposed itself in colonial times with elite merchants of communities such as Boston trafficking contraband into the colonies. It again came to the forefront during the Embargo of 1809 and continued through the War of 1812, the Civil War, nineteenth century filibustering, the Mexican Revolution, and Prohibition. The author also shows that the years of illegal opium trade with China by American merchants served as a precursor to the later smuggling of opium into the United States.

The author confirms that each period of smuggling was a link in the continuing chain of white-collar crime in the 150 years prior to Sutherland's assertion of corporate criminality.

Lawrence Karson is currently an assistant professor of criminal justice at the University of Houston-Downtown. He retired from the U.S. Customs Service, where he served in the investigation division managing a fleet of aircraft and vessels used to pursue and apprehend drug traffickers smuggling contraband into the United States by air or sea.

Routledge Advances in Criminology

American Smuggling as White Collar Crime

Lawrence Karson

Routledge
Taylor & Francis Group
New York London

First published 2014
by Routledge
711 Third Avenue, New York, NY 10017

and by Routledge
2 Park Square, Milton Park, Abingdon, Oxon OX14 4RN

First issued in paperback 2017

*Routledge is an imprint of the Taylor & Francis Group,
an informa business*

Library of Congress Cataloging-in-Publication Data

Karson, Lawrence.
   American Smuggling as White Collar Crime/by Lawrence Karson.
      pages cm. — (Routledge Advances in Criminology; 17)
   Includes bibliographical references and index.
   1. Smuggling—United States—History.   2. White collar crime—United States—History.   I. Title.
HJ6690.K37   2014
364.1'3360973—dc23
2014004576

ISBN 13: 978-1-138-50685-5 (pbk)
ISBN 13: 978-1-138-79207-4 (hbk)

Typeset in Sabon
by Apex CoVantage, LLC

In memory of George Reyes Saenz
father, husband, brother, son . . . customs pilot
1955–1989

Contents

Acknowledgments

Individualism isn't and solitary works aren't …

Thank you.

David Anderson

Steve Barnes

Barbara Belbot

Saul Broussard

Chris Butler

Nick Doucet

Alan Downer

Colin Eldridge

Roger Garland

Kelsey Harmon

Jim Harter

Alice Lewis

Pat Magee

Marilyn McShane

Jennifer Morrow

Max Novick

Beth Pelz

Harv Pothier

Paulette Purdy

Robert Shail

Jeremy Smith

Hsiao-Ming Wang

Bryn Willcock

Trey Williams

Cindy, Steve, and Dave

Renata Corbani

Portions of Chapter 3 appeared as 'Cotton, Congress, and White Collar Crime: A Historical Narrative' in the *Journal of the American Studies Association of Texas*, 44, 35–56.

Portions of Chapters 1, 2, 3, 6, and 7 appeared as 'American Smuggling and British White-collar Crime: A Historical Perspective' in *Papers from the British Criminology Conference*, 12, 25–40.

Introduction

In 1939, the president of the American Sociological Society, Edwin H. Sutherland, gave a presentation at a joint meeting of the society and of the American Economic Society. That presidential address was later published in the society's journal as 'White-Collar Criminality', and still later developed into a book titled *White Collar Crime*. Defining white-collar crime as 'a crime committed by a person of respectability and high social status in the course of his occupation',[1] Sutherland brought to the public's attention that 'respectable or at least respected business and professional men'[2] were involved in criminal activities that were otherwise unrecognized as such, introducing the concept of white-collar crime both to sociology and to the general public. He also pointed out that these same elites had the influence and power to define crime so as not to necessarily encompass their activities within the penal code. He would later identify the activities of these white-collar criminals as a form of organized crime, recognizing both formal and informal organizations, which allowed for organized restraint of trade, the influence over both criminal and civil legislation, the limitation of enforcement through restricted funding, and the development of a consensus among the involved businessmen as their objective.[3]

The purpose of this monograph is to demonstrate that white-collar crime, as conceived by Sutherland, has a historical lineage in America dating back at least to the founding of the Republic and that the presence of white-collar crime is reflected in the violation of the nation's smuggling laws. Distinctively, 'persons of respectability and high social status in the course of their occupation' conspired at various times in American history to smuggle a variety of contraband into or out of the United States, or into other countries, in contravention of 'regulatory norms', to obtain a profit in an attempt to achieve the American Dream, whenever an 'excess of definitions' were favorable to the violation of law.[4] The economic version of that dream, as defined by the sociologist Robert Merton, was a striving for success by all members of society, whatever their station and by whatever means may be necessary.[5]

Sutherland believed that the explanation for white-collar crime could be found in his theory explaining the general process of criminality: differential association. It was Sutherland's premise that criminal behavior is learned through interaction with other persons as is any other behavior, and that learning criminal behavior takes place in intimate personal groups where, besides the techniques of committing a crime, the motives, drives, rationalizations, and attitudes in support of criminal behavior are also learned. As Robert Merton described the premise, 'individuals learn to engage in criminal behavior by associating with others, principally in face-to-face groups, who prefer and practice such behavior'.[6] It was Sutherland's belief that criminal behavior takes place when 'the specific direction of motives and drives is learned from definitions of the legal codes as favorable or unfavorable', varying by interrelationships assessed on 'frequency, priority, duration, and intensity',[7] or as De Fleur and Quinney express:

> Overt criminal behavior has as its necessary and sufficient conditions a set of criminal motivations, attitudes, and techniques, the learning of which takes place when there is exposure to criminal norms in excess of exposure to corresponding anticriminal norms during symbolic interaction in primary groups.[8]

In short, Sutherland's position was that criminal behavior is based on the values an individual receives from interactions with others, including with those whom a person associates in a business or a political environment. When the weight of those values supports activity in violation of a specific law, that law will be ignored.[9] Sutherland also recognized that while differential association explained a person's initiation into criminal activity, the premise of social disorganization explained crime from 'the point of view of society', appearing in the form of a 'lack of standards or conflict of standards'.[10] In the former, '[i]n any period of rapid change, old standards tend to break down and a period of time is required for the development of new standards'.[11] In the latter, when the political will is not effectively organized against business interests that violate the law, that social disorganization allows for white-collar crime.[12]

When Robert Merton wrote his paper 'Social Structure and Anomie', he had just witnessed perhaps the greatest period of communal criminality in the history of America, the years of American Prohibition. His paper, published a year before Sutherland's speech in one of the earliest volumes of the American Sociological Society's (later known as the American Sociological Association) journal, sought to explain how a society that placed a high emphasis on economic success, such as America, led some to use the most expedient methods, including crime, to achieve their financial goals. He recognized that '[t]he extreme emphasis upon the accumulation of wealth as a symbol of success in our own society militates against the completely effective control of institutionally regulated modes of acquiring a fortune'.[13] In particular his typology of adaptations to the possible conflict between the cultural goals of a 'prestige-bearing' financial success and the institutionalized means available identified some as choosing 'innovation', the concept of 'relinquishing the institutional means and retaining the success-aspiration', to deal with the conflict.[14] These individuals recognized that the traditional, approved paths to success were not necessarily available and the rationally chosen, alternative path to success through crime was an achievable path.

Some years later Merton further developed his original work, including an extended description of the success-theme in American culture, recognizing that the goal of monetary success was embedded in the nation's culture. Though the pursuit of money was not limited to Americans, in referring to his earlier paper Merton believed that there was a difference in degree:

> But what makes American culture relatively distinctive in this regard and what was taken as central to the analysis of this case in the foregoing chapter is that this is 'a society which places a high premium on economic affluence and social ascent for *all* its members'. [. . .] The distinctive nature of this cultural doctrine is twofold: first, striving for success is not a matter of individuals *happening* to have acquisitive impulses, rooted in human nature, but is a socially-defined expectation, and second, this patterned expectation is regarded as appropriate for everyone, irrespective of his initial lot or station in life.[15]

Because success is appropriate for all, failure is easily considered a personal character flaw, even a moral flaw. 'The moral mandate to achieve success thus exerts pressure to succeed, by fair means if possible and by foul means if necessary'.[16] It would be this success theme that was distinctive to America and would, at times, dominate the moral compass of many Americans and those linked with them, leading to 'innovation' during times of social disorganization throughout the history of the nation. As one of the founders of the Republic commented, 'We have one material which actually constitutes an aristocracy that governs the nation. That material is wealth. Talents, birth, virtues, services, sacrifices are of little consequence to us'.[17]

Merton's success theme had earlier been famously expressed by historian James Truslow Adams in his *The Epic of America*. For Adams, the American Dream was 'that dream of a land in which life should be better and richer and fuller for everyone, with opportunity for each according to ability or achievement [. . .] It is not a dream of motor cars and high wages merely, but a dream of social order in which each man and each woman shall be able to attain to the fullest stature of which they are innately capable, and be recognized by others for what they are, regardless of the fortuitous circumstances of birth or position'.[18] It was a dream beyond material possessions and the demands of a consumer-driven society, but Adams acknowledged that the material was, as Merton later remarked, 'prestige-bearing', stating that 'so long as wealth and power are our sole badges of success, so long will ambitious men strive to attain them'.[19]

Yet the phrase had been used earlier, if not in quite the same affirmative view, still as an embodiment of a dream of financial achievement for the nation, as mentioned in an 1893 article on U.S. banking written by W. R. Lawson in *Bankers', Insurance Managers' and Agents' Magazine*. In remarking about the Chicago World's Fair of 1893, Lawson described it to be 'the greatest and grandest of all World's Fairs—a year of over-flowing prosperity, bonanza crops, heavy exports and universal boom [. . .] proving to [European tourists] by ocular demonstration how far ahead the New World had got of the Old. Such was the American dream of eighteen hundred and ninety-three'.[20] Though a less nuanced view of the American Dream than was Adams' later iteration, this banker's idea of prosperity and profit is an easy fit into the Andrew Carnegie model of rags-to-riches American achievement and, again, as a reflection of the 'prestige-bearing' financial goals defining the 'innovation' typology of Merton.

The American Dream, an ambiguous concept that easily morphs into a variety of adaptations depending on those interpreting it, has had numerous other readings, including the idea of agrarianism, also termed the pastoral ideal, 'the theme of withdrawal from society into an idealized landscape'.[21] It would be reflected in the works of 'Cooper, Thoreau, Melville, Faulkner, Frost, [and] Hemingway', serving as a catalyst to each author's 'imagination'.[22] In the political sphere a Jeffersonian ideology of 'rural virtue' would mirror the theme.[23] Jim Cullen describes a variety of other versions of the Dream, including the dream of liberty (seeing the Declaration of Independence as the dream's 'charter'), upward mobility, minority equality, home ownership, and personal fulfillment, recognizing that his list was 'suggestive rather than exhaustive' of the Dream's numerous manifestations.[24] It was a dream not limited by geography, extending at times south across the Rio Grande and northward to Canada. 'The American Dream has danced on the horizon for generations of Canadians, a wagon or train trip away in earlier times, a car or plane ride in more recent times.'[25] Though referring to Canadian emigrants the comment is no less true of those who stayed north and trafficked in contraband southward.

One of the earliest iterations, and one of the most durable, was the dream of religious expression unencumbered by the mandates of society or state. From the earliest Puritans to later Quakers, Lutherans, and Jews, numerous individuals risked all and ventured across the North Atlantic to a New World for the opportunity to practice their chosen faith as their spirit determined; for many their Dream was simply one expressed as a 'liberty of conscience'.[26] Yet some versions of that religious faith may have contributed to an attitude of acceptance for later white-collar criminality. More than one theorist has suggested that the Protestant work ethic born of the Calvinistic foundations of various Protestant denominations and exemplified by the Puritans of New England may well have offered a religious justification to extensive monetary acquisition and contributed to the materialistic culture some later identified as part and parcel to American society.[27]

Steve Messner and Richard Rosenfeld also recognized that American crime, and by extension white-collar crime, were intrinsic in the nation's very social structure:

> [T]he American Dream itself and the normal social conditions engendered by it are deeply implicated in the problems of crime. In our use of the term 'the American Dream' we refer to a board cultural ethos that entails a commitment to the goal of material success, to be pursued by everyone in society, under conditions of open, individual success, and they are encouraged to believe that the chances of realizing the Dream are sufficiently high to justify a continued commitment to this cultural goal. These beliefs and commitments in many respects define what it means to be an enculturated member of our society. The ethos refers quite literally to the *American* dream.[28]

Their position was that though beneficial for society, the American Dream had a dark side that led to an excessive willingness to succeed financially at any cost, that created a weakening of community and its ability to control deviant behavior through social structural mechanisms, and that only allowed a limited acceptance of other forms of personal and professional success.[29]

Albert Cohen, Richard Cloward and Lloyd Ohlin, and Robert Agnew would build on Merton's work.[30] Yet 'Merton's theory of anomie is still among the most influential of all criminological theories [. . .] continuing to draw commentary and research'.[31] Both Merton and Sutherland concurred that their separate theories—anomie theory and the theory of differential association—were complementary, applying to both ordinary and white-collar crime.[32]

Sutherland, in establishing his concept of white-collar criminality, supported his argument by providing a variety of examples of the various types of crimes to which he was referring and of the types of businesses involved. Restraint of trade, discriminatory rebate practices, patent infringement, advertising misrepresentation, unfair labor practices, fraudulent financial manipulations, embargo circumventions and neutrality violations were all included.[33]

Yet Sutherland, his contemporaries, and those academics who followed them directed their research toward examples of modern corporations and other organizations that were involved in activities that qualified as white-collar criminality with minimal research looking back to historical examples. Though much has been written in recent years about the history of crime and of criminal justice,[34] little has been addressed at the 'intersection between history, biography and social structure' as it relates to white-collar crime.[35] Sutherland himself recognized the historical precedent, having remarked that the 'unscrupulous American business entrepreneurs', latter known as the 'robber barons' of the late nineteenth century, were within his definition of white-collar criminals.[36] Prior to Sutherland's *White Collar Crime* and a precursor to his work, the muckrakers of the early twentieth century had developed a reputation for exposing business malfeasance. Two of the more notable examples were Ida Tarbell revealing the business practices of John D. Rockefeller—one of those characterized as a 'robber baron'—and his Standard Oil Company's attempts to monopolize the oil industry, as well as Upton Sinclair revealing the plight of factory workers striving for the American Dream and the abominable health hazards of the meat packing industry.[37] Again, with the exception of the 'robber barons' of the late nineteenth century, there has been limited discussion of other historical examples of white-collar crime in America.[38] The purpose of this monograph is to demonstrate that white-collar crime, as conceived by Sutherland, has been a tradition in America since the nation's founding as reflected in its history of smuggling. That tradition provides ample evidence that Sutherland's premise that 'persons of the upper socioeconomic class engage in much criminal behavior' has actually been a practice throughout American history and that 'this criminal behavior differs little from the criminal behavior of the lower socioeconomic class'.[39]

Shortly after Sutherland presented his original paper on white-collar crime, Frank Hartung published his own paper on white-collar offenses in the Detroit wholesale meat industry, Robert Lane circulated his study of national labor law violations, and Marshall Clinard released his research of the American black market during World War II.[40] A decade later, Earl Quinney followed with his study of social structure and its relationship to the criminal behavior of retail pharmacists.[41] Soon after, Gilbert Geis looked at the criminal case history of the heavy electrical equipment antitrust cases against senior executives of General Electric and Westinghouse Electric.[42] Fifty years later, the Enron debacle became one of the more infamous examples of white-collar criminality, documented by Bethany Mclean and Peter Elkind, among others.[43]

These classic criminology studies, which concentrated on then contemporary offenses, paralleled the effort of researchers focused on the history of American crime and criminal justice. Roger Lane's history of the eighteenth-century Boston police department, Eric Monkkonen's monograph on urban policing in the late nineteenth and early twentieth centuries, and James Richardson's study of New York policing from colonial times to the twentieth century are examples of organizational histories giving an understanding of the development of modern policing.[44] Wilber Miller and Michael Hindus achieve a similar goal with their comparative studies of the New York police and London bobbies, and of slave-holding South Carolina's and industrial Massachusetts' justice systems, respectively.[45] Frank Prassel addresses the activities of western lawmen, while Frederick Calhoun focuses his work on the U.S. marshals and their deputies.[46] Carl Prince and Mollie Keller address U.S. Customs history while Irving King achieves the same for the Coast Guard through a series of works.[47] Other work looked at various offenses. For example, Robert McGrath studied violence in the West while Eric Monkkonen attempted to understand historical homicide rates in New York and Los Angeles, as did Douglas Eckberg for post-Reconstruction South Carolina homicides.[48]

This work seeks to approach that 'intersection between history, biography and social structure' where evidence related to historical white-collar criminality is found,[49] looking at the violations, the violators, and the social culture that seemingly condoned much of this behavior. It follows in the interpretational work of Gilbert Geis, who offered a historical perspective of white-collar crime, asserting that '[t]he record shows that there has been a long-standing ancient tradition, passed on to the Judeo-Christian world, that associated commerce with fraud and avarice and that held that such endeavors were a potential source of moral corruption and decay'.[50] Geis held that food shortages in ancient Greece and Rome allowed for the manipulation of the market to the seller's advantage, and the communities enacted various laws to control market conspirators, thereby allowing commodities to be available to all at reasonable prices. Geis extended his argument into the European Middle Ages, identifying various theologians and intellectuals who condemned predatory marketers. He argued that forestalling, regrating, and engrossing, all techniques used to artificially raise the market price of food— were early European examples of white-collar criminality. He also recognized that the muckraking movement of early twentieth-century America contributed to the public exposure of predatory business practices.[51] The white-collar smuggling found throughout the history of America is simply a more evident continuation of Geis' recognition of a history of white-collar criminality.

This work also builds on and substantiates Michael Woodiwiss' argument that the United States has a long history of organized criminal activity, the white-collar criminality found in many types of organized smuggling being one extensive example supporting his position. Woodiwiss observed that criminality extended beyond foodstuffs in ancient history, and that '[c]riminal enterprise was itself embedded in the machinery of Roman law and government'.[52] Viewing crime across history as organized and embedded in the social structure of various cultures, he identified the robber barons of feudalism as a continuation of the powerful controlling the law to serve their own ends. He further identified early modern European business crime, in particular the stock frauds perpetrated by the South Sea Company and the Mississippi Company in the early eighteenth century, 'as spectacular antecedents of modern organized business crime'.[53] He extended his survey of organized business criminality into the fraudulent land deals of the American founding fathers that originally contributed to the nation's expansion westward and into the organized slave smuggling into the South after 1807, finally transitioning from the rural to the urban by identifying the corruption, party politics, and gangs as different aspects of one problem: organized criminality. This work further substantiates Woodiwiss' recognition that business was integral to the organized crime of Prohibition.[54]

Much of the literature in the last fifty years related to white-collar crime has focused on developing a definitive meaning of the very term 'white-collar crime'. One of the earliest challenges to Sutherland's work was Paul Tappan's legalistic argument that without a conviction, a person could not be considered a criminal whether the violation was business related or otherwise.[55] Yet Sutherland himself had addressed that limited view in his article 'Is "White-Collar Crime" a Crime?' by arguing that the failure of the state to choose to prosecute a criminal action, instead utilizing a civil process for redress, did not mitigate the criminality of the offense.[56] The discussion continued with many trying to further clarify its meaning by developing a typological approach. Eventually 'Clinard and Quinney put forward what has become a widely accepted distinction in scholarship on white-collar crime, that between (1) occupational criminal behavior and (2) corporate criminal behavior', separating crimes of employees related to their occupations from the crimes of corporations and corporate officials to benefit the corporation itself.[57] A general typology came to also include governmental/ state sponsored crime, financial crime, computer crime, and various hybrids of these violations.[58]

Gary Potter and Larry Gaines would later view white-collar crime as less of a definitional issue than as a social construct and a 'heuristic device guiding the study or analysis of crimes by certain actors in certain social settings', similar to the use of the terms 'street crime' or 'juvenile crime', a view that informs this monograph.[59]

In 1931, Americans were presented with a view of crime that identified the purveyors of illicit alcohol as organized business entities encompassing 'combinations of illicit distributors, illicit producers, local politicians, corrupt police and other enforcement agencies, making lavish payments for protection and conducting an elaborate system of individual producers and distributors'.[60] The report regarding the enforcement of the Prohibition laws in the United States, widely known as the *Wickersham Report*, contributed to an image that was personalized by Hollywood and the news media. For Hollywood, the gangster of Prohibition became a simplified personification of the American Dream, a success story exemplifying the Andrew Carnegie rags-to-riches model of American achievement, if somewhat perverted still not beyond recognition or approval.

The acceptance and approval of Americans for the framing of the American Dream in a gangster/Horatio Alger narrative was demonstrated time and again at the box office as Americans crowded theatres to witness the successes of the gangster on the silver screen in the 1920s and 1930s. Only national censorship prevented the gangster from achieving long-term financial success without the requisite denouncement at the end of the last reel.[61] The classic gangster films of the 1930s invented the media hood, taking portrayals from the silent era of films and turning him into a 'central cultural figure', an individual who wanted 'to be somebody' and who embodied the competitive and individualistic ideals of American capitalism to achieve that nebulous ambition.[62] As Fitzgerald said of his title character in the quintessential American novel *The Great Gatsby*, 'Gatsby believed in the green light, the orgastic future that year by year recedes before us. It eluded us then, but that's no matter—tomorrow we will run faster, stretch out our arms further . . . and one fine morning—So we beat on, boats against the current, borne back ceaselessly into the past'.[63] That dream, born out of a fight for survival in a new world and the merger of religious Puritanism with that selfsame frontier spirit, opened the doors to the idea that 'worldly achievement and business success, physical energy and activity, and with it youth and virility' would become 'the real objects of adulation' in America.[64] That same energy and vitality coupled with the democratic ideals that helped establish the nation, would also allow an acceptance of a degree of lawlessness that at times would equal its reported respect for the laws of society.[65] Caesar Enrico Bandello (Edward G. Robinson) of *Little Caesar*, Tom Powers (James Cagney) of *Public Enemy*, and Tony Camonte (Paul Muni) of *Scarface* all helped both to buttress the American myths of individual accomplishment and to establish the modern myth that would define the gangster and, by extension, the world's view of organized crime for generations.[66] This early cycle of gangster films also created a genre in cinema that would shape the public's view of the organized criminal underworld with politicians, police, and business only being considered 'mere *associates* of the *real* crooks'.[67] This perspective constructed a view of organized crime that defined it as an alliance of gangsters who represented a 'threat to the nation's institutions'.[68] The imagery of Prohibition and the illegal production and distribution of alcohol, with over seventy-five films being made in the 1920s using smugglers and bootlegging as an aspect of the plot, only further reinforced what journalists were producing as daily copy for the newspapers.[69] These images would eventually lead to the popular view, cultivated by politicians and law enforcement and sustained by the media, that organized crime was synonymous with the mafia in America.[70]

For this work, organized crime is seen instead as 'systematic illegal activity and part of the social, economic, and political systems'.[71] As such it incorporates Sutherland's premise of white-collar criminality as also being organized crime, recognizing that 'a substantial portion of [business] violations are deliberate and organized'.[72]

When writing a qualitative work premised on extending the sociological concept of white-collar criminality across an extensive timeline of previously documented smuggling, the works of Edwin Sutherland and those criminological theorists in the field who followed are the mandated starting point. Yet in conducting any historical research on illegal activities related to white-collar crime, the very nature of the subject matter can itself be a critical problem. Criminals—at least the successful ones—generally avoid leaving documentary evidence accessible. As John Tyler remarked, 'Smugglers do not ordinarily leave behind elaborate records of their transgressions.'[73] The problem is exacerbated when the crime is perpetuated by those of higher social status, an integral component of white-collar criminality, who may also conceal their illicit actions from their peers in an attempt to maintain their 'good name' within the community.

A second major difficulty in writing about contraband trafficking is that geography had an influence on smuggling throughout the country's history; the documentary records related to over a century and a half of smuggling in the United States are scattered across a nation over three thousand miles wide and with almost twenty thousand miles of land, lake, and sea borders as the venue for violations. National records alone are archived in almost two dozen centers, spread across the states and the District of Columbia, filed within the individually stored material of at least half a dozen government agencies. The time period encompassing the first 150 years of American history that is the core of this work was intentionally chosen in order to avoid the quagmire inherent in researching the contemporary narcotics 'war' that has already provided enough data for writers to stock the shelves of a small library with monographs and dissertations, many of which have already been written.

In order to supply a background to American smuggling since 1789 and its associated white-collar criminality, this work reviews the evidence of trafficking ventures, including those in the colonial era, using various secondary resources that have, individually, already effectively documented smuggling during explicit eras in American history and in geographically specific smuggling locales. For early nineteenth-century smuggling, the American State Papers and local newspapers provided further information, offering both an official response and a local viewpoint respectively, particularly regarding public attitudes toward filibustering.

Congressional papers, *The War of the Rebellion: A Compilation of the Official Records of the Union and Confederate Armies*, and the *Official Records of the Union and Confederate Navies* give an understanding of the contraband trade during the Civil War and an official military response toward it. Treasury records, including the Annual Reports of the Secretary of the Treasury, the records of the U.S. Customs Service, Record Group 36, of the National Archives, Washington, D.C., of Seattle, Washington and of Fort Worth, Texas, and the Bureau of Prohibition, Record Group 56 of the Seattle office provided background and individual smuggling case information.[74] Federal district court cases also offered details of specific criminal cases related to liquor trafficking, gunrunning, and narcotics smuggling.

During the Prohibition years, various newspapers, including the *New York Times*, provided extensive coverage of smuggling violations, both liquor and narcotics, with the investigative reporting skills of the early muckrakers coming again into play with the reporters of various news articles. Possibly the more interesting sources about trafficking during this same period were the autobiographies by assorted smugglers, such as James Barbican's (a pseudonym of Eric Sherbrooke Walker) *The Confessions of a Rum-runner*, Gertrude 'Cleo' Lythgoe's *The Bahama Queen*, Alastair

Moray's *The Diary of a Rum-runner*, and Fraser Miles' *Slow Boat on Rum Row*, all of which chronicle their years in the trade.[75] A reader quickly realizes that the smuggling trade was simply one more business concerned with the bottom line. Though at times dangerous, the work was, as it was for many of their contemporaries, monotonous and boring. Being a seaman on either an illegal rumrunner or a legitimate coastal freighter still entailed the same problems and maritime dangers. An interview with one former coast guardsman who served in their aviation fleet during the Prohibition years was also utilized, offering a first-person background of government aviation activities in south Texas at the time.

The trafficking in human beings, either as smuggled slaves after 1807 or illegal immigrants after the passage of the Chinese Exclusion Act in 1882, is considered beyond the scope of this work, which limits its discussion to actual goods found in trade and considered subject to tariff. Relevant works addressing the illegal trafficking in slaves include David Eltis' *Economic Growth and the Ending of the Transatlantic Slave Trade*, Warren Howard's *American Slavers and the Federal Law, 1837–1862*, and Hugh Thomas' *The Slave Trade: The Story of the Atlantic Slave Trade, 1440–1870* while Erika Lee speaks to Chinese illegal immigration in *At America's Gates: Chinese Immigration During the Exclusion Era, 1882–1943*.[76] Peter Andreas' *Smuggler Nation: How Illicit Trade Made America* also discusses human trafficking in his history of American smuggling.[77]

Frauds against the revenue, such as making false statements or submitting fraudulent invoices as to the value or nature of goods entering the United States to minimize or avoid paying duty is also generally beyond this work's reach, which focuses primarily on smuggling, the clandestine introduction of contraband. For many, including Customs, these frauds were at times seen as sharp business practices subject to civil action instead of being viewed as a crime. Even U.S. law tends to treat the two separately, with fraud currently codified as 18 USC 541—Misclassification of Goods and 18 USC 542—Entry of Goods by Means of False Statements while smuggling is categorized as 18 USC 545—Smuggling Goods into the United States. Though misclassification and false statements can also qualify as a form of white-collar criminality, the differences between fraud and the popular view of smuggling offer the potential for two distinct analyses. This monograph focuses on the popular interpretation of smuggling though some are persuaded otherwise. Andreas touches on customs frauds in *Smuggler Nation* as does Andrew Wender Cohen in 'Smuggling, Globalization, and America's Outward State, 1870–1909', for example.[78]

White-collar crime as embodied by American smuggling can be visualized as a continuing criminal enterprise throughout the history of the nation, divided into six major periods when political, legal, and business interests intersected to allow business to participate in organized smuggling to achieve occupational success. Each chapter in this monograph provides evidence that white-collar crime dates back from the time of Sutherland's original conception to the very founding of the Republic. The earliest of these historical periods, addressed in Chapter 1, is the precursor to American smuggling—the trafficking by colonial merchants in a time when enforcement was rudimentary at best. These merchants, including possibly the most famous signatory of the Declaration of Independence, were the economic elite of the colonies in a period when manufacturing had yet to supplant the successful trader in status, and many of these merchants did not hesitate to avail themselves of the financial advantages of contraband trafficking prior to the Revolutionary War. Thirty years after the American Revolution, the political landscape caused the Jefferson Administration to initiate an embargo on American shipping in an attempt to minimize the potential for hostilities against the new nation, only to compel a new generation of traders comprised of America's business elite back into the contraband trade for simple financial survival.

Chapter 2 documents this first period of American smuggling with the great merchant houses of America's seaports challenging the government's foreign policy by evading the law and smuggling presenting itself as an opportunity. Yet later, even after the declaration of war against Britain, some of these same community leaders and merchants continued in the smuggling trade, trafficking with the British. For some, even war would not be allowed to interfere with business, substantiating Sutherland's position that the motivations of these business elite was their own self-interest and little would be allowed that interfered with their financial success. Instead, they would consciously exploit the nation's difficulties as a path to personal profit.

Chapter 3 surveys the smuggling by both sides of the American Civil War, focusing on the trade by Northern merchants with the South in violation of law. If the fog of war can bring uneasiness to commanders in combat, it serves as a cloak of comfort for those profiting from the confusion of conflict. Though business would once again take their profit with the doleful turn of politics—for war is but an extension of the political process—seeing it as a path to enrichment, this conflict would also reveal a level of corruption that was unheard of prior to the hostilities. A U.S. senator and a Union general would personify the venality to which white-collar criminality can lead some to succumb in achieving their objective of financial success by any means necessary.

Yet some smuggling prospects—unlike those of the embargo and the War of 1812, and later, the Civil War—were not limited to a short time frame of opportunity. Filibustering, private military actions attempting to overthrow a friendly government often—but not always—to the consternation of Washington, extended over the entire nineteenth century and into the twentieth, and the smuggling of arms and munitions out of the United States in support of these exploitive adventures was condoned by some in power, as described in Chapter 4. For many, their financial dream was to be found in support of the nation's own dream of Manifest Destiny, offering a justification for numerous entrepreneurs in favor of white-collar criminality committed in support of their goals. Mexico, Central America, and Cuba were all continuing targets for Americans in search of financial success, and all offered opportunities for businesses to profit from these adventurers.

The same white-collar criminality that in the earlier years of the Republic allowed businesses to profit from war and revolution carried over to their business dealings with insurrectionists during the Mexican Revolution of 1910. Again, as shown in the nation's earlier conflicts, profit was put before patriotism and the national interest, with American business trafficking in munitions to the armies revolting in Mexico in violation of the neutrality laws of the United States. The smuggling of arms and ammunition, as documented in Chapter 5 further supports the thesis that white-collar criminality continued to be part and parcel of American history, showing that some business interests again focused on achieving profit and financial success by whatever means necessary, if the opportunity presented itself.

Ten years later politics, the law, and opportunity would once again intersect when the United States passed legislation prohibiting intoxicating liquors, and business responded to customer demand by smuggling millions of gallons of distilled spirits and brewery goods into America by land, by sea, and even by air, leading to the most famous era of smuggling in American history. The business interests involved were little different from legitimate business in many cases, continuing in their distillery or brewery endeavors with the consent of government after Prohibition was repealed. During the thirteen years of Prohibition, however, they manifested all of the traits of white-collar criminality that Edwin Sutherland would describe but a few years later, when referring to contemporary corporations. Chapter 6 describes smuggling in the Detroit area, separated from a large contingent of Canadian distilleries and breweries simply by a mile-wide river that allowed easy passage of contraband across the international boundary, the corruption that went hand-in-glove with successful liquor smuggling, and the reach of Merton's success-theme version of the American Dream northward. Chapter 7 continues by describing the organizational aspects of this white-collar criminality during Prohibition, substantiating Sutherland's contention that white-collar crime is organized crime.

Chapter 8 reverts back in time to the early 1800s in documenting the trafficking of opium illegally into China by the elite owners of the merchant houses of the Northeast sailing in the wake of British China traders, the organized smuggling of opium into the United States at the end of the nineteenth century, and business involvement in the smuggling of narcotics in the early twentieth century. It closes by describing drug smuggling related money laundering in the late twentieth and early twenty-first centuries, providing a final link in establishing a historical precedent to Sutherland's concept of white-collar criminality.

White-collar crime is not simply a twentieth-century corporate phenomenon in America. Each chapter of this work offers a link in the continuing chain of white-collar criminality, utilizing the nation's historical record of organized smuggling as evidence that Edwin Sutherland's conception of white-collar crime preceded even the 'robber barons' of the late nineteenth century. From its days as a British colonial holding, America's businessmen have been willing and able to achieve by whatever means necessary a corrupted version of James Truslow Adams' American Dream, in the process substantiating the thesis that white-collar crime has a historical lineage in America dating back at least to the founding of the Republic.

NOTES

1. Edwin H. Sutherland, *White Collar Crime: The Uncut Version* (New Haven, CT: Yale University Press, 1983), p. 7. There have been numerous critiques of Sutherland's definition of white-collar crime (as well as, for that matter, his theory of differential association), but for the purposes of this work Sutherland's definition is treated as authoritative. See Gilbert Geis, *White-collar and Corporate Crime* (Upper Saddle River, NJ: Person Prentice Hall, 2007), pp. 121–178.
2. Edwin H. Sutherland, 'White-collar Criminality', *American Sociological Review*, 5 (February, 1940), 1–12 (p. 1).
3. Sutherland, *White Collar Crime*, pp. 229–230.
4. Edwin Sutherland, *Principles of Criminality*, 4th edn (Philadelphia, PA: J. B. Lippincott, 1947), pp. 6–7; Sutherland, *White Collar Crime*, p. 7.
5. Robert K. Merton, *Social Theory and Social Structure* (New York: The Free Press, 1968), p. 221.
6. Robert K. Merton, 'On the Evolving Synthesis of Differential Association and Anomie Theory: A Perspective from the Sociology of Science', *Criminology*, 35 (1997), 517–525 (p. 519).
7. Sutherland, *Principles of Criminality*, pp. 6–7.
8. Melvin L. De Fleur and Richard Quinney, 'A Reformulation of Sutherland's Differential Association Theory and a Strategy for Empirical Verification', *Journal of Research in Crime and Delinquency*, 3 (1966), 1–22 (p. 7).
9. Frank P. Williams III and Marilyn D. McShane, *Criminology Theory*, 5th edn (Upper Saddle River, NJ: Prentice Hall, 2010), pp. 63–75.
10. Sutherland, *White Collar Crime*, p. 255.
11. *ibid.*, p. 255.
12. *ibid.*, pp. 256–257.
13. Robert K. Merton, 'Social Structure and Anomie', *American Sociological Review*, 3 (October 1938), 672–682 (p. 675).
14. *ibid.*, pp. 679–682.
15. Merton, *Social Theory and Social Structure*, p. 221.
16. *ibid.*, p. 223.
17. John Adams, as quoted in Michael Woodiwiss, *Organized Crime and American Power: A History* (Toronto: University of Toronto Press, 2001), p. 58.
18. James Truslow Adams, *The Epic of America* (Boston, MA: Little, Brown and Company, 1931), p. 404.
19. *ibid.*, p. 415.
20. W. R. Lawson, 'United States Banking in 1893', *Bankers', Insurance Managers' and Agents' Magazine*, 56 (1893), 371–388 (p. 371).
21. Leo Marx, *The Machine in the Garden: Technology and the Pastoral Ideal in America* (New York: Oxford University Press, 1964), p. 10.
22. *ibid.*, p. 10.

23. *ibid.*, p. 126.
24. Jim Cullen, *The American Dream: A Short History of an Idea that Shaped a Nation* (New York: Oxford University Press, 2003), pp. 8–9.
25. Jeffrey Simpson, *Star-Spangled Canadians: Canadians Living the American Dream* (Toronto: HarperCollins, 2000), p. 14.
26. Alan Taylor, *American Colonies: The Settling of North America*, (New York: Penguin, 2001), pp. 181, 321.
27. Max Weber, *The Protestant Ethic and the Spirit of Capitalism*, trans. by Talcott Parsons (New York: Charles Scribner's Sons, 1976); Mark Valeri, 'Calvin and the Social Order in Early America: Moral Ideals and Transatlantic Europe', in *John Calvin's American Legacy*, ed. by Thomas J. Davis (New York: Oxford University Press, 2010), 19–41.
28. Steven F. Messner and Richard Rosenfeld, *Crime and the American Dream*, 4th edn (Belmont, CA: Thomson Wadsworth, 2007), p. 6.
29. *ibid.*, p. 10.
30. Robert Agnew, 'A Revised Strain Theory of Delinquency', *Social Forces*, 64 (1985), 151–167, 'Building on the Foundation of General Strain Theory: Specifying the Types of Strain Most Likely to Lead to Crime and Delinquency', *Journal of Research in Crime and Delinquency*, 38 (2001), 319–361. Richard Cloward and Lloyd Ohlin, *Delinquency and Opportunity: A Theory of Delinquent Gangs* (New York: The Free Press, 1960); Albert Cohen, *Delinquent Boys: Culture of the Gang* (Glencoe, IL, The Free Press, 1955).
31. Williams and McShane, *Criminology Theory*, p. 83.
32. Merton, 'On the Evolving Synthesis of Differential Association and Anomie Theory', p. 519.
33. Sutherland, *White Collar Crime*, pp. 63–191.
34. Samuel Walker's *Popular Justice: A History of American Criminal Justice*, 2nd edn (New York: Oxford University Press, 1998) is but one of the better examples of a general history from over five hundred titles currently offered by one online booker seller, and Frederic E. Wakeman's *Policing Shanghai, 1927–1937* (Berkeley: University of California, 1995) is an excellent example of a localized police history—as are examples identified in footnotes 37 through 40—from a selection of over four hundred titles on policing history also being offered by the same retailer.
35. John A. Conley, 'Historical Perspective and Criminal Justice', *Journal of Criminal Justice Education* 4 (1993), 349–360 (p. 351).
36. Sutherland, *White Collar Crime*, pp. 7–8.
37. Ida M. Tarbell, *The History of the Standard Oil Company* (New York: McClure Phillips, 1904); Upton Sinclair, *The Jungle* (New York: Doubleday, Page, 1906).
38. British scholars, on the other hand, have recognized a historical context to white-collar crime prior to the violations referred to in the groundbreaking work of Sutherland. See, for example, Peter Johnstone, 'Serious White Collar Fraud: Historical and Contemporary Perspectives', *Crime, Law and Social Change*, 30 (1999), 107–130; John P. Locker and Barry Godfrey, 'Ontological Boundaries and Temporal Watersheds in the Development of White-collar Crime', *British Journal of Criminology*, 46 (2006), 976–992; George Robb, *White-collar Crime in Modern England: Financial Fraud and Business Morality, 1845–1929* (Cambridge: Cambridge University Press, 1992).
39. Sutherland, *White Collar Crime*, p. 7.
40. Frank E. Hartung, 'White-collar Offenses in the Wholesale Meat Industry in Detroit', *American Journal of Sociology*, 56 (1950), pp. 25–34; Robert E. Lane, 'Why Business Men Violate the Law', *Journal of Criminal Law*,

Criminology, and Police Science, 44 (1953), 151–165; Marshall Clinard, *The Black Market: A Study of White Collar Crime* (New York: Rinehart, 1952).

41. Earl R. Quinney, 'Occupational Structure and Criminal Behavior: Prescription Violation by Retail Pharmacists', *Social Problems*, 11 (1963), 179–185.

42. Gilbert Geis, 'The Heavy Electrical Equipment Antitrust Cases of 1961', in *Criminal Behavior Systems*, ed. by Marshall Clinard and Richard Quinney (New York: Holt, Rinehart & Winston, 1967) 139–150.

43. Bethany McLean and Peter Elkind, *The Smartest Guys in the Room: The Amazing Rise and Scandalous Fall of Enron* (New York: Penguin, 2004).

44. Roger Lane, *Policing the City: Boston, 1822–1885* (Cambridge, MA: Harvard University Press, 1967); Eric H. Monkkonen, *Police in Urban America, 1860–1920* (New York: Cambridge University Press, 1981); James F. Richardson, *The New York Police: Colonial Times to 1901* (New York: Oxford University Press, 1970).

45. Wilbur R. Miller, *Cops and Bobbies: Police Authority in New York and London, 1830–1870* (Columbus: Ohio State University Press, 1973; repr. 1997); Michael Stephen Hindus, *Prison and Plantation: Crime, Justice, and Authority in Massachusetts and South Carolina, 1767–1878* (Chapel Hill: University of North Carolina Press, 1980).

46. Frank Richard Prassel, *The Western Peace Officer: A Legacy of Law and Order* (Norman: University of Oklahoma Press, 1972); Frederick S. Calhoun, *The Lawmen: United States Marshals and their Deputies, 1789-1989* (Washington, D.C.: Smithsonian Institution Press, 1989).

47. Carl E. Prince and Mollie Keller, *The U.S. Customs Service: A Bicentennial History* (Washington, D.C.: U.S. Customs Service, 1989); Irving King, *George Washington's Coast Guard: Origins of the U.S. Revenue Cutter Service, 1789–1801* (Annapolis, MD: Naval Institute Press, 1978), *The Coast Guard under Sail: The U.S. Revenue Cutter Service, 1789–1865* (Annapolis, MD: Naval Institute Press, 1989), and *The Coast Guard Expands, 1865–1915: New Roles, New Frontiers* (Annapolis, MD: Naval Institute Press, 1996).

48. Roger D. McGrath, *Gunfighters, Highwaymen and Vigilantes: Violence on the Frontier* (Berkeley: University of California Press, 1984); Eric H. Monkkonen, 'Estimating the Accuracy of Historic Homicide Rates', *Social Science History*, 25 (2001), 53–66; Douglas Eckberg, 'Stalking the Elusive Homicide', *Social Science History*, 25 (2001), 67–91.

49. Conley, 'Historical Perspective and Criminal Justice', p. 351.

50. Geis, *White-collar and Corporate Crime*, p. 51.

51. *ibid.*, pp. 49–75.

52. Woodiwiss, *Organized Crime and American Power*, p. 16.

53. *ibid.*, p. 23.

54. *ibid.*, pp. 15–67, 170–202.

55. Paul W. Tappan, 'Who Is the Criminal?', *American Sociological Review*, 12 (1947), 96–102.

56. Edwin H. Sutherland, 'Is "White-collar Crime" Crime?', *American Sociological Review*, 10 (1945), 132–139.

57. Gilbert Geis, 'White-collar Crime: What Is It?', *Current Issues in Criminal Justice*, 3 (1991), 9–24.

58. David O. Friedrichs, *Trusted Criminals: White Collar Crime in Contemporary Society*, 3rd edn (Belmont, CA: Thomson Wadsworth, 2007), p. 7.

59. Gary Potter and Larry Gaines, 'Underworlds and Upperworlds: The Convergence of Organized and White-collar Crime' in *Definitional Dilemma: Can and Should There Be a Universal Definition of White-collar Crime*, ed. by

James Helmkamp, Richard Ball, and Kitty Townsend (Morgantown, WV: National White Collar Crime Center and West Virginia University, 1996), 30–52 (p. 31).

60. National Commission on Law Observance and Enforcement, *Report on the Enforcement of the Prohibition Laws of the United States* (Washington, D.C.: Government Printing Office, 1931), p. 37.

61. Thomas Doherty, *Pre-code Hollywood: Sex, Immorality, and Insurrection in American Cinema, 1930–1934* (New York: Columbia University Press, 1999), p. 157.

62. David E. Ruth, *Inventing the Public Enemy: The Gangster in American Culture, 1918–1934* (Chicago: University of Chicago Press, 1996), p. 3.

63. F. Scott Fitzgerald, *The Great Gatsby* (New York: Scribner, 1925; repr. 1995), p. 189; Steven Mintz and Randy Roberts, *Hollywood's America: United States History through Its Films* (St. James, New York: Brandywine Press, 1993); Jonathan Munby, *Public Enemies, Public Heroes: Screening the Gangster from Little Caesar to Touch of Evil* (Chicago: University of Chicago Press, 1999); Ruth, *Inventing the Public Enemy*; Andrew Bergman, *We're in the Money: Depression America and Its Films* (New York: New York University Press, 1971).

64. Esmond Wright, *The American Dream: From Reconstruction to Reagan* (Cambridge: Blackwell Publishing, 1996), p. 32.

65. *ibid.*, p. 33.

66. *Little Caesar*, dir. by Mervyn LeRoy (First National Pictures, 1931); *The Public Enemy*, dir. by William A. Wellman (Warner Bros. Pictures, 1931); *Scarface*, dir. by Howard Hawks and Richard Rosson (The Caddo Company, 1932).

67. Donald R. Liddick, *An Empirical, Theoretical, and Historical Overview of Organized Crime* (Lewiston, NY: Edwin Mellon Press, 1999), p. 1.

68. Woodiwiss, *Organized Crime and American Power*, p. 10.

69. Tise Vahimagi, *The Untouchables* (London: BFI Publishing, 1998), p. 65.

70. Liddick, *An Empirical, Theoretical, and Historical Overview of Organized Crime*, pp. 8–9, 12. Forty years later Hollywood would continue the tradition of offering an image of organized crime and gangsters in the *Godfather* trilogy. *The Godfather*, dir. by Francis Ford Coppola (Alfran Productions, Paramount Pictures, 1972); *The Godfather, Part II*, dir. by Francis Ford Coppola (Paramount Pictures, The Coppola Company, 1974); *The Godfather, Part III*, dir. by Francis Ford Coppola (Paramount Pictures, Zoetrope Studio, 1990).

71. Woodiwiss, *Organized Crime and American Power*, p. 10.

72. Sutherland, *White Collar Crime*, p. 239.

73. John W. Tyler, *Smugglers and Patriots: Boston Merchants and the Advent of the American Revolution* (Boston, MA: Northeastern University Press, 1986), p. 13.

74. As a minor side-note, it was found that the investigative reports of the federal customs agents in the late nineteenth century read little different from a contemporary investigative report, the most obvious difference being that it was handwritten in a legible and generally handsome penmanship, another talent deemed of little consequence in this contemporary electronic communication era.

75. James Barbican, *The Confessions of a Rum-runner* (New York: Ives Washburn, 1928); Gertrude C. Lythgoe, *The Bahama Queen: The Autobiography of Gertrude 'Cleo' Lythgoe* (Mystic, CT: Flat Hammock Press, 2006); Alastair Moray, *The Diary of a Rum-runner* (London: Phillip Allan and

Company, 1929); Fraser Miles, *Slow Boast on Rum Row* (Madeira Park, B.C., Canada: Harbour Publishing, 1992).

76. David Eltis, *Economic Growth and the Ending of the Transatlantic Slave Trade* (New York: Oxford University Press, 1987); Warren Howard, *American Slavers and the Federal Law, 1837–1862* (Berkeley, University of California Press, 1963); Hugh Thomas, *The Slave Trade: The Story of the Atlantic Slave Trade, 1440–1870* (New York: Simon and Schuster, 1997). Erika Lee, *At America's Gates: Chinese Immigration During the Exclusion Era, 1882–1943* (Chapel Hill: University of North Carolina Press, 2003).

77. Peter Andreas, *Smuggler Nation: How Illicit Trade Made America* (New York: Oxford University Press, 2013), pp. 130–153.

78. *ibid.*, pp. 177–190; Andrew Wender Cohen, 'Smuggling, Globalization, and America's Outward State, 1870–1909', *Journal of American History*, 97 (2010), pp. 371–398.

1 The New World

When Edwin Sutherland first discussed white-collar crime, he stated that even prior to the modern corporations, white-collar criminality was present in America, the predatory business leaders of the nineteenth century known as the 'robber barons' being one major example.[1] He also recognized that '[c]ontrary to the assumption of later commentators, the modern gangster predated his bootlegger incarnation'.[2] The characterization of that modern gangster also includes the concepts of white-collar criminality and organized crime.[3] 'From earliest times, landlords, merchants, and holders of administrative and executive power have used the relative immunity that their status gave them to engage in or sponsor activity that today would be described as organized crime'.[4] Those earliest times date at least to the early European and Mediterranean traders where many of the techniques for illicitly improving a merchant's personal profits carried across the centuries to the North American shores years later.

Smuggling, defined as the illicit import or export of goods, can be inferred historically at least from the time of the Old Testament.[5] In Ezra 7:24, King Artaxerxes declares that 'it shall not be lawful to impose tribute, custom or toll upon any one of the priests, the Levites, the singers, doorkeepers, the temple servants, or other servants of this house of God' in reference to the taxes or fees that local nobles levied upon merchants to increase their own revenue.[6] With the imposition of tribute and customs or tolls, it was only a matter of time before their handmaidens, fraud and smuggling, followed.[7] The earliest English record of merchant ships paying customs duties dates to AD 742.[8] Customs would later be referred to in the Magna Carta with the Crown claiming its 'ancient and rightful customs' in the payment of its due for imported goods.[9] Indeed customs funds could have the potential to make a kingdom quite wealthy; '[t]owards 1600 the coffers of the Venetian state treasury were overflowing with money; seven or eight hundred ships went in and out of her port every year'.[10] The state's ability to serve as an economic catalyst and developer was achieved in the sixteenth century as much as in the nineteenth century through those funds. That income led to a concern for smuggling, not so much to prevent the entry of illicit goods as for the effective collection of customs duties on taxed goods.[11]

As early as the sixteenth century, the techniques later used by colonial and American smugglers caused consternation to legitimate merchants trading on the Baltic. To control trade and to prevent smuggling by English merchants trafficking with Poland, traders were required to post a bond and declare that all tolls would be paid; failing to do so leading to the forfeiture of the bond.[12] The bonds' objective was to protect fellow merchants from 'reprisals and losses should one of their number be caught evading tolls in the Danish Sound, at the Pillau entrance to the Frisches Haff, or in Elbing itself'.[13] Yet much to the embarrassment of the merchants of England, even with the bonding system in place, frauds against Polish customs were identified by representatives of the government. The practice of passing expensive cloth off as cheaper material with the intent of lowering the duty paid to the Polish Crown was the most common fraud reportedly practiced, possibly in collusion with local customs officials.[14] These merchants, organized as a trading company to control the traffic, were an early reflection of the formal and informal organizations that Sutherland referred to where techniques, justifications, and rationalizations for smuggling may be acquired in the day-to-day interactions of their members.

Even specie itself became contraband. With silver from the New World supporting Spanish imperialism, Spanish policy was to guard against the export of its precious metals. Yet merchants throughout Europe needed specie, leading inevitably to the smuggling of specie out of Spain. 'A French boat, *Le Croissant* of St.-Malo for instance, was seized in Andalisa for illegal traffic in silver; another time, two Marseilles *barques* were stopped in the Gulf of Lions and found to be laden with Spanish coins'.[15] In 1554, passengers leaving Catalonia for Italy were searched and seventy thousand ducats, primarily from Genoese merchants, were seized. In 1567, nine hundred thousand ducats, four hundred thousand of which were gold coins, had been determined to have entered Lyons from Aragon, the coins being smuggled in bales of leather.[16] At one point, of an estimated ten million ducats worth of bullion shipped to Spain yearly, six million were then exported while the remaining four million stayed in Spain or were smuggled out by a variety of travelers.[17]

Spain's continued policy of commercial restriction extended to the New World as well as to the Old. That policy meant, however, that others would profit from Spain's own failure to supply the needs of her colonies. In 1661, the contraband trade by the English and Dutch with the port of Buenos Aires led to the establishment of an *Audiencia* responsible for civilian and military affairs of the Rio de la Plata in an attempt to stifle smuggling.[18] The British South Sea Company, thanks to the Treaty of Utrecht, obtained an agreement, known as the *Asiento*, in 1713 to trade with various Spanish settlements in the New World, 'opening possibilities for unloading merchandise that ultimately became a main source of smuggling' with the endorsement of their chartering government and the involvement of the local English factors in collusion with various Spanish officials.[19] The company was another example of a formal organization offering an opportunity for the development of a consensus among all concerned parties to successfully achieve their objective: successful contraband trade. Eventually the Spanish government would counter with the creation of the *guarda-costas*, private sailing vessels licensed to serve as a maritime customs preventive force.[20]

The Dutch, besides being a nuisance to the Spanish trade in the New World, had to cope with their own smuggling concerns in New Netherland. As early as the 1620s, both colonists and employees of the Dutch West India Company—yet another formal organization involved in circumventing the law—were smuggling furs out of New Netherland in company ships, one case identified the company supercargo sharing in the profits. Many seemed to be following the advice of their fellow countryman, Gerhard Mercator, whose text of a map of the known world closed with the counsel, 'Fare wel, and make thy proffyt'.[21] Smuggling had reached such a level that by 1637, the company had strengthened established penalties for employees to include forfeiture of wages, personal trade goods, and personal belongings. Yet as with future colonial smuggling laws, their effect was questionable due to the limited ability to enforce them. Though restrictions also applied to free colonists, many continued to trade contraband furs with company sailors in an attempt to fulfill their own economic American Dream.[22] The English eventually conquered New Amsterdam to suppress, among other justifications, the contraband trade of goods to and from English possessions.[23]

As Spanish sea power declined in the seventeenth century, Holland, France, and England would continue to engage in contraband traffic. As trade became synonymous with politics, the English government itself would condone and protect contraband trade to the Spanish colonies to further its perceived economic interests—which were viewed as one and the same as its political interests. After its seizure from Spain, Jamaica was used as a base for extending British economic interest through illegal trade in the Caribbean. In time all involved in the carrying trade would demand a greater free trade policy; eventually even the definition of free trade would evolve from being a catch phrase against company monopolies such as the South Seas Company to a term encompassing smuggling itself.[24] All would help lead England into becoming the commercial empire of the eighteenth century and all would be a precursor to the concept of state crime—in this case the state supporting the illegal trade with Spain in the interest of its own national policy.

By the early eighteenth century, foreign merchants were operating over one hundred vessels off the Caribbean coast of New Granada, many with the connivance of local Spanish authorities. Smuggling was a critical component of the political economy not only of the Caribbean but of the New World itself.[25] All were the precursors of modern organized white-collar crime. As Grahn states:

> As an alternative to the trans-Atlantic mercantilist economy, smuggling competed with legal trade for available market shares and corollary

market niches for the buying and selling of controlled, or regulated, commodities. Conversely, it complemented licit commerce and cultural systems. It allowed consumers to obtain both common goods and scarce commodities at relatively reasonable prices, thus promoting purchasing power parity. It gave both producers and merchants another outlet of exchange that avoided Spanish taxation and regulation, thus enhancing market efficiency. It also quickened trade by increasing sellers' profits, thus reinforcing capitalist tendencies. In a very real way, then, smuggling served a useful socioeconomic function and so strengthened the political economy of the colony.[26]

His appraisal is no less applicable to the organized entrepreneurs of the future United States.

COLONIAL AMERICA

With the arrival of the Puritans in the New World in 1630, their version of the American Dream would eventually allow those who followed the opportunity to achieve their own.[27] In a short time revenue replaced religion for many as the American Dream. 'In Massachusetts itself the commercial spirit was steadily growing, and with it went a decline in religious fervor'.[28] The idea of trade and profit, that which had sustained both New Netherland and the Spanish exploration in the Western Hemisphere, once again came to the forefront. As Barrow remarked, 'In pursuit of profits, idealism receded in importance'.[29] Within a short time, the English Crown pursued its own profits. The notion of profit eclipsing idealism foreshadows Merton's concept of anomie and the rationalizations of Sutherland's white-collar criminals.

By 1621 the Privy Council ordered that all tobacco and other commodities from Virginia be landed first in England and that appropriate customs duties be paid.[30] With the Atlantic isolating the colonies geographically from the European and Caribbean trade, regulatory control was primarily a maritime concern for the British. Thirty years later, the first Navigation Act directed that all produce landed in England, Ireland, or any English possession be transported in English hulls with English crews.[31] This was followed in 1660 by the further restrictions limiting trade to or from English lands to only English, Irish, or Welsh ships. Other restrictions incorporated in the Act of 1660 required that hulls in colonial trade be three-quarters English manned with an English master. Though most goods could be shipped directly to or from the colonies to a foreign port in English vessels, the Act restricted colonial sugars, tobacco, indigo, and other enumerated goods from being exported other than to England or its possessions.[32] In an attempt to effectively enforce the Act, the Royal Navy was given the authority to seize foreign vessels trading in English seas. Naval powers were further expanded in 1687, when they were deputized as customs officers. By

1663, even shipments from foreign ports were required to be transshipped through England, allowing further duties to be collected for the Crown. The Act also both required that a manifest of the cargo be given within twenty-four hours of entry to appropriate British officials and prohibited the commencement of loading or unloading until entry was made and proof of English ownership and crews was given.[33]

Yet these regulations had little impact on intra-colonial shipping, allowing restricted goods to be exported under cover of domestic trade. The Act of 1673 attempted to address this shortcoming by requiring a bond for the movement of enumerated goods between the colonies, as well as requiring a duty, with the objective of preventing these restricted commodities from being illegally exported to the detriment of England.[34] Oversight of these regulations, the responsibility of the colonial governments, was questionable at best and eventually led to the appointment of the first royal customs officer in 1671. By 1673, officers were designated for Maryland, the Carolinas, and Virginia, each being compensated with a percentage of the total receipts collected. The New England colonies followed in 1678, with much discussion in England regarding New England ships still 'purchasing European goods directly from Holland and France and distributing them throughout all the colonies with no stopover in England'.[35]

The intent of these series of regulations was twofold. They assisted in the perpetuation of mercantilism, allowing English-based merchants to gain financially at the expense of colonial traders. They also allowed the Exchequer, though only in limited measure, to increase its own revenues. Yet by 1688, the enforcement of the Navigation Acts was honored more in the breach. A period of 'salutary neglect' in England's management and oversight of the colonies eventually developed offering a rationalization and attitude for a general acceptance of violation and neglect, much to the benefit of the commercial interest of the colonies, as well as to those nations opposed to the British lock on colonial trade and commerce.[36] The first link in a continuing chain of white-collar criminality throughout the history of America had been established.

Throughout the late seventeenth century, the Scots became active partners with the Chesapeake tobacco growers in smuggling out tobacco to the European markets, due to the Scots exclusion from active participation in direct English commerce. With the Navigation Act of 1660 declaring them aliens and their vessels and crews ineligible for service in the colonial trade, more than one Scot threw his lot in with the smugglers. In 1670, a ship was seized and condemned in Barbados for violating the Act by not having an appropriate number of English crew. Later reports told of Scots unloading tobacco in Glasgow prior to clearing in England and of various other vessels being identified as sailing directly to Maryland without transiting England. With family ties in the Chesapeake area thanks to relatives having been previously transported to the colonies following the English Civil

War, Scotsmen reportedly became a major scourge on the customhouse.[37] In 1693, Scotsmen and New Englanders were specifically identified as illegally trading directly with Scotland from Maryland. The following year eight vessels were claimed to have been improperly cleared direct for Scotland.[38] The surveyor-general of customs for the colonies eventually identified thirteen ships as involved in illegal trade, eleven connected to Scotsmen. English customs estimated a national loss of £50,000 due to free traders that year. Not until the Act of Union in 1707 did violations involving the Scots seriously dwindle, but as late as 1723, they continued to be accused of involvement in frauds against the British revenue.[39]

Southern states' tobacco, besides entering Scotland via Glasgow, also was indirectly part of the Irish-American trade. The tobacco would travel through the Isle of Man, Guernsey, or France en route to Ireland. Some was English-exported tobacco that was falsely documented as being shipped to Spain or France in order to receive the drawback, but was then transported to Ireland instead. Both rum and limited quantities of tobacco were also dispatched from inbound or transit vessels prior to landing and declaring the remainder of the ships' cargo. Irish manufactured goods, including shoes, woolens, silks, poplins, needles, books, clocks, and watches, as well as East India tea, were part of the contraband trade bound to the colonies in return; the unhindered flow was so great that the amount of smuggled Irish woolens, for example, inundated the market in some years.[40]

New England traders were even more heavily involved in the illegal shipment of tobacco from the colonies, again in some cases in exchange for contraband goods. 'Not only did the northerners habitually break the law, but they apparently did so with a degree of impunity'.[41] That impunity was fed by the merchants' influence with both local officials and with the popular courts, reflecting Sutherland's concept of white-collar crime with elites using their groups' influence to manipulate litigation and enforcement activity to their personal benefit. In a two-year period, for example, the collector of customs located in Boston seized thirty-six vessels, cases that eventually went to trial, yet all but two were acquitted. At least one captain initiated a civil suit against the collector.[42] At one point the collector recommended 'fitt persons' be appointed to curtail the 'Illegal Trade carried on by Scotchmen & others in vessels belonging to New Eng^d & Pennsylvania, from those provinces, to Scotland, Carasaw, & other unlawful places' insinuating that some previous appointees had obviously been 'unfitt'.[43] Business had compromised the political and legal interests of the state.

'Carasaw', or Curacao, was a West Indies Dutch entrepôt of trade and a prime destination of New England merchantmen. Exchanging illegally exported tobacco and other enumerated American products such as pitch and tar for sugar, molasses, French wines and brandies, silk, linen, and various manufactured goods, the new cargoes would then be fraudulently entered into the English continental colonies shortly afterwards.[44] However, with the warehouse inspection system established in Virginia to maintain tobacco market quality in 1730, to be followed by a similar system in Maryland in 1747, tobacco smuggling declined only to be replaced in later years with a trade in grain and sugar. Exporting corn, pork, and beef in exchange for molasses and sugar was made illegal whenever Anglo-French animosities flared prior to 1733, but a profitable trade, especially one with few alternative customers, is hard to break, in particular a trade that, with so few enforcement tools available to the Crown, offered so many opportunities to circumvent the restrictions.[45] Similar New England trade with Suriname was also seen as a threat to the British sugar plantations.[46] In line with Sutherland, an 'excess of definitions' favorable to violating the law rather than complying with the law continually existed.

By the mid-eighteenth century, more than 80 percent of the sugar production in the Western Hemisphere occurred in the islands of the West Indies. French planters, in shipping more semi-refined sugar than the British, had a surplus of molasses, a byproduct of the refining process. Both the molasses and inexpensive French rum were sought by merchants of the British North American colonies.[47] In an attempt to favor the British sugar-producing islands and their indigenous rum industry and to stop French island trade, the importation of foreign molasses was tariffed prohibitively with the passage of the Molasses Act of 1733.[48] Throughout the following years, the rum-distilling business in the British sugar islands was also given special legal perquisites, which limited shipping and distribution expenses and encouraged the development of island distillers over distillers in New England. This preferential treatment reduced the availability of molasses for exportation to the continental colonies.[49]

New England shipping interests and American grain farmers, avoiding what would have been a disastrous duty—six pence per gallon versus the one penny per gallon for British West Indies molasses—placed upon their livelihood by the British mercantilists and others with concerns in the Caribbean, known collectively as the 'West India Interest', and chose to evade what would be a poorly enforced law.[50] Again, finding an 'excess of definitions' favorable to violating the law while placing their own economic interest above the Crown's, merchants utilized a variety of techniques to maximize and retain their earnings. One early method was accomplished by having their vessels clear from Jamaica, empty except for unfilled sugar casks, but having claimed a full cargo of Jamaican sugar on board. Inward bound for the colonies they surreptitiously called at Santo Domingo and took on a full cargo of sugar, casks already being available onboard for loading. The most common method of import, however, was through the connivance of colonial customs officers who allowed only a small portion of an imported sugar or molasses cargo to be declared while also permitting a smaller duty to be paid on what was actually declared. In a documented acknowledgment of the practice, one Salem merchant admitted to expecting to pay six pence per gallon on one eighth to one tenth of the actual cargos, which was more than twice what he had given prior to 1758.[51] Later the neutral Dutch islands of the Lesser Antilles, as well as the British Virgin Islands, were utilized for transshipment of the prohibited goods through the use of various fraudulent papers.[52]

'Especially daring and ingenious in pursuit of profit were the import-export merchants who dominated enterprise in the colonial ports'.[53] Even with legal trade, when opportunity presented itself, some could not refuse. James Dick and his son-in-law Anthony Stewart, Maryland import-export merchants, purchased the brig *Peggy Stewart* in partnership with a Baltimore merchant with the intent of shipping corn, wheat, flour, and beans to Madeira. After the cargo was sold, the profit was returned to the colonies as wine with Dick and Stewart advising the master of the *Peggy Stewart* to avoid revealing its cargo to anyone upon landing, their intent being to circumvent the payment of import duties on the wine and to increase their profit margin.[54] The *Peggy Stewart* later met a famously inglorious demise in 1774 when she was burned by a mob after bringing tea into Annapolis in contravention of the colonial tea embargo.[55]

The house of Hancock typified the colonial traders—Sutherland's informal business groups[56]—who were found throughout the seaports of British North America and who were the foundation of white-collar crime in the colonies. Thomas Hancock, one of Boston's gentry and uncle of the Declaration of Independence signatory John Hancock, in an early attempt at an overseas triangle trade, shipped dried fish to Spain in 1731. Eventually some lemons were taken aboard in Spain on one of the vessels bound directly to the colonies in violation of the Navigation Acts.[57] From the seed of those small lemons, the contraband trade of Hancock grew. By 1736, Hancock and his associates were instructing the captain of one vessel to return to Boston from Spain by way of Suriname.[58] The cargo, identified as 'taffeta, velvet, raisins, "handkers," French linen, Holland duck, broadcloth, calico, sweet oil cordage, [and] gloves' was considered contraband because it had not been re-exported through England prior to being shipped to North America,[59] and its source could be concealed as originating legally from the Dutch colony by having their vessel transit Suriname en route to Boston. The shipment was successful and, one assumes, profitable for all concerned.[60] Later in an unsuccessful venture, the brigantine *The Three Friends*, traveling to Newfoundland to sell off its cargo of New England goods, was seized and condemned for illegally having on board eight barrels of tobacco and some coffee.[61]

When war broke out with Spain in 1740, Thomas Hancock developed a triangular trade with the West Indies and Holland in violation of colonial and British law. Vessels traveled south carrying fish and sold or exchanged the cargo for 'bills [of sale] on London or Holland, logwood, lignum vitae (source of a valuable drug), indigo, or molasses, et cetera; any empty space was to be filled with freight to Europe'.[62] If the trade link to Europe was not forthcoming, appropriate goods of profit were smuggled into Boston. Over the next four years the contraband trade for Hancock was highly profitable—this while at the same time being a member of the community's elite, becoming a selectman of Boston, part of the town's governing board, and later being appointed to supervise the construction of military fortifications in the city among other community duties, easily fulfilling Sutherland's definition of white-collar criminals being a 'respectable or at least respected business and professional men'.[63]

The French entry into the war in 1744 led the British to impose an embargo on the New England colonies to prevent trade with the enemy; Hancock altered his trade route by having Dutch goods, including paper and tea, shipped via St. Eustatius then onward to New England where the European goods were illicitly landed prior to a ship's formal entry at Boston. Return trips to the Caribbean were with cargoes of cod, as likely sold to the enemy as to British colonials.[64] After the war Hancock was elected to the governing council of the colony while contraband tea continued to add to Hancock's profits, again being shipped through his agent in St. Eustatius; his traffic reportedly led to the development of packing the tea in lead-lined solid casks, both for protection and concealment.[65] This innovation reflects Hancock's own extensive immersion in the smuggling trade, since those with limited involvement in any practice tend not to be the innovators within that arena and is a reflection of Sutherland's recognition that the diffusion of illegal practices is evidence of differential association.[66]

With hostilities occurring once again between England and France, in 1757 the export of grain from the colonies was allowed only to other British possessions. Faced with only a limited market and recognizing the profits available in illicit trade for French sugar, colonial vessels sailed for Monte Christi in Spanish Santo Domingo. After picking up Spanish crews, masters, and papers, the vessels then sailed west along the coast to Cap Francois in French Santo Domingo and traded grain for sugar, returning to the 'Mount' to once again exchange their crews and hence back to the colonies. The tactic became so common that traffic climbed from fourteen colonial vessels being documented in Cap Francois during a seven month period in 1757 to more than two hundred colonial vessels believed to have traded in Monte Christi in 1759 after a British sloop found twenty-nine ships in Monte Christi upon its own arrival in the harbor. The trade lasted another five years until it was finally censored by the French.[67] Contraband trade was also found between Holland and New York with tea, linen, guns, and powder moved by vessel to Sandy Hook and off-loaded to smaller boats with the ocean-going vessel continuing into New York empty of contraband. When the governor initiated pressure to stop the illegal practice, the traffic only moved to Connecticut with the goods then being transshipped via the Long Island Sound.[68]

As with many monopolies that successfully control a given commodity, the East India Company's monopoly of tea, in conjunction with the British government's objective of heavily taxing tea to increase revenues, led to a smuggling trade in the Asian beverage. Prior to 1767, every pound of 'irregular' tea brought ashore evaded an extra shilling of expense—in some years, up to three shillings of extra expense. With Dutch islands in the West Indies importing tea 'practically free of duty' the opportunity to profit from tea smuggling was offered to the same vessels transporting sugar and molasses in inter-colonial trade throughout the eighteenth century. The trade's hub was Boston, and, as Sutherland characterized in his description of white-collar criminals, it 'involved some of the leading merchants'.[69] Thomas Hancock, for example, had continued contraband tea shipments via St. Eustatius though 'not more than three casks were to be risked on any one ship'.[70]

THE AMERICAN REVOLUTION AND SMUGGLING

The practices and techniques of the American merchant-smugglers of the nineteenth century were developed by colonial merchants of the eighteenth century. For those traders, '[y]ears of lax enforcement of customs regulations had also habituated many of [Boston's] residents to illicit trade. Smuggling was a violation of law but nothing out of the ordinary'.[71] Those habits applied no less to other town traders throughout the colonies. At the onset of the French and Indian, or Seven Years, War Britain cracked down on colonial smuggling with the navy being brokered as the preventive officers at sea.[72] This was the end of 'benign neglect': trade restrictions were enforced and new trade laws, along with new taxes, were created with the intent of increasing the Crown's revenue flow to cover the cost of the war. British calculations of illicit trade from Europe to North America were estimated at between five hundred thousand pounds and seven hundred thousand pounds per annum, equaling 16 to 33 percent of all European goods imported into North America.[73] This was enough for the Grenville to 'fear that trade outside the empire would lead inevitably to demands for colonial independence'.[74]

The merchants of the colonies, particularly those in Boston, reacted as one might expect of anyone whose income was threatened. Boston's merchants, increasing from approximately 200 in the mid-1760s to almost 350 before the start of the Revolution, were an influential group within the community.[75] Of the group, at least twenty-three have since been confirmed as smugglers by Tyler's research of the records of one of the agents for a Dutch merchant in Boston as well as the records that survived of one of the four Boston marine insurers. Recognizing the probability of the other three marine insurers also profiting from the illicit trade, in theory the number of smugglers within the Massachusetts merchant community could be as high as one out of four traders.[76] As Tyler points out:

> The significance of the smuggling group does not lie in their numbers but in their political importance. Like the merchants trading to southern

Europe (four of the merchants belonged to both groups), the smugglers served on many of the most important committees. John Rowe, perhaps one of Boston's most active smugglers, was always at the center of merchant deliberations despite his political trimming. Dutch traders Solomon Davis and William Molineux became the special *betes noirés* of lieutenant governor Thomas Hutchinson because of their radical political activities and their easy rapport with the urban crowd [. . .] These men's opinions were guaranteed a hearing because they dominated certain key posts in the patriot hierarchy. The smuggler Edward Payne, in his capacity as secretary of the Boston Society for Encouraging Trade and Commerce, drafted and redrafted most of the memorials sent to Parliament petitioning for redress from the burdensome restrictions of the Grenville program. Another smuggler, William Cooper, the secretary of the Boston town meeting, stood in close association with Sam Adams and the other members of the radical junto. In brief, the illicit traders enjoyed an influence out of all proportion to their numbers.[77]

As Sutherland had identified white-collar crime as organized crime, the smuggling merchants of Boston had 'organized formally for the control of legislation, selection of administrators, and restriction of appropriations for the enforcement of laws which may affect themselves'.[78] Economic self-interest was the handmaiden of ideology. A Hancock would be in the forefront—this time John Hancock, a nephew by birth and a son by adoption of Thomas.

In 1768, John Hancock's ship the *Lydia* arrived from London.[79] Suspected of possible violations, no doubt based upon earlier comments made by Hancock dismissing the authority of British customs and suspecting that dutiable goods were on board, tidesmen from the customs office boarded the vessel. After Hancock reportedly directed the ship's captain to prevent the tidesmen from going below deck, the crew physically removed one of the tidesmen found below the following night, April 9. The affront to the King's customs was immediately directed to the attorney-general of Massachusetts but, after much consideration, no prosecution was forthcoming.[80]

Within the month, and while the outcome of the *Lydia* case was still undecided, Hancock again challenged the authority of the colonial customs when his sloop the *Liberty* arrived in Boston from Madeira. Again tidesmen boarded and, on May 10, stated under oath that the cargo had been undisturbed during the night; the cargo of twenty-five casks of wine was entered with duty paid.

During the following month, the *Liberty* both unloaded her original cargo and was laden with a new one outbound. Then on June 9 one of the tidewaiters informed his superiors that he had been forcibly confined below decks while the *Liberty* had been illegally unloaded with the greater part of its cargo of wine on the night of its entry into Boston. When finished 'they released the Tidesman but with such Threats and Denunciations of

Vengeance Death and Destruction in Case he divulged the Affair' that the official had failed to report either the smuggling or the threats until the following month.[81]

The following day the *Liberty* was again boarded and seized, with the collector of customs filing suit two weeks later claiming that twenty barrels of tar and two hundred barrels of oil were found on board at the time of the seizure, yet no bond had been posted and no permit to load had been obtained. The collector's action led to the formal confiscation and seizure of the vessel.[82] Eventually Hancock, along with five other merchants, was served with a personal suit for their actions upon the original entry of the *Liberty* into Boston Harbor and the offloading of a reported one hundred pipes of wine. Though the suit against Hancock and the other merchants eventually was withdrawn, the *Liberty* was retained by the customs service; cruising the Long Island Sound in the following year, a mob scuttled her after she had seized two other vessels and brought them into Newport Harbor.[83] Dickerson later described the supposed venality and greed of the customs officials as 'racketeering', a term in common use in describing modern organized crime at the time of his original writing.[84]

As time went on an 'increasing tendency in the newspapers to defend some types of smuggling as a positive good' developed.[85] That tendency condoned the behavior of those interested in profiting from violations of the law and eventually presaged the idea that 'undue restrictions on trade are an unwarranted interference in the rights of personal property'.[86] Of greater concern was the idea that 'a few smuggling merchants who enriched themselves[. . .], finding themselves too narrowly watched, have had the art to make a mere mercantile affair, a subject of general and public complaint'.[87] As Tyler states, 'Leading patriots, to serve their own self-interest, had pushed the colonies into war'.[88] Trade and the consummate smuggling that went hand in hand with the British Crown's mercantilist beliefs and that eventually contributed to rebellion throughout the colonies, led to the creation of a nation built, at least for a substantial minority of its merchant class, on organized white-collar criminal activity in the fulfillment of the merchants' own version of the American Dream—a dream of wealth. Even as the war progressed American merchants gladly sold ship masts to the Royal Navy in exchange for British goods. The Passamaquoddy area of Maine was described as a 'hotbed of smuggling' during the Revolutionary War with contraband trade between Americans and British loyalists condoned by both.[89]

These smuggler-merchants epitomized Sutherland's description of white-collar crime when he later characterized the criminality of corporations. His specifications are just as applicable to the Boston smugglers of the mid-eighteenth century. First, they were persistent: 'a large proportion of offenders [were] recidivists', running more than one cargo of contraband.[90] John Hancock's *Lydia* and *Liberty* are but two examples; another is his uncle's own extensive record of smuggling. Second, 'the illegal behavior is much more extensive than the prosecutions and complaints indicate'.[91] Repeated communications to England identified the colonial problem, yet little was done to address it until the years immediately prior to the Revolution.[92] Third, 'the businessman who violates the laws which are designed to regulate business does not customarily lose status among his business associates'.[93] As Thomas Hancock exemplifies, even after the seizure of one of his vessels, he still was offered a position in the Governor's Council. Fourth, 'businessmen customarily feel and express contempt for law, government, and for governmental personnel'.[94] The actions at Hancock's direction toward the customs personnel who boarded his vessel *Lydia* were but one obvious example. The actions over the years prior to the Revolution against customs personnel in general in the Boston area further substantiate that the merchants had little respect for the law or the personnel enforcing it. Fifth, '[w]hite collar crimes are not only deliberate, they are also organized'.[95] In Boston, the merchants formed the Boston Society for Encouraging Trade and Commerce with the intent of addressing British trade restrictions against their financial interests.[96] Their organization allowed a consensus to develop with many of the participants in the smuggling trade able to influence political events in the community. In a city with a population of approximately 15,000, though only about 1,500 adult males met the property requirements for voting, the merchants of Boston, totaling between 200 and 350 at any given time in the immediate years prior to the Revolution, tended to dominate the political process of the community, as well as the legislation and courts of the colony.[97] Finally, the 'businessman [. . .] thinks of himself as a respectable citizen and, by and large, is so regarded by the general public'.[98] For years the penalties for smuggling were against the goods and vessels involved—not the citizen-smuggler—which differentiated smuggling for many in the community from the stereotypical crimes against a person and the smugglers from the 'common' criminals, thereby helping to protect the self-image and public image of the merchants involved in the traffic. The merchants of Boston not only thought of themselves as respectable, but many thought themselves patriots as the Revolution approached. Sutherland may have been referring to corporations 150 years later, but the colonial merchants of America served as the precursor to his modern corporation and to his concept of white-collar crime.[99]

THE BIRTH OF AMERICAN CUSTOMS—AND AMERICAN SMUGGLING

With the end of the Revolutionary War and the eventual ratification of the Constitution, the U.S. government formally was granted the ability to finance its responsibilities through the auspices of the customs. The previous guiding document of the federal government, the Articles of Confederation, left the collection of customs duties in the hands of the individual sovereign states, leading in some cases to individual states collecting duties on domestic goods shipped interstate. With Section 8 of the Constitution's first article stating that Congress shall have power 'To lay and collect taxes, Duties, Imposts and Excises [. . .] but all Duties, Imposts and Excises shall be uniform throughout the United States' the new federal legislature wasted little time in formally approving the creation of an organization to initiate the collection of duties. The Tariff Act of July 4, 1789,[100] the Tonnage Act of July 20,[101] and the subsequent statute of July 31[102] establishing fifty-nine customs districts in eleven states (Rhode Island and North Carolina had yet to ratify the Constitution) formed the foundation of the original Customs Service, its operations primarily marine based. Not until March 2, 1799 and the passage of the Customs Administration Act would a land border be of serious concern.[103]

With the creation of the Department of Treasury,[104] the executive department overseeing the subsidiary customs shortly after its own establishment, along with the appointment of Alexander Hamilton as the secretary of the Treasury and the official responsible for the development and management of the nation's finances and of customs, the principle source of income for the emergent nation, the intent of Congress finally would be fulfilled.[105] Hamilton's view of the new republic, as a 'great commonwealth' of economic development in partnership with the affluent demonstrated an acceptance of an American Dream of economic prosperity, was fully supported by the merchants of the seaport communities of America,[106] and led to the creation of a symbiotic customs organization both supporting the trade and merchant community while also building the financial foundation of the nation from the fees and duties collected from them. Within days of Hamilton's appointment, the merchants expressed their own feelings regarding contraband trade and its potential harm to the new order in the *Gazette of the United States*, Philadelphia, September 19, 1789:

> We, the subscribers, Merchants and Traders of the city of Philadelphia, do hereby pledge ourselves to each other, and to our fellow-citizens at large, that we will not be concerned directly or indirectly in any trade contrary to the revenue laws of the United States; but will; by every effort of our power, discourage such illicit practices, by not employing, or by dismissing from our service, any master or Mate of a vessel, or any Pilot, who shall be engaged in a contraband trade, or in aiding or abetting others in such collusive employments.[107]

Hamilton, believing that '[e]xorbitant duties on imported articles would beget a general spirit of smuggling',[108] also recognized that after years of evasion, traders would be inclined to continue past illicit practices if economically feasible. James Madison recommended a low general tariff of 5 percent to 15 percent ad valorem, which was incorporated in the Tariff Act of 1789. The tariff was low enough to prevent avoidance when balanced against the penalties, which could include the seizure and forfeiture of the offending vessel. Instead of being primarily a protective duty, new tariffs became a revenue enhancing mechanism, with 88 percent of the nation's revenue deriving from the Customs Service in the first ten years.[109]

Hamilton's initial focus was on building a unified customs organization staffed in most cases by individuals who were 'rewarded for their services during the Revolutionary War'[110] with many having served as state customs officers under the Articles of Confederation.[111] The positions within the service—from collectors, surveyors, and naval officers to the tide waiters and land waiters—mimicked what had already been in place before independence and carried down through the individual states into the new republic. Yet within a year, on August 4, 1790, the first preventive force to be created to frustrate potential smuggling—instead of being responsible for the collection of the revenue—was authorized with the passage of 'An Act to Provide more Efficiently the Collection of Duties'.[112] This act further developed a set of laws that framed the boundaries of the unacceptable and deviant from the respectable and legal. It also became the genesis of the revenue cutters of the republic and of the future Coast Guard. Though the Act of July 31, 1789, imposed penalties, including forfeiture, for the concealment of goods subject to duty—the classic definition of smuggling—without such a preventative force 'the many creeks and inlets [and] the great number of small craft [were] great inducements to evil disposed people to attempt evading the laws'.[113]

Historically numerous techniques were used to circumvent the customs laws. For ships entering and clearing through customs, simply declaring a lesser quantity of manifested goods reduced any duties proportionately. For a boarding officer, sifting through the hold of a merchant vessel was both a difficult and hazardous responsibility, at best. For those ports where the potential for actual inspection was greatest, disguising a high duty or contraband cargo in the container used by a low duty or legal cargo was not unusual. If cargo was taxed by weight, heavier containers were concealed at the bottom of cargo holds, while the lighter ones were stacked on the upper layers of cargo, and were therefore more easily available to the customs officials who calculated the total weight of the cargo and its respective duty. If duty was based on the number of casks instead of weight, larger casks would be surreptitiously built and used to ship the cargo. Forged papers were another method used to conceal cargoes, ports of embarkation, and bond postings. All of the proceeding techniques were forms of misrepresentation and under the new republic, a fraud upon the revenue.[114] The system developed by Hamilton was one designed to address these frauds, as well as directly addressing those vessels—and captains—who smuggled simply by concealing goods and attempting to land them in port. Correspondence between Hamilton and the collector of Boston, Benjamin Lincoln, identified one scheme: the use of a smaller 'hovering vessel' to offload a shipment of fish from the schooner *Bee* and land it without the payment of duty prior to the *Bee* actually entering port.[115] For those vessels attempting to run goods into the new republic without formally entering and clearing, the ten original cutters became a primary method of suppression, if for no other reason than that their very presence made the profit in non-taxed goods not worth the expense when compared to the potential in fines, penalties, and forfeitures.

Yet with the implementation of a tariff acceptable to the merchants while also having a system in place that minimized the benefits of commercial smuggling as celebrated during the colonial years, the government was able to unite the wants of the merchants with the needs of the new government. Revenue cutters, originally built and manned with the intent of interdicting smugglers, turned, with what one can only assume was a lack of employment, to other tasks including charting and coastal survey, and in aiding in the enforcement of local quarantine and health laws of the different states.[116] The attitude of the captains of the various revenue cutters toward preventing smuggling reached a point that it was considered to be 'almost degrading'.[117] Annual receipts from fines, penalties and forfeitures to the United States would total only $657 over the next eight years.[118] 'Thereafter, from approximately 1792 through the end of Hamilton's secretaryship, [smuggling] incidents and patterns largely disappear from the correspondence record [of the Treasury]. What remains is almost completely the minutiae of a smoothly running system'.[119]

When Edwin Sutherland described the concept of white-collar crime, though he was referring to the businessmen of his own generation, he also recognized that the 'robber barons' of the previous century provided a historical linkage to his contemporary corporate criminals. His own ideas built on Robert Merton's explanation of how American society placed a high emphasis on economic success, identified as the American Dream for many, that led some to use the most expedient methods to achieve their objectives. That extreme emphasis upon wealth as the symbol of success led some to 'innovation' in order to achieve their financial goals by methods in conflict with society's approved means.

Sutherland's premise postulated that criminal behavior is learned through interaction, taking place in intimate groups, such as those found in business settings, and that when the weight of those learned values supports activity in violation of a specific law, that law will be ignored. One group of laws violated by the colonists prior to the birth of the United States was the English Crown's smuggling statutes. Profit drove the trade between the colonies and various European and Caribbean markets, avoiding English duties and circumventing embargos on numerous occasions. The business partnerships of the colonial traders—Sutherland's intimate business groups—were the fount of white-collar crime in the colonies. Eventually the 'benign neglect' of the British government ended, leading to a concerted enforcement of the revenue laws and straining the relationship between the Crown and her colonies, finally becoming a contributory cause of the revolution and the creation of the United States of America.

Over the first 150 years of the new nation's existence, a level of social disorganization presented some members of the business community with an 'excess of definitions' in favor of violating the nation's smuggling statutes, believing money, whatever its source, was the defining symbol of success. It would only take twenty years for these same merchants who had circumvented the revenue laws while colonists to return to their past practices when put under financial strain by their new government, a government threatening their own personal wealth and thereby what they perceived as their economic success and social status within their communities. Once again, the political, legal, and business interests would intersect to the detriment of the nation.

NOTES

1. Edwin H. Sutherland, 'White-collar Criminality', *American Sociological Review*, 5 (February 1940), 1–12 (p. 2).
2. David E. Ruth, *Inventing the Public Enemy: The Gangster in American Culture, 1918–1934* (Chicago: University of Chicago Press, 1996), p. 45.
3. Michael Woodiwiss, *Organized Crime and American Power: A History* (Toronto: University of Toronto Press, 2001), pp. 227–311.
4. *ibid.*, p. 7.
5. Alan L. Karras, *Smuggling: Contraband and Corruption in World History* (Lanham, MD: Rowman and Littlefield, 2010), p. 49.
6. Ezra 7:24, *The New Oxford Annotated Bible with the Apocrypha, RSV* (New York: Oxford University Press, 1977), p. 581.
7. One of the inherent difficulties of understanding the extent of smuggling is the lack of records documenting the crime. As Barrow states, 'Illegal trade does not leave official records'. Because of this limitation, in many cases 'only general, and undoubtedly controversial, conclusions may be offered' when discussing the extent of the problem. Different stakeholders may have different and sometimes opposing agendas in making conclusions based on the same available data. See Thomas C. Barrow, *Trade and Empire: The British Customs Service in Colonial America, 1660–1775* (Cambridge, MA: Harvard University Press, 1967), p. 143; John W. Tyler, *Smugglers and Patriots: Boston Merchants and the Advent of the American Revolution* (Boston, MA: Northeastern University Press, 1986), p. 13.
8. Graham Smith, *King's Cutters: The Revenue Service and the War against Smuggling* (London: Conway Maritime Press, 1983), p. 7.
9. Peter Gillman with Paul Hamann, *The Duty Men: The Inside Story of the Customs* (London: BBC Books, 1987), p. 76.
10. Fernand Braudel, *The Mediterranean and the Mediterranean World in the Age of Philip II, Volume I* (New York: Harper Colophon, 1976), p. 391.
11. *ibid.*, p. 449; Ethan A. Nadelmann, *Cops across Borders: The Internationalization of U.S. Criminal Law Enforcement* (University Park: Pennsylvania State University Press, 1993), p. 19.
12. Eastland Company, *The Acts and Ordinances of the Eastland Company*, ed. by Maud Sellers (London: Royal Historical Society, 1906), pp. 15–16, 61.
13. J.K. Fedorowicz, *England's Baltic Trade in the Early Seventeenth Century: A Study in Anglo-Polish Commercial Diplomacy* (Cambridge: Cambridge University Press, 1980), p. 57.

14. *ibid.*, pp. 133, 146–147.
15. Braudel, *The Mediterranean*, p. 478.
16. *ibid.*, p. 478.
17. *ibid.*, p. 496.
18. C.H. Haring, *The Spanish Empire in America* (New York: Harcourt, Brace and World, 1963), p. 89.
19. Rafael Donoso Anes, 'Accounting and Slavery: The Accounts of the English South Sea Company, 1713–22', *European Accounting Review*, 11:2 (2002), 441–452 (pp. 443–445).
20. Lester D. Langley, *America and the Americas: United States in the Western Hemisphere* (Athens: University of Georgia Press, 1983), p.13; N.A.M. Roger, *The Command of the Ocean: A Naval History of Britain, 1619–1815* (New York: W.W. Norton, 2004), p. 234.
21. Gerhard Mercator, *Orbis Terrae Compendiosa Descripitio* [Amsterdam, 1637?], Map Division, John H. Levine Bequest 97–7397, New York Public Library, New York, NY, URL: http://digitalgallery.nypl.org/nypldigital/dgkeysearchdetail.cfm?strucID=773787&imageID=1524650#_seemore [Date accessed: December 25, 2013].
22. Oliver Rink, *Holland on the Hudson: An Economic and Social History of Dutch New York* (Ithaca, NY: Cornell University Press, 1986), n90, pp. 133, 144.
23. Carl Lotus Becker, *Beginnings of the American People* (Boston, MA: Houghton Mifflin, 1915), p. 131.
24. Peggy K. Liss, *Atlantic Empires: The Network of Trade and Revolution, 1712–1826* (Baltimore, MD: Johns Hopkins, 1983), pp. 2–10.
25. Lance Grahn, *The Political Economy of Smuggling: Regional Informal Economics in Early Bourbon New Granada* (Boulder, CO: Westview Press, 1997), p. 27.
26. *ibid.*, pp. 4–5.
27. Jim Cullen, *The American Dream: A Short History of an Idea that Shaped a Nation* (Oxford: Oxford University Press, 2003), p. 13; Alan Taylor, *American Colonies: The Settling of North America*, ed. by Eric Foner, The Penguin History of the United States, I (New York: Penguin, 2001), pp. 301–323.
28. Herbert S. Osgood, *The American Colonies in the Seventeenth Century*, 3 vols. (New York, 1904–1907), III, 310, cited in Barrow, *Trade and Empire*, p. 33.
29. Barrow, *Trade and Empire*, p. 33.
30. W. L. Grant and J. Mason, (eds), *Acts of the Privy Council of England, Colonial Series*, 6 vols (London: Anthony Brothers, 1908–1912), I, No. 77; Barrow, *Trade and Empire*, p. 5.
31. C.H. Firth, R.S. Rait (eds),'October 1651: An Act for Increase of Shipping, and Encouragement of the Navigation of this Nation', Acts and Ordinances of the Interregnum, 1642–1660, British History Online, www.british-history.ac.uk/report.aspx?compid=56457.
32. 12 Charles II, c. 18 (Eng.).
33. Barrow, *Trade and Empire*, pp. 5–6, 12–13; 15 Charles II, c. 7 (Eng.).
34. 25 Charles II, c.7 (Eng.).
35. Barrow, *Trade and Empire*, pp. 14–15.
36. J. W. Fortescue (ed), "America and West Indies: August 1696, 17–31," Calendar of State Papers Colonial, America and West Indies, Volume 15: 1696–1697, British History Online, www.british-history.ac.uk/report.aspx?compid=70866; Edmund Burke cited in Jerome R. Reich, *British Friends of the American Revolution* (Armonk, NY: M.E. Sharpe, 1998), XV, p. 5.

37. Samuel G. Margolin, 'Lawlessness on the Maritime Frontier of the Greater Chesapeake, 1650–1750' (unpublished doctoral dissertation, College of William and Mary, 1992), pp. 93–95.
38. J. W. Fortescue (ed), "America and West Indies: August 1696, 17–31," Calendar of State Papers Colonial, America and West Indies, Volume 15: 1696–1697, British History Online, www.british-history.ac.uk/report. aspx?compid=70866
39. Margolin, 'Lawlessness on the Maritime Frontier', pp. 95–100.
40. J. W. Fortescue (ed), "America and West Indies: February 1686," Calendar of State Papers Colonial, America and West Indies, Volume 12: 1685–1688 and Addenda 1653–1687, British History Online, www.british-history.ac.uk/ report.aspx?compid=70499; Thomas M. Truxes, *Irish-American Trade: 1660–1783* (Cambridge: Cambridge University Press, 1988), pp. 43–45.
41. Margolin, 'Lawlessness on the Maritime Frontier', p. 92.
42. Barrow, *Trade and Empire*, p. 31.
43. Edward Randolph, *Edward Randolph 1676–1703, Including His Letters and Official Papers from the New England Middle and Southern Colonies in America*, ed. by Robert N. Toppan and Alfred T. Goodrick, 7 vols (New York: Burt Franklin, 1967), V, 135, as cited in Margolin, 'Lawlessness on the Maritime Frontier', p. 111.
44. Margolin, 'Lawlessness on the Maritime Frontier', pp. 105–110.
45. *ibid.*, p. 159; Arthur Pierce Middleton, *Tobacco Coast: A Maritime History of Chesapeake Bay in the Colonial Era* (Baltimore, MD: Johns Hopkins University Press, 1984), pp. 209–210.
46. Cecil Headlam (ed), "America and West Indies: February 1714," Calendar of State Papers Colonial, America and West Indies, Volume 27: 1712–1714, British History Online, www.british-history.ac.uk/report.aspx?compid=73930 &strquery=.
47. Cecil Headlam (ed) and Arthur Percival Newton (introduction), "America and West Indies: October 1724, 16–31," Calendar of State Papers Colonial, America and West Indies, Volume 34: 1724–1725, British History Online, www.british-history.ac.uk/report.aspx?compid=72399&strquery=.
48. 6 George II. c. 13 (Eng.).
49. Oliver M. Dickerson, *The Navigation Acts and the American Revolution* (Philadelphia: University of Pennsylvania Press, 1951), p. 16; Jan Rogozinski, *A Brief History of the Caribbean* (New York: Plume, 2000), pp. 108–111; 6 George II, c. 13 (Eng.); 15 George II, c. 25 (Eng.); 33 George II, c. 28 (Eng.); 6 George III, c. 47 (Eng.).
50. K. G. Davies (ed), "America and West Indies: March 1737, 1-15," Calendar of State Papers Colonial, America and West Indies, Volume 43: 1737, British History Online, www.british-history.ac.uk/report.aspx?compid=72900&strquery=; Middleton, *Tobacco Coast*, pp. 220–221.
51. Timothy Orne to George Dodge, July 18, 1758, Timothy Orne manuscripts, Essex Institute, Salem, MA, as referenced in Barrow, *Trade and Empire*, p. 142.
52. Dickerson, *The Navigation Acts*, p. 17.
53. Charles Sellers, *The Market Revolution: Jacksonian America, 1815–1846* (New York: Oxford University Press, 1991), p. 21.
54. James Dick and Stewart Company, Letter Book, 1773–1781, Duke University Library, Durham, NC, pp. 14, 17, 19, 20, 29, 34, 68, and 82, as cited in Edward C. Papenfuse, *In Pursuit of Profit: The Annapolis Merchants in the Era of the American Revolution, 1763–1805* (Baltimore, MD: Johns Hopkins Press, 1975), pp. 46 n.24, 47 n.26.
55. Arthur M. Schlesinger, *The Colonial Merchants and the American Revolution* (New York: Columbia University, 1918), pp. 388–392.

56. Edwin H. Sutherland, *White Collar Crime: The Uncut Version* (New Haven, CT: Yale University Press, 1983), pp. 229–230.

57. William T. Baxter, *The House of Hancock: Business in Boston, 1724–1775* (Cambridge, MA: Harvard University Press, 1945), pp. 53–54.

58. Letter book, August 12, 1736, Greene, October 22, 1736, Checkering, Hancock Family Papers, Baker Library, Harvard Business School, Cambridge, MA, as cited in Baxter, *The House of Hancock*, p. 54 n.34.

59. Letter book, October 22, 1736, Checkering, December 20, 1736, Storke, as cited in Baxter, *The House of Hancock*, p. 55 n.35.

60. Baxter, *House of Hancock*, pp. 54–55.

61. Letter book, August 11, 1740, Wilks, as cited in Baxter, *The House of Hancock*, p. 73 n.46.

62. Baxter, *House of Hancock*, p. 85.

63. Baxter, *House of Hancock*, pp. 85–86; *Boston Post-Boy*, June 21, 1742, p. 3; *A Report of the Record Commissioners of the City of Boston Containing the Records of Boston Selectmen, 1736–1742* (Boston, MA: Rockwell and Churchill, 1886), p. 227; Sutherland, 'White-collar Criminality', p. 1.

64. Letter book, 1745–1748, as cited in Baxter, *House of Hancock*, p. 94 n. 17.

65. Letter book, April 17, 1755 and May 27, 1755, Hopes, as cited in Baxter, *House of Hancock*, p. 117, 117, n.27; *Boston Evening Post*, June 1, 1761, p. 1; *Boston Evening Post*, May 31, 1762, p. 3; *Boston Weekly News-Letter*, May 29, 1760, p. 1; *Boston Weekly News-Letter and New-England Chronicle*, May 31, 1764, supplement, p. 1.

66. Sutherland, *White Collar Crime*, pp. 246–250.

67. Barrow, *Trade and Empire*, p. 162; Middleton, *Tobacco Coast*, pp. 212–213.

68. Virginia D. Harrington, *The New York Merchant on the Eve of the Revolution* (Gloucester, MA: Peter Smith, 1964), p. 255.

69. Dickerson, *The Navigation Acts*, pp. 88–91; Sutherland, 'White-collar Criminality', p. 1.

70. Baxter, *The House of Hancock*, p. 135.

71. Tyler, *Smugglers and Patriots*, p. 26.

72. Liss, *Atlantic Empires*, pp. 30–31, 39–40.

73. Treasury official Henry McCulloh offered the lower figure while Thomas Whately, George Grenville's secretary, claimed the latter in *The Regulations Lately Made Concerning the Colonies and the Taxes Imposed Upon Them, Considered* (London: J. Wilkie, 1765), as noted in Tyler, *Smugglers and Patriots*, p. 77, n.25.

74. Tyler, *Smugglers and Patriots*, p. 78.

75. *ibid.*, p. 8.

76. *ibid.*, pp. 8–16.

77. *ibid.*, pp. 16–17.

78. Sutherland, *White Collar Crime*, p. 229.

79. *Boston Chronicle*, April 4 to April 11, 1768, p. 151.

80. Baxter, *The House of Hancock*, pp. 260–261.

81. D. H. Watson, 'Joseph Harrison and the *Liberty* Incident', *William and Mary Quarterly*, 3rd ser., 20 (1963), 585–595, (p. 589).

82. *Boston Weekly News-Letter and New-England Chronicle*, June 23, 1768, p. 2; *Providence Gazette and Country Journal*, September 23 to September 30, 1769, p. 1.

83. Baxter, *The House of Hancock*, pp. 262–268; Dickerson, *The Navigation Acts*, pp. 231–250; Neil R. Strout, *The Royal Navy in America, 1760–1775: A Study of Enforcement of British Colonial Policy in the Era of the American Revolution* (Annapolis, MD: Naval Institute Press, 1973), p. 140; *Newport Mercury*, July 24, 1789, p. 3.

84. O.M. Dickerson, 'John Hancock: Notorious Smuggler or Near Victim of British Customs Racketeers?', *Mississippi Valley Historical Review*, 32 (1945–1946), 517–540 (pp. 532–534).
85. Tyler, *Smugglers and Patriots*, p. 90.
86. *ibid.*, p. 91.
87. *Massachusetts Gazette and Boston Post-Boy*, March 2, 1775, as cited in Tyler, *Smugglers and Patriots*, p. 234.
88. Tyler, *Smugglers and Patriots*, p. 235.
89. James S. Leamon, *Revolution Downeast: The War for American Independence in Maine* (Amherst, MA: University of Massachusetts Press, 1993), pp. 178, 138–139, cited in Joshua M. Smith, 'The Rogues of 'Quoddy: Smuggling in the Maine-New Brunswick Borderlands, 1783–1820' (unpublished doctoral dissertation, University of Maine, 2003), p. 36.
90. Sutherland, *White Collar Crime*, p. 227.
91. *ibid.*, p. 228.
92. Barrow, *Trade and Empire*, pp. 163–164.
93. Sutherland, *White Collar Crime*, pp. 228–229.
94. *ibid.*, p. 229.
95. *ibid.*, p. 229.
96. Tyler, *Smugglers and Patriots*, pp. 19–20.
97. *ibid.*, p. 8.
98. Sutherland, *White Collar Crime*, p. 230.
99. Barrow, *Trade and Empire*, p. 154; Sutherland, *White Collar Crime*, pp. 227–235; Tyler, *Smugglers and Patriots*, pp. 145, 174.
100. 1 *Stat.* 24, c. 2 (1789).
101. 1 *Stat.* 27, c. 3 (1789).
102. 1 *Stat.* 29, c. 5 (1789).
103. 1 *Stat.* 627, c. 22 (1799).
104. 1 *Stat.* 65, c. 12 (1789).
105. *Senate Executive Journal*, 1st Cong., 2nd sess., September 11, 1789.
106. David Hackett Fischer, *Liberty and Freedom: A Visual History of America's Founding Ideas* (New York: Oxford University Press, 2004), p. 199.
107. Roger P. Vance, 'The First Federal Customs', *U.S. Naval Institute Proceeding*, March 1976, p. 50, as cited in Michael N. Ingrisano, Jr., *A History of Enforcement in the United States Customs Service, 1789–1875* (Washington, D.C.: U.S. Customs Service, 1988), p. 15.
108. Alexander Hamilton (as Publius), *Federalist No. 35* (1788).
109. Carl E. Prince and Mollie Keller, *The U.S. Customs Service: A Bicentennial History* (Washington, D.C.: U.S. Customs Service, 1989), p. 36.
110. Michael N. Ingrisano, Jr., *The First Officers of the United States Customs Service: Appointed by President George Washington in 1789* (Washington, D.C.: U.S. Customs Service, 1987), p. 4.
111. Vance, 'The First Federal Customs', p. 48 as cited in Ingrisano, *A History of Enforcement*, p. 13.
112. 1 *Stat.* 145, c. 35 (1789).
113. Florence Kern, *James Montgomery's U.S. Revenue Cutter, General Green*, (Washington, D.C.: Alised Enterprises, 1975), pp. 6–7, as cited in Ingrisano, *A History of Enforcement in the United States Customs Service*, p. 16.
114. Margolin, 'Lawlessness on the Maritime Frontier', pp. 70–78.
115. Benjamin Lincoln to Alexander Hamilton, October 20, 1791, in *Correspondence of the Secretary of Treasury with Collectors of Customs, 1789–1833*, 39 rolls (National Archives Microfilm Publications), microcopy no. 178, as cited in Robert Copeland Ayer, 'Shifty Seafarers, Shifting Winds: Government Policies toward Maritime Smuggling in North America from

Colonization to the War of 1812' (unpublished doctoral dissertation, Tufts University, 1993), p. 189.

116. *Impartial Herald*, January 26, 1796, p.1; *Massachusetts Mercury*, May 20, 1796, p. 2.
117. *Sun*, May 3, 1802, p. 1.
118. American State Papers: Finance 1:665.
119. Ayer, 'Shifty Seafarers', p. 193.

2   The Embargo of 1807–1809 and the War of 1812

When Sutherland presented his concept of white-collar crime, he argued 'that persons of the upper socioeconomic class engage in much criminal behavior; that this criminal behavior differs from the criminal behavior of the lower socioeconomic class principally in the administrative procedures which are used in dealing with offenders; and that variations in administrative procedures are not significant from the point of view of causation of crime'.[1] The merchants of the newly established United States formed the core of Sutherland's 'upper socioeconomic class' in the major communities along the eastern seaboard. Having become the hub of American trade, developing business links throughout the maritime trade routes, their business success gave them wealth and social position little changed from colonial times.[2] Boston and like-minded merchant towns were places where 'everybody was at work trying to make money and money was becoming the only real avenue to power and success both socially and in the regard of your fellow-man'.[3] By 1830, that entrepreneurship led to two-thirds of the richest Boston citizens being merchants.[4]

Operating out of small counting houses with minimal staff, these merchants nonetheless developed intricate and large networks of partnerships requiring both trust and vigilance. That trust was reinforced through social interaction among their peers and through marriages tying the various families together. By 1835 more than 70 percent of the seventy-nine wealthiest families of Boston were related.[5] Their influence carried over to the political arena with the merchant elite supporting the Federalist Party. The party's ideology of a strong, central government was believed to offer political and financial stability, and financial growth through a managed public debt and a national bank, both of which were seen as beneficial to business.[6] This party support allowed like-minded individuals to be appointed to the revenue and judicial positions that had a direct impact on the enforcement of the smuggling and neutrality statutes of the federal government. Half of the Federalist appointments of which an informed determination can be made were gentry, elite, or upper class.[7] As Sutherland suggests, their influence paid dividends in how these elites were affected by government regulation. In 1802, the collector of customs at Plymouth, Massachusetts, was accused of being a ' "bitter federalist" in customs business, one who "winked at the fraud of [merchant followers in] his party" '.[8] Secretary of the Treasury Alexander Hamilton advised Jeremiah Olney, the collector of the Providence, Rhode Island, port, that he was considered by some to be in 'some instances too *punctilious* and not sufficiently accommodating' and that '[t]he good will of the Merchants is very important in many senses, and if can be secured without any improper sacrifice or introducing a looseness of practice, it is desirable to do it'.[9] It was these business and social elites who pursued smuggling as their source of wealth and, by extension, their source of success as an era of social disorganization developed in Europe capable of reaching across the Atlantic.

With the passage of the Tariff Act of July 4, 1789, primarily designed to fund the new republic by instituting a moderate tariff rate on imported goods, smuggling was no longer the problem it was during the colonial period. Some domestic smuggling, however, would be reported in the local newspapers, such as furs from Nova Scotia seized in Boston, puncheons of rum off-loaded from a Jamaican sloop prior to docking in New Jersey, a small quantity of broadcloth from a British packet ship in New York being confiscated, and jewelry valued at over four thousand dollars in Charleston forfeited with a local jeweler being fined four hundred dollars.[10] Yet American merchants and vessels continued to be involved in smuggling throughout the greater Atlantic area, the smuggling not being into the United States but into the harbors and coasts of other sovereign nations and their possessions. These organized smuggling and fraud ventures of American traders included contraband into and out of such locations as the Canadian provinces,[11] England,[12] Bermuda,[13] and Spanish Havana.[14]

European wars offered many an opportunity for trade both in Europe and throughout the Caribbean. For the merchants of America, wherever a profit could be turned, so it seemed they would venture. 'Colonial Americans pursued wealth more freely than Europeans because they were not overshadowed and hemmed in by aristocrats and post feudal institutions. And they pursued wealth more avidly because it made them the American equivalents of aristocrats'.[15] With warring states' own merchant fleets subject to seizure, belligerents turned to neutral American shipping in order to fill the void.[16] As fresh opportunities presented themselves, new entrepreneurs would enter the market for their own chance at success. Prosperity was on an exceptional rise, attested to in the growth in value of exports and re-exported goods from $2.5 million in 1790 to almost $165 million in 1807, and the value of imports climbing from $23.8 million to $144.7 million in the same period; earnings from shipping also increased from almost $6 million to over $42 million.[17] Numerous ancillary services developed in support of this commerce and major seaports doubled and, in the case of New York, almost tripled in population between 1790 and 1810.[18] As statistician James Seybert commented, '[T]he most adventurous became the most wealthy'.[19] The profits and adventure of this period led one maritime historian, Robert Albion, to call this the 'heroic age' of the U.S. merchant marine.[20]

With no American laws in place preventing an American bottom (vessel) from profiting in the trade to belligerent parties nor in the smuggling of goods into a third country, many availed themselves of the opportunities presented. The difficulty, however, was that once a practice of smuggling into a European nation's territory was considered acceptable for a new generation of merchants and seamen, it was but a short sail to use the same techniques, if circumstance required, into or out of the United States. As Sutherland stated in his theory of differential association, criminal behavior is learned, and when an excess of definitions favors violating the legal code, the law is ignored.[21] The time for American mercantilists to not only violate the laws of other nations but also federal law as well was fast approaching.

In 1801, when Thomas Jefferson became the third president, he attempted to address the partisanship of the previous decade and to unite the differing parties. Successful among the populous during his first years in office and having carried all of the states except Connecticut and Delaware in 1805, Jefferson achieved numerous political successes.[22] By his second term, however, Jefferson's foreign policy opened the door to a level of defiance against the government by farmers and merchants alike unheard of since the British ruled the Atlantic seaboard. Jefferson's foreign policy was also the catalyst to the second great smuggling era in North America. As Smith remarked in his seminal work on borderlands and smuggling, referring to smugglers and governments in conflict world-wide, '[T]his struggle was linked to an increasing commercial impulse related to the rise of capitalistic economic systems, and the growing needs for the state to control its borders to tax and regulate commerce'.[23] In pursuit of an economic version of the American Dream, from the initiation of the embargo in 1807 until after the termination of war in 1815, American commerce ignored the demands of Jefferson, Madison, and the national government for its own 'worldly achievement' and, once again, deliberately organized to successfully circumvent the federal law for individual and corporate profit, innovating—in both the traditional sense and in Merton's use of the phrase—when few other opportunities presented themselves.[24]

The precursor to the War of 1812 was found in American maritime trade and its conflict with British economic interests—and in Jefferson's failure to secure an accommodation with the most formidable sea power in the world, even when the opportunity presented itself. The United States profited from trade as a neutral nation while Britain and France continued their hostilities, increasing its exports to $108 million in 1807 from $54 million in 1803, however, British courts would enforce a maritime doctrine that prevented the United States from transshipping trade goods from France through the United States and then on to French colonies in the Caribbean.[25] Though most of the estimated three hundred to four hundred ships seized by the British navy under the *Essex* decision were ultimately released, not until

May of 1806 did government action eventually overrule the admiralty court decision. With insurance on cargo increasing by a factor of four, the loss to American merchants in the meantime would be 'staggering'.[26]

The impressment of seamen aboard American flagged vessels was another issue of consequence in the relationship between the U.S. and British governments. Because Britain had been at war for an extended period, the need for seamen to serve on her naval vessels was extreme. With American merchant vessels paying better than British vessels, besides not putting their crews in harm's way, as many as one-half of American sailors involved in foreign trade were estimated to hold British citizenship.[27] British naval crews would stop and board both private and public American vessels, even in some cases within American territorial waters, in order to determine the nationality of the crews and impress any they suspected of holding British citizenship— the firing upon, boarding, and impressments of crewmembers of the U.S.S. *Chesapeake* by the H.M.S. *Leopard* being the most flagrant example. In early 1808, Congress estimated that in excess of 4,200 American seamen had been impressed by the British since the renewal of European war in 1803, noting that impressments took place even while in neutral ports.[28]

Other grievances concerned the seizure of contraband goods shipped via American bottoms and 'paper' blockades of belligerent ports in lieu of physical confinement of enemy harbors with British enforcement taking place in contravention of international law. The definition of contraband conflicted between the two states with Britain taking a more expansive position on what was considered contraband.[29]

In 1806, France entered the fray with the Berlin Decree, stating that any neutral vessel that called at a British port was denied entry to French harbors and that all British manufactured goods were contraband, regardless the ownership. The British responded with a series of Orders in Council creating a 'paper' blockade of all ports that denied entry of British goods and directing that all neutrals attempting trade with those ports must clear through a British port prior to landing in a 'blockaded' port. France countered with the Milan Decree, informing all that any vessel compliant with British regulations was forfeit. Attempting trade with either warring party by American neutral vessels was, in theory, a legal impossibility. As with many such laws and regulations both warring states only enforced the various decrees when immediately advantageous, Britain issuing special licenses and France granting exemptions whenever doing so was beneficial.[30]

Though Jefferson authorized diplomatic action in an attempt to address these on-going grievances (as demonstrated by the Monroe-Pinkney Treaty) and though the British formally denounced the violent and forcible boarding of the *Chesapeake* and the seizure of four British deserters, offering reparations and the release of three of the deserters believed to be American citizens, Jefferson eventually declined the opportunity to accept a treaty with Great Britain. Instead, he attempted to force the hand of Britain with economic sanctions. 'All the United States had to do, the Republicans believed, was to turn the economic screws and the European belligerents would be brought to terms, if not to their knees'.[31] To the chagrin of the administration, the sanctions did more long-term damage to American mercantile interests, and to Americans' own acceptance of the rule of law, and the needs of a centralized government than they ever did to British or French will.[32]

The first of a series of non-importation and embargo laws was passed in early 1806 in an attempt to influence the British by limiting the importation of various non-critical manufactured goods; with ongoing diplomatic trade discussions with Britain, the law was, but for one short period, not implemented until late in the following year.[33] But by the end of the year, Jefferson and the Republican Congress passed the first embargo law, one of draconian wording for American commerce. The law prohibited all ships and vessels from clearing for a foreign port and demanded the payment of a bond equal to double the value of the vessel and cargo in order to guarantee that those vessels with cargoes claiming to be bound for another domestic harbor would, in fact, re-land the cargo in some port of the United States.[34] Jefferson's political agenda, originally enforced by this sequence of restrictive maritime laws (as the British had previously attempted), brought his administration into direct conflict with the business interests of the economic elite of the American Northeast.

The embargo legislation was followed by two more laws, tightening the loopholes in the original statute. Licensed coastal traders, fishing, whaling, and other small vessels were incorporated into the embargo requirements with fishing and whaling vessels required to post a bond at four times the value of the vessel and cargo, and licensed vessels 'confined to rivers, bays and sounds' posting a bond of three hundred dollars per ton of vessel. The statute also designated penalties for violating the embargo, including forfeiture of vessel and cargo for departing without a permit or for being involved in any prohibited foreign voyage. The master or any other persons concerned with the trade were subject to a fine of one thousand to twenty thousand dollars, with the owner liable for twice the value of the ship or vessel and cargo if the vessel was not seized. Foreign vessels were also prohibited from shipping 'specie or any goods, wares or other merchandise', they also being subject to seizure and forfeiture. The next law limited the length of time a coastal trader was allowed to complete its journey to four months, and it addressed the smuggling traffic to and from Canada by authorizing the seizure of land conveyances of contraband goods and penalties of up to ten thousand dollars for those involved, setting bonds for foreign vessels domestically re-landing cargo to four times the value of the vessel and cargo, lowering to two hundred dollars per ton for vessels 'confined to rivers bays, sounds and lakes'. It also eliminated bonds for vessels not masted or, if masted, not decked and confined to rivers, bays, and sounds in areas not adjacent to foreign territory. Finally, the president was authorized to grant permission to citizens of the United States to send vessels in ballast to recover and import property held outside the United States prior to December 22, 1807.[35]

The fourth and fifth laws continued to address various maneuvers around the original law by requiring 'vessel(s) of any description whatsoever' to be incorporated under the statutes (not including packets, ferry-boats, and vessels exempted from the obligation of giving any bond whatever) decreasing transit time for coastal traders in half with minor exceptions, and establishing penalties for unauthorized departures and for failure to provide a certificate of landing in the appropriate time frame. Restrictions upon Mississippi River marine traffic were also specified. Revenue cutters, revenue boats, public armed vessels (naval vessels), and gun boats of the United States were all authorized to enforce the embargo with the statute specifying that they were authorized to board any vessel 'which there may be reason to suspect' was in violation of the embargo acts. These laws also prohibited foreign vessels from participating in the coasting trade. The local collector of customs was given further authority to 'detain any vessel ostensibly bound with a cargo to some other port in the United States' merely based on the suspicion that 'the intention [was] to violate or evade' the embargo. That policing authority also carried over to detaining 'any unusual deposits of provisions, lumber, or other articles of domestic growth or manufacture' in any port adjacent to foreign territory, pending the posting of a bond guaranteeing the goods would be delivered to some other port within the United States.[36] Each individual law was an attempt to minimize, if not eliminate, Sutherland's conception of an 'excess of definitions' favorable to violating the law.

The passage of each individual law became de facto documentation of the merchant communities' methods and attempts at circumventing the previous statutes. The Enforcement Act, passed January 9, 1809, was the culmination of the Jefferson Administration's and the Republican Congress's attempts at addressing the violators by national edict.[37] Fines increased to four times the value of the cargo and the forfeiture of the ship or wagon involved, bonds increased to six times the value of vessel and cargo, permits and the presence of a revenue officer became required to load a vessel, legal defenses against seizure and forfeiture such as capture by a hostile vessel or distress due to weather (if due to negligence) were eliminated, and masters, mates, mariners, and crew were all subject to presentation at any trial. To assist in identifying smugglers, informers were entitled to one-half of all fines collected. To further address the enforcement of the embargo, the president was also authorized to employ the army and the militia, besides the customs and the navy. Their duties extended to 'preventing and suppressing any armed or riotous assemblage of persons' opposing the embargo.[38]

When on Christmas Day 1807, the owners of almost three hundred ships at anchor in New York harbor received news that Congress had passed the first embargo, they immediately sent word to their vessels to depart posthaste. The control of those vessels was 'concentrated into a few blocks of brick countinghouses near the tip of Manhattan Island'; Sutherland's 'intimate personal groups' of merchants and owners quickly circulated the news of the embargo allowing a timely, though illegal, response to the quarantine.[39] Ships sailed half-manned, with or without cargo. In an attempt to prevent their sailings in violation of the law, customs sent gunboats and revenue cutters to thwart their departure.[40] Like the earlier colonials, with the passage of each statute, '[a] complicated regulatory and enforcement scheme that involved gray areas and uncertain interpretations and uneven enforcement almost guaranteed that Americans would follow their keen profit-seeking sense into questionable activities and then deploy all their favorite political, economic and legal arguments to defend their acts'.[41]

When Sutherland conceived his theory of white-collar crime, he was responding to the dominant criminological theories of the early twentieth century that postulated, based on offender case histories and statistical analysis of residential areas, that poverty was entwined with both social and personal pathologies and that these pathologies explained criminal behavior. He disagreed. In challenging these early general theories of criminal behavior, Sutherland believed that the premise of these theories biased the outcome as it excluded business crime. Sutherland theorized that the choice of criminal behavior was not pathological, but a rational decision determined by a businessman (and in his time corporate business was primarily a male field of endeavor) when the 'definitions' favored violating the legal code. No better example could be found than the response of the businessmen whose vessels fled the waters and legal reach of the United States on Christmas Day.[42]

For many merchants a generation removed from the Revolutionary War, this became their time to fight. Instead of fighting for a nation's independence, they fought for their own economic survival. In an attempt to weather the disastrous measures initiated by Jefferson, measures that could lead to bankruptcy for those without the financial wherewithal required to survive almost fifteen months of lost commerce, numerous methods were utilized to circumvent the various trade restriction acts.[43] The methods dated back to colonial times, and many were brought back into play by a new generation of free traders. As the British had remarked years earlier, American merchants 'had commonly undertaken those voyages which afforded the greatest prospect for gain, without any further regard for their illegality'.[44] They would do so once again.

The most obvious method employed was also a risky one: bribery. By bribing a customs official many a regulation could effectively be evaded with minimum inconvenience to all concerned, the trader having secured, as Sutherland described it years later, 'special privileges'.[45] The difficulty was that one never knew if the officer approached was of a temperament to accept an offer, and if accepted, whether higher charges would eventually be required for the same level of 'personal' service.[46]

The notion of misrepresentation was a broad category of historically evading the revenue and one that would again be used to evade the embargo. Misrepresentation included misstating the particulars of a given cargo, either as to the actual product being shipped, its true weight, or its total volume, whichever would be financially advantageous to the owner or master of a vessel. Other forms of misrepresentation included stating that a specific voyage was intended for an approved port or place and off-loading cargo at a proscribed foreign location while in transit, claiming prohibited entry due to the necessities of weather, or declaring to have been seized by a hostile vessel with the objective of recovering any posted bonds or surety. In some cases, ships entered prohibited lands under the guise of exchanging prisoners while at the same time offloading or acquiring any cargo otherwise proscribed. In other cases, counterfeit documents, false seals, and blank certificates were obtained at obliging ports to assist a smuggler in completing a journey.[47]

Evasion included loading or off-loading a sea-going ship utilizing the services of shallower and smaller craft outside of a customs port and out of sight of revenue officials with an interest in enforcing any statutes. If inbound, the ship would then enter and clear without the presence of dutiable or contraband cargo. If outbound, clearance papers were already in hand. The contraband would be unladed prior to reaching the designated destination. Even a ship's identity was concealed to prevent overseas representatives of a given state from notifying anyone of the ship's illicit activities.[48] All of these methods were used by American merchants in an organized attempt to circumvent the intent of the president and of the Congress. In many cases these methods, which persisted throughout the War of 1812, bordered on treason.[49] More than one historian framed these entrepreneurial merchants as versatile and resourceful in the face of adversity.[50] In exhibiting these attributes, these international traders epitomized Robert Merton's theory of anomie and social adaptation—the achievement through innovation of the societal goal of material success denied via legitimate means by, in this case, the embargo. They would turn to criminal behavior against the state to achieve their own economic ends.[51] They would turn to organized smuggling.

The extent of diffusion of these illegal practices among the American merchants attests to Sutherland's premise that white-collar crime is due to differential association. Sutherland's position was that '[b]usiness firms have the objective of maximum profits. When one firm devises a method for increasing profits, other firms become aware of the method and adopt it'.[52] Individuals learn these techniques in interaction with others in the trade, including within the 'intimate personal groups' of their professional community.[53]

Whatever method was used to achieve commercial success, for many who owned vessels in foreign commerce that had not left U.S. ports prior to the embargo, the first requirement was to enroll their vessels for coastal American trade. By doing so, deep water vessels otherwise secured against departure by the government were afforded the opportunity to return to service. Providence, Rhode Island, for example, had 'a 25 percent increase in vessels newly enrolled for the coastal trade' with 60 percent of the fleet having been previously registered for foreign trade in 1808, up from 40 percent in the year prior to the embargo.[54] In New London, Connecticut, over 60 percent of the vessels in foreign trade (twenty-eight vessels) surrendered their registrations with thirteen then enrolling as coastal craft.[55] These newly enrolled vessels had the opportunity to profit from domestic shipping in lieu of rotting dockside or, if considered advantageous, to move contraband goods south to Saint Mary's, Georgia, 'the southern smuggling entrepot'. From Saint Mary's, American products could be transferred into Spanish Florida or north to Passamaquoddy and the coast of Maine, for later smuggling into New Brunswick and onward, in both cases, to the traditional markets of the West Indies or the Atlantic.[56] Though prior to the embargo, sporadic ships had sailed from Maine to Providence with timber, 10 percent of Providence's coastal entries and clearances in 1808 were to eastern Maine ports.[57] Unlike the colonial era, when smuggling required that ships travel to Europe or the Caribbean, trading partners were now also located immediately adjacent to both the northern and southern frontiers of the United States.

Of all the American ports, Boston's was the most infamous for illicit trade with the Passamaquoddy area, because it was the nearest major seaport to the northern borderlands. Within weeks of the passage of the Embargo Act, three vessels were seized while departing illegally from Boston, and two more successfully evaded detention. For the next eight years Boston was a breeding ground for smuggling and for evasion of the embargo, non-intercourse, and revenue laws of the nation.[58]

The men implicated in these adventures included the merchants involved in maritime commerce from throughout the Northeast. They were the same individuals that opposed Jefferson and his Republican Party and its attempts at restricting commerce and free trade. Nathan Appleton, a merchant of Boston, was but one example. Having joined his brother in trade as a clerk, he eventually became a partner in what was known later as the S. & N. Appleton Company, trading both domestically and abroad while also investing in various vessels. The brothers in turn were connected to the Boston mercantile elite through business and social connections, a network that carried over in circumventing the embargo. When the embargo was rumored to be in the offing for example, the *Brutus*, owned by the Jacksons and the Lees of Boston and carrying Appleton cotton, quit Boston harbor ahead of its enforcement.[59]

Others that traveled to the borderlands of Passamaquoddy called New York, Philadelphia, Salem, and Portsmouth home. Estimates indicated that over one hundred merchants from New York and other places engaged in smuggling at Passamaquoddy. The geography of the region, with numerous remote islands and limited roads, favored the smuggling trade, as did a continuous political discourse regarding the exact location of the international border.[60] One of the merchants, James Colles, was born of a prosperous

New York family and, while working for Hugh Kennedy Toler of New York, traveled to Eastport in 1812 with the objective of moving contraband goods from Canada into the United States. Working in collusion with local merchants in Eastport as well as a cadre located in St. Andrews, St. Johns, and Halifax, Colles arranged for Toler's goods to be smuggled into Eastport and turned over to a customs official, who would then seize the primarily British-made goods, and arrange for them to be sold at a court-ordered auction. After also arranging for the goods to be under-appraised by customs, Colles bought back his employer's goods at a fraction of their true value while also claiming 25 percent of the auction price as an informant's reward. The goods, now legally entered into domestic commerce, were then shipped to New York for a handsome profit, even after the costs of repurchasing them at auction and expenses to obliging customs officials, thanks to high demand for contraband goods. Colles eventually became the president of the Bank of New Orleans and extremely wealthy in later years.[61]

Another such merchant was Jabez Mowry of Lubec, formerly of Eastport. Involved in the importation of gypsum at the beginning of the decade, he eventually owned warehouses and docks at Eastport. Working in collusion with the collector of customs, Lemuel Trescott, the seized gypsum was undervalued by as much as 75 percent. Mowry then arranged for the payment of the bond and took custody of the now legally admitted merchandise, which was then turned over for a profit. In 1812 about one-quarter of all seized plaster belonged to Mowry. In the same year he also successfully shipped over fifty thousand dollars in supplies to the British in Halifax. In 1813, James Colles, working with Mowry and Trescott, attempted to arrange for a load of British manufactured goods transported on the sloop *Polly* to be seized by collector Trescott on a tip from Mowry. His misfortune was having the military intercept the vessel and formally seize it before Trescott could intervene. When the case landed in district court, the goods were condemned and auctioned off for approximately one hundred thousand dollars. Colles obtained his goods and sold them still at a profit with Trescott and Mowry each receiving twenty-five thousand dollars as their legal share of the seizure, and Mowry eventually returning his portion to Colles.[62]

These adventurers, the white-collar criminals of a new nation, like John Hancock before them, had little regard for the laws that prevented them from fulfilling their version of the American Dream—one of financial wealth and security born of market economies. The smuggling was, for many, 'a major, well-organized operation in which profits were exchanged either in cash or on paper balance sheets by British and American merchant houses'.[63] In the years from 1807 to 1815, conspiring with various fortune-hunters, government officials, fellow merchants, ship masters, and others, numerous methods would be utilized to achieve their goals, even as the enforcement of the nation's sovereignty, and by extension, control of its borders, became more effective as time passed.

SMUGGLING DAYS AND SMUGGLING WAYS

H. N. Shore's 1892 book on English smuggling, *Smuggling Days and Smuggling Ways*, is as applicable to America in the early 1800s as it was to the smuggling found across the North Atlantic.[64] Thanks to the complexity of the various embargo and non-intercourse laws, and also to their constant change by the Jefferson and Madison administrations, numerous methods to contravene the laws came into play. One of the simplest was merely ignoring the statutes. As mentioned earlier, more than one ship simply departed port upon obtaining news of the passage of the embargo. Once out to sea, a ship could trade between foreign ports without the worry of American interdiction, while awaiting the law to be repealed or modified to return to an American port. Another method was simply to sell the vessel and its cargo overseas, thereby negating the difficulties of returning to the United States. The schooner *Hannah*, though having had her canvas and rigging secured by the local customs collector in an attempt to prevent her departure, managed to sail from Plymouth on a stormy night thanks to a second set of gear from another vessel. The same captain, Charles C. Dolton, under cover of a second storm, took the brig *Hope* out of Provincetown, while being chased by a local revenue cutter. He eventually sold the brig and its cargo in St. Lucia for twenty-five thousand dollars in Spanish doubloons, smuggling the specie back home sewed into his clothing.[65]

In 1808, New York customs officials seized numerous vessels for attempting or departing without clearance. Examples included the schooners *Richmond Packet* (carrying butter and flour), *Morning Star, Mary Ann, Venus* (also carrying flour), as well as the sloops *Black Fish* and *Young Connecticut*, with papers found on the *Venus* actually identifying St. Croix as her true destination.[66] By the end of the embargo seventy-two vessels were eventually seized for violations at the port of New York alone.[67]

An unsuccessful attempt was made by the *Good Intent*. Having tried to leave Boston with a cargo of flour, beef, and other provisions, the owner, Asa Nichols, was sued for twenty thousand dollars for violating the Embargo Act. An acquiescent jury decided that the embargo had not been violated.[68] The brigantine *Betsey* was seized later in the year for sailing from Boston and landing at Barnstable to surreptitiously load a cargo at night. Another compassionate jury acquitted the captain, Samuel S. Newell.[69] From March 1808 (the start of the first new term of the district court in Boston for 1808) until December 1809, 135 embargo violations were decided by the courts, including 'libel actions (*in rem* proceedings), bond violations, and failures of merchants or ship owners to obtain clearances to leave port (both *in personam* proceedings)' with the enforcement decisions 'divided equally between a federal judge and federal juries'.[70] Juries decided sixty-five *in personam* cases. Juries acquitted in nineteen cases in 1808 and another thirty-four in 1809 for a total of fifty-three out of sixty-five cases. The district judge handled another seventy *in rem cases* with twenty-six convictions and twenty pleading no contest. The failure of juries to convict persons charged substantiates the premise that the embargo was not only unpopular, but also unenforceable without the further intercession of the federal government.[71]

As the embargo continued to be ignored, Congress authorized the use of the navy in fulfilling the intent of the law and used vessels such as the naval frigate *Chesapeake* to deter the merchant-smugglers. During August 1808, the *Chesapeake* seized thirteen vessels alone, twelve from the New England area bound for the West Indies.[72] By the end of 1808, few vessels were actually being apprehended smuggling in Boston, but many were being seized upon their return from abroad, with a major group having been given clearances for domestic ports in the Southern states but instead sailing for the West Indies and claiming that weather or foreign flagged privateers were at fault.[73] One that claimed to have been seized was the *Short Staple*, a brig that sailed from Boston to Baltimore for a cargo of 1,315 barrels and 200 half-barrels of flour purchased at five dollars a barrel. Reputedly returning to Boston, she was captured by the British privateer *Ino* and taken to Haiti where she was abandoned while a second captured prize was transported to Jamaica. The captain sold the cargo, still in his possession, for thirty-five dollars a barrel, and then loaded salt at Turk's Island, eventually returning to the United States where the *Short Staple* was seized for violating her bond. At court the captain's story was considered suspect, and the brigantine was forfeited as the *Ino* had been under repairs in Boston when the *Short Staple* was docked there, their respective captains had been seen together and the suggestion that a privateer would abandon such a cargo was not credible. Yet, in the end, the voyage was still profitable. After subtracting the value of the vessel and the bond forfeited (equal to double the value of the purchase price of the cargo plus the vessel's value), the owner still turned a profit estimated at fifteen thousand to twenty thousand dollars less crew salaries and insurance premium.[74] With the West Indies historically being a major foreign destination for Boston shipping (with over 376 arrivals and 187 departures in 1807 alone), many attempted to continue their past profitable dealings with the islands.[75]

By spring of 1808, President Jefferson granted permission—under the authority of the third embargo law, the supplementary Act of March 12, 1808—for merchants to send vessels, in ballast, foreign to pick up cargo and property that had been purchased prior to the passage of the Embargo Act.[76] Nationally 550 vessels were granted permission with 385 returning with cargo by December 1808.[77] This became another legal loophole for American merchants. One of the more famous incidents was of John Jacob Astor obtaining permission for his ship, the *Beaver*, to depart for Canton, China, after eventually claiming that a Chinese merchant acquaintance was a Mandarin requesting permission to return to China with his personal possessions. It returned with a cargo of tea, silk, and nankeens, realizing a profit of two hundred thousand dollars for Astor. Others were not so lucky. The brig *Washington* and the ship *Cotton Planter* were both seized for concealing illegal cargo while reportedly departing in ballast.[78]

THE BORDERLANDS

Many a cargo of foodstuffs was shipped north by coastal traders to the Passamaquoddy region of Maine for eventual transfer across the frontier to New Brunswick. Within a five day period alone in May 1808, 19,000 barrels of flour, 2,700 barrels of pork and beef, 1,700 barrels of bread, 3,059 barrels of naval stores, 4,500 bushels of corn and butter, lard, etc. were reported as landing in Passamaquoddy.[79] The merchants of 'Quoddy were tied to the British commercial system as a matter of survival, and those ties eased the establishment of smuggling routes for American agricultural goods into the Maritimes and to the rest of the British Empire.

Yet the relationship went beyond the commercial ties with Britain. Borderlands theory as presented by Smith describes an area where different political communities 'blend into each other, especially in economic terms, where they meet at a boundary'.[80] This allows communities on both sides of the frontier to interact successfully for mutual gain despite any ideological distinctions, violating those rules that hamper the accord and making their own when appropriate. That pragmatism led Passamaquoddy and northern New York to become central corridors for the merchants of Boston, New York, and beyond, and was another example of Sutherland's contention that when criminal behavior is learned, the learning includes 'motives, drives, rationalizations and attitudes' that offer an 'excess of definitions favorable to violation of law'.[81]

The passage of the supplementary Act of March 12, 1808, the third embargo law, was further evidence of the initiative shown by merchants in using a legal loophole to circumvent the embargo. The original statute focused on the merchant fleet and its related maritime commerce but ignored the minor commercial traffic by land into Canada. That ignorance was recognized in a short time by both the British and by Jefferson's administration. The British and New Brunswick officials took whatever actions they could to undermine the embargo, directing British vessels intercepting American ships to allow their passage with or without documentation if bound to or from British colonies in the Caribbean or South America, conspiring with merchant-smugglers, and offering asylum for those reshipping in British bottoms or selling contraband goods in the province. The Treasury recognized the problems of Passamaquoddy and authorized staffing increases, directed federal troops and naval personnel—along with gunboats—northward, reassigned a revenue cutter to the region, and passed further legislation allowing customs officers to seize questionable provisions shipped to the area.[82] Yet even with the expanded enforcement effort, 'definitions' for the traffickers were favorable enough for the smuggling to continue.

From the passage of the Supplementary Act in March through August of 1808, Lewis Delesdernier, the collector of customs for the Passamaquoddy customs district, filed approximately fifty cases with the federal district court and by November at least twenty-eight seized vessels would be advertised for auction by the U.S. marshal.[83] Yet social pressure from the borderlands community evidently caused Delesdernier to take no court action after August. Eventually he was replaced by Lemuel Trescott, a local merchant and former war hero who, as discussed earlier, facilitated trade to his own personal benefit.[84]

In northern New York, attitudes toward smuggling coincided with 'Quoddy, but instead of provisions being moved by coastal vessels to the border area only to later be smuggled across the water to New Brunswick, the goods were moved via trails through the wilderness forests to the frontier. In northwestern New York, the contraband was transferred, when convenient, to boats and rafts to move it across the St. Lawrence River or Lake Ontario. In northeastern New York, Lake Champlain served as a hundred mile north-south expressway for the maritime smugglers as its northern terminus was north of the Canadian border. In winter, sleds moved barrels of potash, wheat, and other provisions; in summer, rafts (one reputedly a half-mile long) and sloops were utilized. By spring, Burlington merchants reportedly had over four hundred thousand dollars of potash and timber awaiting shipment to market in Canada, having been advanced funds prior to the embargo's enactment. By April, the president declared a state of insurrection in the Champlain area.[85]

The most famous seizure on Lake Champlain was of a former forty-foot ferry boat, the *Black Snake*, on August 3, 1808. While anchored near Burlington, Vermont, with a load of potash, the revenue cutter *Fly*, with state militiamen onboard, attempted to seize the *Black Snake*. Two members of the militia, a tiller man, and a bystander on shore were killed in the action and the militia commander, Lieutenant Daniel Farrington, was wounded. Eventually one of the smugglers was hanged for murder and four others were convicted of manslaughter and sentenced to one hour in the pillory, fifty lashes, and ten years in prison, serving three before being pardoned.[86]

Further west near Sacketts Harbor on Lake Ontario, Barnet Dundas, the brother-in-law of George Scriba, a wealthy merchant of New York, property owner, and land jobber, invited Scriba's participation in moving a load of salt to the area under the guise of marketing it locally only to later pass it over to Kingston, in Lower Canada. As Scriba was known to allow smugglers to use his buildings for storage of contraband, one might easily assume Dundas knew of his own relative's proclivities for profit whatever the source.[87] John Banker, Jr., another New Yorker, successfully obtained a commission from the collector of the port of New York for a privateer, *The Lark*, to operate on Lake Champlain. Armed with only a couple of muskets, the small sailboat, working in collusion with the smugglers, 'seized' contraband vessels loaded with provisions and, utilizing a prize crew, later marketed them in Canada if the goods were northbound, and in New York if southbound, retaining a percentage of the profits after reimbursing the original cargo owners.[88] Canadian records for the Champlain area show that, even with a closed American frontier for trade, the value of northbound commodities increased 31 percent from 1807 to 1808 (from £116,000 to over £140,000). All the president's men, vessels, and artillery could not prevent the success of men determined to pursue their economic dreams.[89]

St. Mary's, Georgia, in the South was little different, with wheat flour and meat as the outbound contraband cargo.[90] Small boats also ferried cotton out to ocean going vessels all along the Georgia coast. Being the American port closest to the West Indies, coastal craft would obtain clearances for St. Mary's only to be blown off course or claim emergencies to justify foreign landings.[91]

With the repeal of the embargo in March 1809, a new Non-Intercourse Act came into effect, limiting trade only with Britain and France.[92] With ships being granted permission to sail foreign, the opportunities to divert to Britain (Liverpool was recognized as a prime destination) or to the British West Indies became easier than ever. The schooner *Antelope* was seized for an illicit trip to the British West Indies though having cleared for the Brazils; the court case was eventually dismissed years later. Other vessels with cargos from Labrador and Halifax were also seized shortly after the detention of the *Antelope*.[93]

The Non-Intercourse Act was suspended in 1810, only to have a new Non-Intercourse Act instituted in March 1811, addressing only British commerce.[94] By June 1812, the United States was at war with Britain and trade—or at least unauthorized trade—became treason. To keep American farmers supportive of the war, the attorney general and the Treasury under Madison, who had replaced Jefferson, allowed American grain to be shipped to Spain to feed the British troops located on the Iberian peninsula, but prohibited any exports to Canada or maritime trade with the Empire, interpreting that the Enemy Trade Act was not violated by this trade.[95] This limiting of trade, allowing some to benefit while preventing others from the similar opportunities closer at hand, could only become a self-serving justification for the persistence of smuggling by the merchants otherwise being financially damaged by the extensive restrictions. Many continued to organize and supply the British fleet sailing off the United States as well as British subjects in Canada and the West Indies while also importing prohibited goods in exchange.[96] John Jacob Astor in collaboration with his Canadian corporate associates had a large quantity of furs that shipped south from Montreal shortly after the declaration of war, moving 2,700 wolf skins through one route with the aid of a local smuggler and another 2,693 wolf skins along with 148 beaver pelts via a second route.[97]

Vessels flagged as neutral, with some American captains obtaining Swedish nationality to achieve that status, obtained British goods in the Maritimes for import into the United States.[98] Other vessels cleared for a neutral port but then diverted into Canada. The *Rebecca*, a schooner out of New York bound for Cadiz, Spain, with 570 barrels of flour, was captured off of the West Quoddy Lighthouse headed for Halifax.[99] The administration again pushed through laws to attack this trade, recommending 'new restrictions: (1) an embargo prohibiting all American ships and goods from leaving port; (2) a complete ban on the importation of certain commodities customarily produced in the British Empire, such woolen and cotton goods and rum; (3) a ban against foreign ships trading in American ports unless the master, supercargo and at least three-quarters of the crew were citizens or subjects of the flag flown by the ship and (4) a ban on ransoming ships' in late 1813.[100]

Yet the frauds continued. The Providence, Rhode Island, *Patriot* of December 10, 1814, reported that a neutral Swedish vessel legally transported goods back and forth between Hampden, Maine, and Castine, Maine—held by the British, twenty miles downstream on the Penobscot River. With winter, the river would freeze allowing even easier trade across the line.[101] Two-thirds of the British army in Canada was living on beef from Vermont and New York.[102] Moses and Guy Catlin of Burlington, Vermont, worked with Montreal businesses, trading in furs and British manufactured goods for smuggling into the United States with provisions from the Lake Champlain area being shipped northward. Account records show Guy Catlin purchasing cloth, including broadcloth, calico, flannel, and linen, along with clothing accessories, china, and various other goods from C. P. Lester and Company in Montreal, over a six-month period during the war. Working on commission for Horatio Gates of Bellows and Gates and Company, Catlin also received $9,916.20 in payment for goods shipped to Montreal.[103]

Besides being used in sham endeavors to 'seize' friendly vessels, allowing legal entry of high-valued goods into the country, privateers also were known to depart port loaded with supplies manifested as crew provisions, only to sell them foreign later.[104] If a method to circumvent the various non-importation or embargo laws could turn a profit thanks to the demand for goods on both sides of the line, some entrepreneur would attempt it. As a privateer operating on the edges of the law, crossing the line into organized white-collar criminality was more of a short step than a long stride.

Even officials assigned to prevent smuggling continued to collude with the malefactors, some for profit and some for the perceived good of the community. Soldiers were bribed to allow seized goods to be rescued;[105] militia both assisted in the movement of merchants' smuggled goods and entered the trade of their own volition.[106] After the war, the collector of customs for the District of Vermont stated that it was common practice for an importer to notify customs of their goods entering the United States, allowing a customs officer to seize the merchandise, to determine its value via invoices, and to add 10 percent to the sum. The merchant would post a bond, claim his merchandise, now legally entered into the United States, and file for a remission of the forfeited bond through the Treasury or the courts, which in many cases was successful. Further, by informing on his own contraband, the merchant was entitled to one-third of the forfeiture, if his remission claim was not approved, thereby minimizing his loss.[107] At least one collector profited personally by using such methods.[108] These techniques were but a continuation of the frauds practiced during Jefferson's earlier embargo and another example of the 'fixing' of white-collar crimes described by Sutherland.[109]

In the new nation, those merchants of the upper socioeconomic class along the Atlantic seaboard who previously had profited from smuggling goods into colonial America had a minimal financial incentive to continue to do so in the recently created United States. For most, thanks to a reasonable tariff, the 'definitions' described by Sutherland were generally considered unfavorable to violating the law. Yet those same merchants found 'definitions' favorable for contraband traffic to other nations and to their overseas colonies.

Jefferson's use of economic sanctions in an attempt to avoid U.S. involvement in the European conflict served only to damage American mercantile interests and Americans' respect for the law. As the law created strain for merchants, they found 'an excess of definitions' to justify disobedience of the new non-intercourse and embargo laws and a return to the smuggling 'innovations' of colonial times. Further, smuggling extended to the Republic's northern land border, where cross-border communities blended together for mutual gain, and violated those rules that hampered their border accord. In some cases the very officers charged with enforcement of the law were themselves compromised by businessmen looking for what Sutherland called 'special privileges'.[110] Over time, new laws were passed to address the weaknesses of previous statutes and regulations that the merchants had identified and had used to circumvent governmental action. Geographical boundaries also became a consideration in future efforts both to initiate smuggling endeavors by business interests and to interdict those efforts by the government.

With the end of the war in 1815, trade once again became legal and the incentive to continue smuggling was eliminated for most. The merchant capitalists of New York, Boston, Baltimore, Philadelphia, New Orleans, and the other seaports of America returned to legitimate maritime trade. Yet for the years of Jefferson's embargo and the War of 1812, these same merchants fulfilled Sutherland's definition of white-collar criminals, the respected businessmen committing crime in the course of their occupation.[111] Many of the merchant traders in the countinghouses of New York, Boston, and Philadelphia, as well as the ship captains in the smuggling trade, fully qualified; they lived in a society that placed a high premium on economic success and defined for many the American Dream. As Thomas Jefferson Coolidge had remarked, 'money was the only real avenue to power and success both socially and in the regard to your fellow man'.[112] To their personal profit, they continued a tradition of finding a need and filling it, providing a product in demand whatever side of the line they served, whatever laws existed to thwart it; Merton's 'innovation' was the typology of the successful merchant. Some had already extended their trade into smuggling opium from Turkey into China (discussed in chapter 8), little questioning the morality of their actions. They were truly white-collar criminals in the commission of organized crime. As the century progressed, industrialists came to the fore-front of the economic elites in the Northern states while another elite social and financial group in the South, the plantation owners and their associ-ates, led the nation into cataclysmic strife, creating yet another environment of social disorganization and, thereby, an opportunity for a new phase of American smuggling to develop.[113]

NOTES

1. Edwin H. Sutherland, *White Collar Crime: The Uncut Version* (New Haven, CT: Yale University Press, 1983), p. 7.
2. Sven Beckert, 'Merchants and Manufacturers in the Antebellum North', in *Ruling America: A History of Wealth and Power in a Democracy*, ed. by Steve Fraser and Gary Gerstle (Cambridge, MA: Harvard University Press, 2005), 92–122 (pp. 94–95).
3. Thomas Jefferson Coolidge, *Thomas Jefferson Coolidge: An Autobiography* (Boston, MA: Houghton Mifflin, 1900), p. 9.
4. Frederic Jaher, *The Urban Establishment: Upper Strata in Boston, New York, Charleston, Chicago and Los Angeles* (Urbana: University of Illinois Press, 1982), p. 73.
5. Jaher, *The Urban Establishment*, p. 73.
6. Beckert, 'Merchants and Manufacturers', p. 104.
7. Carl E. Prince, *The Federalists and the Origins of the U.S. Civil Service* (New York: New York University Press, 1977), p. 274.
8. Henry Warren to Thomas Jefferson, September 5, 1801, and November 10, 1802, Henry Warren entry, Letters of Application and Recommendation dur-ing the Administration of Thomas Jefferson, cited in Prince, *The Federalists*, p. 26.
9. Alexander Hamilton to Jeremiah Olney, April 2, 1793, *The Papers of Alex-ander Hamilton*, ed. by Harold C. Syrett, 27 vols (New York: Columbia University Press, 1969), VIII, pp. 276–277.
10. 1 *Stat.* 24, c. 2 (1789); *Columbian Centinel*, April 30, 1791, p. 54; *Mas-sachusetts Mercury*, December, 5, 1800, p. 2; *New York Herald,* June 11, 1803, p. 2; *Gazetteer;* June 25, 1803, p. 3; *New England Palladium*, August 8, 1803, p. 2.
11. *Western Star*, June, 23, 1795, p. 3; *Morning Chronicle*, May 16, 1803, p. 2.
12. *Newburyport Herald*, June 12, 1801, p. 3 and May 4, 1802, p. 2.
13. *Evening Post*, April 26, 1802, p. 3.
14. *Commercial Advertiser*, April 23, 1802, p. 3 and July 26, 1806, p. 3; *New England Palladium*, July 26, 1803, p. 2; *American Citizen*, December 16, 1806, p. 3.
15. Charles Sellers, *The Market Revolution: Jacksonian America, 1815–1846* (New York: Oxford University, 1991), p. 21.
16. James H. Coatsworth, 'American Trade with European Colonies in the Caribbean and South America, 1790–1812', *William and Mary Quarterly*, 3rd ser., 24 (1967), 243–266 (p. 243).
17. Douglass C. North, *The Economic Growth of the United States, 1790–1860* (New York: W. W. Norton, 1966), pp. 53–54, 221, 228, 249.

The Embargo of 1807–1809 and the War of 1812   59

18. U.S. Census Office, *The Seventh Census of the United States: 1850* (Washington, D.C.: Robert Armstrong, 1853), p. lii.
19. Sellers, *Market Revolution*, p. 23.
20. Robert Greenhalgh Albion and Jennie Barnes Pope, *Sea Lanes in Wartime: The American Experience, 1775–1942* (New York: Norton, 1942), p. 65.
21. Edwin H. Sutherland, *Principles of Criminology*, 4th edn (Chicago: J. B. Lippincott, 1947), p. 6.
22. Charles M. Wiltse, *The New Nation: 1800–1845* (New York: Hill and Wang, 1961), p. 22.
23. Joshua M. Smith, 'The Rogues of 'Quoddy: Smuggling in the Maine-New Brunswick Borderland, 1783–1820' (unpublished doctoral dissertation, University of Maine, 2003), p. 2.
24. Esmond Wright, *The American Dream: From Reconstruction to Reagan* (Cambridge: Blackwell Publishing, 1996), p. 32.
25. Donald R. Hickey, *The War of 1812: A Forgotten Conflict* (Urbana: University of Illinois Press, 1995), pp. 9 and 10. North would claim $55.8 million in exports in 1803. See North, *The Economic Growth of the United States*, p. 221.
26. Anthony Merry to Lord Mulgrave, September 30, 1805; MSS, British Archives, as cited in Henry Adams, *History of the United States during the Administrations of Thomas Jefferson* (New York: Library of America, 1986), p. 669.
27. Albert Gallatin to James Madison, April 13, 1807, *The James Madison Papers*, LC, ser. 2, reel 25, URL: http://hdl.loc.gov/loc.mss/mjm.25_1528_1531 [Date accessed: August 3, 2011].
28. *Annals of Congress*, Senate, 10th Cong., 1st sess., p. 36.
29. Burton Spivak, *Jefferson's English Crisis: Commerce, Embargo, and the Republican Revolution* (Charlottesville: University of Virginia Press, 1979), p. 14.
30. Hickey, *The War of 1812*, pp. 17–19.
31. *ibid.*, p. 20.
32. *ibid.*, p. 21.
33. Christopher Ward, 'The Commerce of East Florida During the Embargo, 1806–1812: The Role of Amelia Island', *Florida Historical Quarterly*, 68 (1989), 160–179; 2 *Stat.* 379, c. 29 (1806).
34. Douglas Lamar Jones, ' "The Caprice of Juries": The Enforcement of the Jeffersonian Embargo in Massachusetts', *American Journal of Legal History*, 24 (1980), 307–330 (p. 311); 2 *Stat.* 451, c. 5 (1807).
35. Jones, ' "The Caprice of Juries" ', pp. 311–312; 2 *Stat.* 453, c. 8 (1808); 2 *Stat.* 473, c. 33 (1808).
36. Jones, ' "The Caprice of Juries" ', pp. 312–313; 2 *Stat.* 499, c. 66 (1808).
37. Albert Gallatin to William B. Giles, November 24, 1808, *Selected Writing of Albert Gallatin*, ed. by E. James Ferguson (Indianapolis, ID: Bobbs-Merrill, 1967), pp. 301–309.
38. Jones, ' "The Caprice of Juries" ', pp. 313–314; 2 *Stat.* 506, c. 5 (1809).
39. Robert Greenhalgh Albion, *The Rise of New York Port, 1815–1860* (Boston, MA: Northeastern University Press, 1939; repr. 1984), p. 260.
40. Harvey Strum, 'Smuggling in the War of 1812', *History Today*, 29 (1979), 532–537 (p. 532).
41. Robert Copeland Ayer, 'Shifty Seafarers, Shifting Winds: Governmental Policies toward Maritime Smuggling in North America from Colonization to the War of 1812' (unpublished doctoral dissertation, Tufts University, 1993), p. 51.

42. Sutherland, *White Collar Crime*, pp. 3–7.
43. Harvey Strum, 'Smuggling in Maine during the Embargo and the War of 1812', *Colby Library Quarterly*, 19 (1983), 90–97 (pp. 90–91).
44. Lawrence Henry Gipson, *The Coming of the Revolution, 1763–1775* (New York: Harper and Brothers, 1954), pp. 59–60, as quoted in Glenn Stine Gordinier, 'Versatility in Crisis: The Merchants of the New London Customs District Respond to the Embargo of 1807–1809' (unpublished doctoral dissertation, University of Connecticut, 2001), p. 2.
45. Sutherland, *White Collar Crime*, p. 93.
46. Samuel G. Margolin, 'Lawlessness on the Maritime Frontier of the Greater Chesapeake, 1650–1750' (unpublished doctoral dissertation, College of William and Mary, 1992), p. 70.
47. *ibid.*, pp. 70–78.
48. *ibid.*, pp. 78–85.
49. *ibid.*, p. 85.
50. W. Jeffery Bolster, 'The Impact of Jefferson's Embargo on Coastal Commerce', *Log of Mystic Seaport*, 37 (1986) 111–123; Gordinier, 'Versatility in Crisis'; H.N. Muller, 'Smuggling into Canada: How the Champlain Valley Defied Jefferson's Embargo', *Vermont History*, 38 (1970), 5–21; Strum, 'Smuggling in Maine', pp. 90–97.
51. Robert Merton, 'Social Structure and Anomie,' *American Sociological Association*, 3 (October 1938), 672–682.
52. Sutherland, *White Collar Crime*, p. 246.
53. Sutherland, *Principles of Criminology*, p. 6; Sutherland, *White Collar Crime*, pp. 246–250.
54. Bolster, 'The Impact of Jefferson's Embargo', p. 113.
55. Gordinier, 'Versatility in Crisis', p. 250; Ward, 'Commerce of East Florida', p. 160.
56. Bolster, 'The Impact of Jefferson's Embargo', p. 120.
57. *ibid.*, p. 120.
58. John D. Forbes, 'Boston Smuggling, 1807–1815', *American Neptune*, 10 (1950), 144–154 (pp. 144–146).
59. Frances W. Gregory, *Nathan Appleton: Merchant and Entrepreneur, 1779–1861* (Charlottesville: University Press of Virginia, 1975), pp. 17–18, 35, and 39.
60. Smith, 'The Rogues of 'Quoddy', p. 59.
61. *ibid.*, pp. 215–220.
62. Joshua M. Smith, *Borderland Smuggling: Patriots, Loyalists, and Illicit Trade in the Northeast, 1783–1820* (Gainesville: University Press of Florida, 2006), pp. 81–82.
63. Ward, 'Commerce in East Florida', p. 171.
64. Henry N. Shore, *Smuggling Days and Smuggling Ways or, the Story of a Lost Art* (London: Cassell & Company, 1892).
65. Samuel E. Morison, *The Maritime History of Massachusetts, 1783–1860* (Boston, MA: Northeastern University Press, 1979), p. 188.
66. Israel Ira Rubin, 'New York State and the Long Embargo' (unpublished dissertation, New York University, 1961), pp. 89–90.
67. *ibid.*, pp. 263–265.
68. District Court, March 1808, p. 383, as cited in Forbes, 'Boston Smuggling', p. 146.
69. Forbes, 'Boston Smuggling', p. 149.
70. Jones, ' "The Caprice of Juries" ', p. 326.
71. *ibid.*, pp. 326–327.

72. Rubin, 'New York State', p. 90.
73. Forbes, 'Boston Smuggling', p. 149.
74. Robin D. S. Higham, 'Port of Boston and the Embargo of 1807', *American Neptune*, 16 (1956), 189–210 (pp. 202–203).
75. *ibid.*, p. 196.
76. 2 *Stat.* 473, c. 33 (1808).
77. Higham, 'Port of Boston', p. 204.
78. Rubin, 'New York State', pp. 103–105.
79. Joseph Whipple to Albert Gallatin, May 22, 1808, Gallatin Papers, as cited in Smith, 'The Rogues of 'Quoddy', p. 263.
80. Smith, 'The Rogues of 'Quoddy', p. 80.
81. Sutherland, *Principles of Criminology*, p. 6.
82. Smith, 'The Rogues of 'Quoddy', pp. 257–262.
83. 'Final Record Book,' National Archives and Records Administration, RG 21, Federal District Court Records, Maine District, Ms. at NARA Northeast, Waltham, Massachusetts, as cited in Smith, 'Rogues of 'Quoddy', pp. 266–267.
84. Smith, *Borderland Smuggling*, p. 73.
85. Muller, 'Smuggling into Canada', pp. 5–21; Rubin, 'New York State', pp. 110–115.
86. John Duffy, Samuel Hand, and Ralph Orth, *The Vermont Encyclopedia* (Burlington: University of Vermont Press, 2003), p. 58.
87. George Shackelford, *Jefferson's Adoptive Son: The Life of William Short, 1759–1848* (Lexington: University of Kentucky Press, 2006), p. 182; Barnet Dundas to George Scriba, June 8, 1808, Scriba Papers and Elizabeth Simpson, *Mexico, Mother of Towns* (Buffalo, NY: J. W. Clement,1949), p. 78, as cited in Rubin, 'New York State', p. 130.
88. Frederic F. Van De Water, *Lake Champlain and Lake George* (Indianapolis, ID: Bobbs-Merrill, 1946), p. 319; Muller, 'Smuggling into Canada', p. 14.
89. Muller, 'Smuggling into Canada', pp. 17–21.
90. James H. Eves, ' "The Poor People Had Suddenly Become Rich": A Boom in Maine Wheat, 1793–1815', *Maine Historical Society Quarterly,* 27 (1987), 114–141 (pp. 125–126).
91. James McCulloch to Albert Gallatin, December 5, 1808, and Albert Gallatin to Thomas Jefferson, December 28, 1808, Microfilm Edition of the Papers of Albert Gallatin, ed. by Prince, roll 18, as cited in Carl E. Prince and Mollie Keller, *The U.S. Customs Service: A Bicentennial History* (Washington, D.C.: U.S. Customs Service, 1989), pp. 77–78.
92. 2 *Stat.* 528, c. 24 (1809).
93. Forbes, 'Boston Smuggling', pp. 149–150.
94. 2 *Stat.* 651, c. 29 (1811).
95. 2 *Stat.* 778, c. 129 (1812); Albert Gallatin to Larkin Smith, July 24, 1812, in Gallatin Papers, reel 25, as cited in Hickey, *The War of 1812*, p. 117.
96. Hickey, *The War of 1812*, p. 117.
97. Pliny Moore MSS, Astor to Moore, Montreal, July 9, 1812, *Moorsfield Antiquarian*, 1: 2 (August 1937), pp. 121–123, as cited in H. N. Muller, 'A "Traitorous and Diabolical Traffic:" The Commerce of the Champlain-Richelieu Corridor during the War of 1812', *Vermont History*, 44 (1976), 78–96.
98. Hickey, *The War of 1812*, p. 169.
99. RG8 IV, 'Nova Scotia Vice-Admiralty Court Prize Records', vol. 94, the *Rebecca*, as cited in Smith, 'The Rogues of 'Quoddy', p. 300.
100. 3 *Stat.* 88, c. 1 (1813); Hickey, *The War of 1812*, p. 172.

101. Eves, ' "The Poor People" ', pp. 131–132.
102. Sir George Prevost to Earl Bathurst, August 5, 1814, included in *Select British Documents Relating to the Canadian War of 1812*, III, pt 1, p. 346, cited in Chilton Williamson, *Vermont in Quandary* (Montpelier: Vermont Historical Society, 1949), p. 273; Edward Brynn, 'Patterns of Dissent: Vermont's Opposition to the War of 1812', *Vermont History*, 40 (1972), 10–27; and Muller, 'A "Traitorous and Diabolical Traffic" ', p. 91.
103. Account with C. P. Lester and Company, September 12, 1815, and Receipt, April 22, 1815, Catlin MSS, Wilbur Collection, Bailey Library, University of Vermont, Burlington, Vermont, as noted in Muller, 'A "Traitorous and Diabolical Traffic" ', p. 93.
104. Henry A. S. Dearborn to William Jones, January 4, 1814, in U.S. Department of Treasury, *Correspondence with the Secretary of the Treasury with the Collectors of Customs, 1789–1833*, (M178), reel 12, as cited in Hickey, *The War of 1812*, p. 173.
105. Deposition of John Stevens, United States v. Sloop *Sally* of Portland May Term, 1813, RG 21/MeDC, as cited in Smith, 'Rogues of 'Quoddy', p. 80.
106. Muller, 'A "Traitorous and Diabolical Traffic" ', pp. 90–91.
107. Deposition of Cornelius Peter Van Ness, March 13, 1818, as noted in Muller, Van Ness MSS, Wilbur Collection, Bailey Library, University of Vermont, as cited in 'A "Traitorous and Diabolical Traffic" ', pp. 86–87.
108. Smith, *Borderland Smuggling*, p. 86.
109. Sutherland, *White Collar Crime*, p. 238.
110. Sutherland, *White Collar Crime*, p. 93.
111. Sutherland, *White Collar Crime*, p. 7; Edwin H. Sutherland, 'White-collar Criminality', *American Sociological Review*, 5, (February 1940), 1–12, (p. 1).
112. Coolidge, *Thomas Jefferson Coolidge*, p. 9.
113. Sutherland, *White Collar Crime*, pp. 255–257.

3   The Civil War

Within two generations of the War of 1812, the expansion of commerce—particularly developments in agribusiness, American manufacturing, and international maritime transportation—offered opportunities unimaginable years earlier for business to profit from the military needs of a nation in civil conflict. The industrial requirements of the armies in the world's first modern war offered unparalleled prospects for white-collar crime and, thanks to the length of the borders between the two warring entities and the close proximity of neutral territory to both, smuggling became one of its major forms.[1]

In his seminal book *White Collar Crime*, Sutherland documented the war crimes of the corporations he had surveyed, including various violations of embargo and neutrality laws and treason, believing that they might offer some insight as to the motivations and mindset of the violators. The evidence, he believed, substantiated the 'proposition that profits take priority to patriotism'.[2] That belief, as documented during the embargo of 1809 and the War of 1812, was no less true during the Civil War years.

With religious security and the growth of commerce through the early 1800s, the American Dream changed and became more secular, eventually incorporating the idea of upward mobility and the concept of the self-made man. Andrew Carnegie and J.P. Morgan, two of the many 'robber barons' of the nineteenth century who personified the new American Dream and who were recognized by Sutherland as white-collar criminals, became the modern day exemplars of the new myth of success and its tie to business interests.[3] Yet it was a war hero and a U.S. senator who came to personify the proposition that profits take priority over patriotism; his smuggling ventures eventually would expose him to the charge of treason.

In the years leading up to secession, the South and Southwest became the major producers of cotton for the Northern textile mills while the North continued to develop its manufacturing capabilities.[4] Industrial output for the South was approximately 10 percent of the North's capability, with most of the iron and flour mills, grain areas, and slaughterhouses within a few days' march from northern borders.[5] Manufacturing eventually matured with Northern entrepreneurs surpassing merchant capitalists in importance to the nation. During the same period, the merchant fleet developed and world shipping achieved 'almost revolutionary changes'.[6] As Northern seaports grew, New York came to occupy the preeminent position in the coastal trade in cotton as well as in general foreign trade.[7] The port of New York served as the predominate apex of the cotton triangle with vessels controlled by New Yorkers regularly trafficking between Sandy Hook and the major cotton ports of the South: Charleston, Savannah, Mobile, and New Orleans. Those ties also extended to England via Liverpool and France by way of Havre. Those same economic ties also carried over to families for many a New Yorker or Yankee settled in the Southern ports to facilitate business.[8] As early as 1800, New Orleans business interests were dominated by northeastern merchants, with the prevailing marine traffic bound for New York and the Chesapeake.[9] Those self-same ties also extended the 'techniques [. . .] motives, drives, rationalizations and attitudes' required of the traders to justify later violation of the laws of two nations in conflict.[10]

The symbiotic trade, and the networks that developed between the South and North to achieve it, were both catalysts and precursors for contraband trade deemed treasonous by the two governments. With the start of the Civil War, both nations passed laws to terminate trade with the opposing force, assuming that any trade only helped the enemy. Lincoln initiated a blockade of the seacoast ports and of the inland waterways of those states that seceded from the Union.[11] The South originally developed polices to prevent trade to enemy ports or seizures by Union vessels but otherwise permitted seaborne commerce.[12] Both denied institutional means in the achievement of cultural goals, opening the door for Merton's concept of 'innovation' to come into play.[13]

With such an extensive land border between the warring factions and with many contiguous Union states supportive of the South and slavery, such as Delaware, Maryland, and Kentucky, the opportunities for illegal commerce were immense. Smuggling was found all along the line with individuals attempting to augment both personal and military needs. Though originally discouraged by both capitals on principle, for both sides politics and policies would tolerate the flow of goods. The acquiescence of both governments to the traffic offered 'definitions' favorable to violations of the law both for opportunists and for those whose survival depended on trade, as it had two generations earlier.

CONFEDERATE GOVERNMENT, TRADE AND BLOCKADE RUNNING

Though the Confederate government was hesitant to permit trade, believing that the trade did not support the greater goal of bringing Britain into the war to maintain the island's needed imports of Southern cotton, Richmond eventually turned a blind eye to its own policy by the middle of 1862. With a poor financial structure based primarily on agriculture, nominal transportation systems, and minimal industry, much of which was within a few days ride from the borders of the free states, the need for external goods became of paramount concern.[14] Salt, not cotton or foodstuffs, would be the catalyst for Southern clandestine trade. Salt was critical to survival both domestically and militarily, as it was used as a preservation technique for meat and fish, much of which was needed by the military. With over three hundred million pounds required yearly and with much of the nation's imported salt going to the South prior to the war, scarcity was inevitable.[15] General Sherman stated that, 'Without money [. . .] they cannot get arms and ammunition [. . .] and without salt they cannot make bacon or salt beef. We cannot carry on war and trade with a people at the same time'.[16] Individual state governments pressured Richmond to allow the trade with at least one governor permitting the exchange of cotton for salt. As with many pragmatic decisions, instead of legalizing the trade, it was simply ignored.[17] The quantities being shipped south were at such a level as to have Sherman write that, 'Cincinnati has sent enough salt to supply all their army for six months'.[18] The trade in salt continued until 1865.[19] Pharmaceuticals, including quinine, were also moved across the line through locations such as Louisville.[20]

Besides developing manufacturing capabilities within the Confederacy, the Ordnance Department also used individuals such as Levi White to travel north and acquire needed military supplies by buying goods from Baltimore and New York and shipping them first through various routes to the Potomac and then into the South by a schooner using a false bulkhead. The quantity of war material is shown by the first shipment totaling two million musket-caps alone. All along the lower Potomac and across the Chesapeake Bay, contraband goods were transported across the line. The Union navy extended its blockade as the Northern troops took control of Virginia soil in an attempt to interdict the traffic. Besides contraband, individuals interested in crossing the lines without interference used these same smugglers and their vessels to move quietly across the frontier. In at least one case the going rate for transport was twenty dollars in gold.[21]

The maritime industry also recognized opportunity in adversity: those in the North shipped manufactured goods to neutral ports for transit to the South and mariners from the Confederacy and neutral countries manned the famed blockade runners and transported needed and wanted goods into Southern ports. It was these blockade runners, carrying both private and government goods, that provided '60 percent of the South's arms, one-third of its lead for bullets, ingredients for three-fourths of its powder, nearly all of its paper for cartridges, and the majority of its cloth and leather for uniforms and accoutrements'.[22]

The interconnections of trade were already at work prior to the initiation of hostilities, with George Alfred Trenholm as the directing partner of Fraser, Trenholm and Company, Liverpool; Trenholm Brothers, New York; and John Fraser and Company, Charleston, South Carolina, having already shipped arms to Charleston via Liverpool. This triangular trade, established during the antebellum period to serve the cotton textile industry of England, would be the template for clandestine trade throughout the war.[23] With the potential for high profits, various companies in England, Scotland, Canada, and the Confederacy joined in the trade.[24] Some English companies even partnered with Southern companies by providing the necessary steamers to the joint enterprise. The E. P. Stringer's Mercantile Trading Company and the Anglo-Confederate Trading Company, associated with Edward Lawrence and Company of Liverpool, were but two examples.[25]

Zachariah Pearson, the mayor of Hull and both a merchant and ship owner, sent seven craft to challenge the blockade. His failure at running the blockade led his operation, Pearson and Company, into bankruptcy. Six of his vessels were captured with a seventh running aground in mid-1862.[26] The Navigation Company of Liverpool was another English venture in blockade running, losing two of her ships to Union forces and another four to maritime accidents.[27] Thomas Sterling Begbie, a shipping merchant from London, united with Peter Denny, a Dumbarton shipbuilder, and controlled the steamer *Memphis*. Offered to investors for blockade running, she was seized en route from Charleston with approximately 1,500 bales of cotton after having run munitions to the South, including 112,000 pounds of gunpowder, eleven thousand small arms, a million percussion caps, twenty-five tons of lead, and other needed goods. The investment was not a total loss as the *Memphis* had been insured for twenty-six thousand pounds.[28] But not all were as unlucky as these endeavors. Henry Lafone of Liverpool teamed with Gazaway Lamar of the Importing and Exporting Company of Georgia to run seven vessels against the blockade. Their first endeavor was a small steamer named *Little Ada* that managed to export 295 bales of cotton to Nassau, which sold for over eight thousand pounds, only to be captured on her return to the South. Another of their vessels, the *Lilian*, managed two successful round trips from Bermuda to Wilmington before she was captured outbound from North Carolina.[29] Over the first two years of the war, over one hundred attempts were made with three-fourths being successful. That success came at a high cost, whatever the high profit that could be earned—twenty-eight out thirty-six vessels that attempted the run were either captured or lost.[30]

All of these merchants, shippers, and speculators were willing to violate the law of a nation, in this case the United States, for profit; the penalty, of course, being the seizures of their goods and the vessels transporting them. 'Without profits, blockade running would not have existed'.[31] In so doing they were a new generation of Americans satisfying Sutherland's definition of white-collar criminality and who, in this case, also 'attempted to use this emergency as an opportunity for extraordinary enrichment of themselves at the expense of others'.[32]

Much of the trade from the Atlantic seaboard transited the British port of Nassau, located in British New Providence. The port was 570 miles from the Southern-controlled harbor of Wilmington, making it more convenient than other British ports on the western side of the Atlantic such as Halifax or Bermuda. With brokerages already established and easy access for Confederate agents, British goods were easily transshipped in exchange for exported Southern cotton, leaving only minimal exposure to Northern seizures. By declaring the goods exported from Britain as Nassau destined, they avoided seizure on the high seas by eliminating any evidence that showed their ultimate destination was to the South. Upon arrival in Nassau, the cargo would be broken and reshipped on the blockade runners.[33] With the concurrence of the islands' governor, Charles John Bayley, whose sentiments leaned (much to the chagrin of Union naval commanders) toward the Southern cause, Nassau became a major hub of blockading activity throughout the war.[34] Besides England, much of the supplies that transited Nassau and the other British colonial ports originated in, of all places, New York. Those goods were smuggled out of New York and the Northeast, and many of the entrepreneurs holding American citizenship were guilty of treason.

NORTHERN MERCHANTS AND SOUTHERN TRADE

With a triangular trade between England, New York, and the Southern states having been established prior to the war, many of the same interconnections would be of use in the smuggling trade. In the cotton port of Mobile, approximately 10 percent of the white population was from the Northeast in 1850.[35] New Orleans, for example, had an extensive commercial population of Northeastern Americans established in the banking, shipping, insurance, and mercantile businesses. With a population of approximately 116,000 in the mid-1800s, 40,000 of which were American-born whites, over 9,000 were from Northern free states with New York providing over 4,000 of this number alone.[36] The New Yorker Charles Morgan developed a shipping line operating between New Orleans and New York that eventually extended its operations into the western Gulf and Texas. His ships' names, which included the *New York*, the *Louisiana*, the *Aransas*, and the *Savannah*, said much as to the ties that bound New York to the South.[37] New York's ties to the South were so strong that the mayor, Fernando Wood, proposed that the city secede from the state of New York and become a free city allowed to continue trading with its historical business partners.[38] Though unsuccessful, he obviously felt enough support to even suggest the idea publicly. Prior to the seizure of Fort Sumter, cotton continued to be shipped north with return shipments of merchandise to Southern ports escalating. Reports of arms and munitions being shipped were met, in some cases, with seizure and legal action but trade continued through early 1861. As late as April, a ship transporting a thousand barrels of gunpowder was seized by federal marshals.[39] For Southern representatives, New York posed few difficulties. As one special agent of the Confederate States Ordnance Department stated,

'In New York I could purchase almost as readily from a Union man as from a "sympathizer." No questions were asked. They had the goods and I had the cash. They took my money and I got the goods'.[40] Years later, Sutherland, described a conference of war-time manufacturers deciding the advantages of publicizing a policy to 'First Win the War', but where one individual reportedly expressed a position better framed as 'First Realize Our Own Interests'. He might just as easily have been recounting a New York merchant's conference in the Civil War years.[41]

With the outbreak of war, many Northern ship owners registered their vessels with a neutral flag to avoid Southern privateers, taking advantage in particular of the ease of British registry. Some used a neutral registry as a way to avoid the seizure of their vessels not by the Confederacy, but instead by Union forces when these same vessels were found carrying merchandise destined for the South. Historically America believed in and endorsed the theory that goods shipped in neutral vessels were neutral goods themselves, no matter the origin. Though this concept would not assist in defending later seizures of vessels actually running the North's blockade of Southern ports (in violation of international law), it served as a legal defense for cargo that was to be transshipped at neutral ports after being carried there via neutral flagged vessels. If stopped en route, the cargo could be defended as one that was both neutral and bound to a neutral port. That allowed only a short sea run from Nassau or Bermuda to the Confederacy without the protection of a neutral flag.[42] Goods such as 'boots, shoes, cloths and clothing, drugs and medicines, blankets, liquors, and provisions, from vessels arriving from New York, Boston, and Baltimore' were shipped to Nassau for transshipment via blockade runners for Southern ports.[43] Even anthracite coal, a prohibited export because of its need by Confederate vessels and blockade runners, was smuggled south to Nassau and other ports.[44]

An example of this trade was suspected by the commanding officer of the U.S.S. *United States* after he boarded the Canadian brig *Isabella Thompson*, outbound from Nassau to Halifax with a cargo of turpentine and cotton. Though seized but later released by a prize court, correspondence found on board alluded to the New York trade with the South. A letter addressed to B. Weir and Company in Halifax discussed the disposal of the original cargo on behalf of Dollner, Potter and Company of New York, with a second letter giving the impression that this was one of a series of clandestine shipments.[45] Halifax served as both a repair station for blockade runners and as a transit port for supplies clearing onward to Nassau, Bermuda, and Havana with Weir and Company supplying the shipping services as needed.[46]

Some chose to ship their contraband directly through the blockade to Southern ports. Charles Van Zandt, a wine and liquor merchant in New York, was compromised by an undercover investigator in mid-1863 in revealing that he was shipping a cargo on the schooner *Niagara* to Hilton Head and Beaufort, South Carolina. Van Zandt put the undercover agent in contact with others involved in blockade running. The case eventually led to the seizure of the *Niagara* and the schooner *Ladies' Delight*, along with multiple arrests.[47] In that same year, Samuel G. Miles, a Baltimore merchant, was in partnership with a Southerner in the schooner *Secretary*. After failing in their attempts to run the blockade, the vessel eventually offloaded a portion of its cargo in Nassau for later shipment by another blockade runner while the *Secretary* was suspected of finally succeeding in running the blockade herself with pork and other foodstuffs.[48]

The blockade-running schooner *Alexander Copper* was seized north of Wilmington, North Carolina, near New Topsail Inlet, in August of 1863; though reportedly bound for Port Royal, South Carolina, a Union blockade re-supply facility since November 1861, after departing New York she was found tied to a local wharf under the protection of the Confederate military.[49] Besides the North Carolina coast, much of the direct trade passed through the lines via the Chesapeake Bay region. Departing from New York and other Northeastern ports and bound for the docks of the communities along the Potomac, including Washington, some off-loaded cargo along the western inlets to the Chesapeake leading inland to the Confederate lines.[50]

The Mexican port of Matamoros on the Rio Grande River was a major port used throughout the Civil War by the South to move cotton and whose use avoided the dangers of the blockade. With the state of Texas having an extensive land border with Mexico, the South had a legal mechanism to circumvent the Northern blockade fleet. The South could simply ship and sell Confederate cotton to Mexican nationals or others and transport the cotton on foreign ships from Mexico to Liverpool or directly to New York or other northeastern ports demanding cotton for the Yankee textile mills. In exchange were all the supplies needed to sustain a nation including munitions and weapons, normally considered the contraband of war, but when reputedly bound for a neutral nation's use, less likely to be seized.

It was not until February 1, 1862, that the Rio Grande was effectively blockaded by the U.S.S. *Portsmouth* with the English-flagged vessel *Labuan* being seized. With 439 bales of cotton that had been lightered to it over the previous month while at anchorage, she had arrived from Havana. The seizure was vigorously protested by the British, leading to the establishment of the rules of engagement for the blockade captains limiting seizures to vessels on their way to a Texas port after being warned of the Northern blockade.[51]

Though small ships ran the blockade from the upper Texas coast to Matamoros in lieu of overland transport, the vessels involved in the Matamoros trade to Europe and the Northeast were not specially designed blockade runners. Instead, they were the merchant fleet of England, including those vessels that were re-registered as English at the start of the war.

In February 1862, ten vessels were found off of the mouth of the Rio Grande, but by April of 1863, reports of up to two hundred vessels, including American ships bound for Union ports, were present.[52] In 1861, one vessel arrived in New York from Matamoros but in 1862, twenty had arrived;

in 1863, seventy-two with another thirty-two in less than ninety days since the beginning of 1864. Within the same period, 152 outbound vessels were cleared for Matamoros from New York with the U.S. consul in Matamoros believing that at least three-quarters of the cargo was primarily bound for Texas.[53] With the growth of the marine traffic, it may be reasonably inferred once again that communication and the diffusion of the illegal practice among maritime and business trade groups circulated the advantages of Matamoros for contraband trade, in accord with Sutherland's theory of differential association.[54]

Charles Stillman was the most infamous example of a trader operating between the Rio Grande and New York. Born in Connecticut, early in his mercantile career he moved to the lower Rio Grande to assist in the family business. With over a decade and a half in commerce prior to the shells exploding over Fort Sumter, he had developed close ties to the New York mercantile firm of J and N Smith and Company, later known as Smith and Dunning, conspiring to move goods such as boots, powder, cloth, flour, coffee, sugar, lumber, etc., south from New York in exchange for northbound cotton. Using John D. Donahue as his New York agent to obtain cargo for shipment and to dispose of inbound cotton, wool, and deer skins, his finances were handled by his longtime associate James Smith. Goods were documented under the names of Jeremiah Galvin in Matamoros and Jose Morell in Monterrey to allow cargo that otherwise would be subject to seizure free movement under the neutrality laws. Ships were placed under the protection of the British red ensign to accomplish the same while river boats operating on the Rio Grande owned in partnership with Richard King (co-founder of the King Ranch) and Mifflin Kenedy flew a Mexican flag of convenience. His sea-borne vessels, including the *Emma Dean*, the *Alice Tainter*, and the *Banshee*, served as the backbone of his profit-making venture. In early 1864, two shipments alone turned an estimated gross profit of over $285,000 for Stillman from almost one thousand bales of cotton. After the war he settled in New York, having received a pardon from President Andrew Johnson.[55]

Stillman and his associates, Donahue and Smith, epitomize those who are involved in white-collar organized crime. Using their business connections and conspiring to circumvent the law, in many cases using a technicality or fortuitous gratuity to assist in completing their transactions, these men became rich violating the law through their business acumen. By any definition, they were the epitome of Sutherland's white-collar criminal.

SENATORIAL TREASON AND THE 'TEXAS ADVENTURE'

One may simply consider Stillman, though profiting from the war, a Southerner supporting the cause of secession by fighting the war on the economic front (though the same rationalization does not necessarily apply to his

New York accomplices). What may be considered the most egregious act of smuggling was done by no less than a Union war hero and former state governor. William Sprague married the daughter of Lincoln's own secretary of the Treasury and future chief justice of the Supreme Court and, while committing treason against the Union, served as a U.S. senator. Outside of the 'robber barons', Sprague may be the definitive exemplar of Sutherland's white-collar criminal during the nineteenth century.

William Sprague was heir to a multi-million dollar Yankee textile empire, the family eventually having a near domination of the print-cloth industry in later years. Considered as 'one of the oldest and wealthiest in the state' of Rhode Island, Sprague had also risen to the rank of colonel in the state militia prior to the initiation of hostilities. Elected governor in 1860, he would be one of the first Union governors to offer personnel, specifically two regiments, along with an artillery unit to the federal government upon Lincoln's request. He eventually led them into combat at Bull Run (Manassas) where, in the grand tradition of heroism, Sprague had a horse shot out from under him. Within two years, he was appointed as a United States senator from Rhode Island, and shortly afterward he married Catherine (Kate) Chase, the daughter of Salmon Portland Chase, secretary of the Treasury under Lincoln and future chief justice of the Supreme Court of the United States.[56] He was truly one of Sutherland's upper socioeconomic class members.

At the start of the war, Harris Hoyt was living in Galveston, Texas, a major seaport for the state of Texas since the days of the Republic. After shipping his family north to Illinois, Hoyt quit Texas himself by a cotton-laden schooner from Sabine Pass, Texas, ten bales of which were Hoyt's to finance his venture. Four weeks later he arrived in Jamaica, sold his cotton, and eventually made his way to New York in early July by steamer via Port au Prince, Haiti.[57]

Hoyt, carrying letters of introduction, attempted to meet with President Lincoln shortly afterward. Though unsuccessful he did obtain at his own request a letter from Lincoln's private secretary, John Hay, stating that Hoyt had been recommended to the president. He also wrote to Secretary of War Edwin Stanton and met with Secretary of the Navy Gideon Welles and Secretary Chase, intent on receiving a permit to authorize running the blockade while reputedly bringing family members and property, including cotton, out of Texas and to assist Union sympathizers with supplies; none was received.[58]

Yet with a portfolio of letters of introduction, including one now from the executive mansion and an introduction from the former governor of Ohio, within days Hoyt was able to arrange a meeting where he presented his ideas to Governor Sprague. A meeting was agreed to in Providence where Hoyt sold his capability to get cotton out of Texas then have it shipped north. Though Governor Sprague was not present at that meeting, his cousin, Bryon Sprague, represented his firm's, A. and W. Sprague, interests. Also present was William Reynolds, a cotton broker and merchant. Eventually the Providence business houses of Orray, Taft, and Company and B.B. and R. Knight joined the adventure, contributing to the financial means necessary to its success: twenty-five thousand dollars, the planned contribution of each house for a total of one hundred thousand dollars. Hoyt brought Charles Prescott into the operation as his own partner. An arrangement was made that those who fronted the finances, including Sprague, Reynolds, Taft, and Knight, would claim half of all profits and 6 percent of interest on the invested funds, with Hoyt and Prescott entitled to the other half. The agreement stipulated that the intent of the partnership was to trade for and ship Texas cotton to New York or other ports, as appropriate. The contract further authorized the purchase of two vessels, one to conduct the trade in Texas and the second, a steamship, to transport the cotton north. This agreement, though never signed by the parties, more truly stated the intentions of the partnership than any statement later offered in mitigation of the actions of those concerned. With no permits or authorization ever being obtained, the plan simply changed to the schooners running the blockade and bringing the cotton acquired to the steamer, which would then transport the bales to New York.[59]

To assist in the venture, Governor Sprague wrote to Secretary Welles again, attempting to obtain a permit allowing Hoyt to negotiate the blockade without consequence while exchanging goods for cotton with Union adherents in Texas. This attempt, like the previous ones by Hoyt, was unsuccessful. In late October, letters were also written to Major General B.F. Butler of New Orleans and Commodore Farragut, commanding the Gulf Squadron, introducing Hoyt as one who was shipping aid to loyal citizens in Texas and who hoped to supply information to the Union. These latter letters were given to Hoyt for his use, as appropriate.[60]

Reynolds authorized Hoyt and Prescott to purchase two small vessels along with their cargo, the funds being paid by the New York agent of Reynolds, James Suydam, drawn on the account of Reynolds and Company. Those vessels were the schooners *Snow Drift*, purchased in Prescott's name at a cost of $3,500 and later transferred to Reynolds' agent H.B. Bradstow, and *Citizen* owned by Reynolds and Taylor. A third vessel, the steamship *Ella Warley*, was also purchased on October 15 for $29,600, drawn from Sprague's New York house of Hoyt, Spragues and Company, having been put up for sale by the U.S. marshal, per court order. Of the purchase price, $1,000 was paid to one N.C. Turnbridge for arranging the transaction. The 220-foot, 1,115-ton, wooden sidewheel *Ella Warley* had been previously used as a blockade runner, completing three runs prior to her seizure while en route to Charleston from Havana the previous April.[61]

With three vessels now under the control of the conspirators, a cargo was acquired for the *Snow Drift*, including machinery for processing cotton (at Hoyt's request for use in Texas), kerosene oil, lard oil, linseed oil, sperm oil, rope, bagging, prints, brandy, claret, bleached goods, nails, soap, butter, twine, medicines, pins, needles, mustard, and copper. Along with the merchants' variety of goods, also included was the contraband of war; at least 124,000 percussion caps, eight colt revolvers, four thousand pistol cartridges, ten Wesson's rifles, and five thousand cartridges for them. Prior to sailing for Havana, the police superintendent of the New York Police Department, John A. Kennedy, seized the weapons. After the sailing of the *Snow Drift*, the weapons were released in bond, only to be shipped south on the *Ella Warley* for transfer back to the *Snow Drift*.[62]

After Hoyt and *Snow Drift*, under Captain Joseph Wilham, cleared New York on November 14, the *Ella Warley* followed a month later, captained by George Schenck, on December 13; its own cargo included the seized weapons that had been released by Kennedy. Instead of being included in the cargo manifest, they were shipped in trunks as passenger baggage. In the interim, the *Snow Drift* had been detained in Havana by the U.S. consul. Upon Prescott's arrival on the *Ella Warley*, it was arranged to change the ownership as shown on the ship's papers from himself to a British straw man and thereby placed the *Snow Drift*, now re-christened *Cora*, under the British flag and out of reach of U.S. oversight. The straw man earned one hundred dollars for his services. The advantages of foreign ownership, besides reputedly preventing the vessel from being seized by Confederate raiders and Union blockading vessels, lessened the opportunity of identifying Northern interests involved in the illegal trade. The *Ella Warley* then returned to New York.[63]

From Havana the newly named *Cora* sailed for Matamoros, arriving January 23, 1863. After a portion of the cargo was lightered to shore, she sailed across the bar of the Rio Grande and anchored at Bagdad. Hoyt sent the cargo upriver to Matamoros, where a portion of it was sold, and twenty bales of cotton were eventually shipped to New York with the assistance of his brother, Horace Hoyt. Another portion of the proceeds assisted Hoyt in shipping his carding machinery and some of the cargo into the interior of Texas.[64]

While the *Snow Drift/Cora* was in transit to the Rio Grande, the *Citizen* departed New York for New Orleans on December 27 with William Whitford, another agent of Reynolds, on board. Not finding a market for her cargo, she was then also dispatched to Matamoros with her cargo under bond and a New York clerk of Reynolds onboard, a Mr. Hyer. H. B. Brastow, serving as general agent to Reynolds, et al., would take possession of her and her cargo at Matamoros.[65]

Prior to traveling to Matamoros, Brastow had been assigned as general agent aboard the *Ella Warley* on her second voyage from New York. Cleared for New Orleans, she departed on February 9, 1863, only to be run down accidently by the steamer *North Star*, owned by 'Commodore' Vanderbilt. Brastow, having survived the collision, was directed to Matamoros as the group's general agent.[66]

Brastow, upon his own arrival in Matamoros on the *Herbert*, found the *Cora* and sold it in exchange for medicines. Those were sold and the funds were then used to purchase Confederate cotton that was shipped on to New York. Upon the arrival of the *Citizen*, it too was sold, along with the majority of its cargo, and the proceeds were converted to Confederate cotton for a New York delivery. That which was not sold was consigned locally with instructions to remit the profit in cotton, again to New York. Within the first two weeks of July, Brastow had arranged to ship 299 bales of cotton, one bale of wool, and a couple of bales of waste rope to New York via British sailing vessels. He departed Matamoros for New York himself that same month.[67]

Hoyt himself returned to New York in January 1864, after having operated his smuggled cotton carding machinery for a significant profit while in Texas; he had sold the equipment, turning the funds into cotton as he had also turned the *Cora*'s cargo into cotton. He had also purchased cotton using counterfeit Confederate currency previously bought for ten cents on the dollar in the North. Hoyt had arranged for shipments of cotton to travel south to Matamoros via the vessel *America*, the three-masted schooner *Lamon*—reportedly with 127 bales—and the vessel *Zaragossa*, though the latter was seized by the blockade and fifty bales were lost. Of the two successful shipments out of Texas, at least several hundred bales made it south for forwarding to New York. These cotton transactions seem to have benefited only Hoyt. Upon his return to the North, he saw Reynolds and was taken to a meeting with Lyman Frieze, representing A. and W. Sprague, Edward Taft, and Robert Knight. Hoyt only mentioned the seized bales and a separate quantity of cotton located up the Rio Grande as having been the shipments for the investors, claiming the rest of the funding had gone to expenses. Yet he was able to convince Reynolds to make a further investment in shipping once again to Matamoros, in this case flour and corn valued at twelve thousand to fifteen thousand dollars, later to be converted into cotton while also giving Hoyt five thousand dollars for cotton purchases. The partners in this smuggling venture, each with one-fourth interest, were Reynolds, Hoyt, Suydam, and an associate of Hoyt's, T. A. Morris. The vessel *Caraccas* was chartered and after arriving at Bermuda due to damage, the cargo was moved to the British-flagged brig *Monarch* for the run to the Rio Grande. The general agent onboard in this venture was Morris himself. Reportedly the *Monarch* was to return to New York in December of 1864 with 160 bales of cotton; 120 bales were consigned for Hoyt while the other 40 bales were for his fellow conspirators.[68] This was but one venture of William Sprague's; both a letter written to Major General Dix during an investigation of the Texas Adventure and congressional testimony allude to other Sprague adventures to obtain cotton, including using British possessions to run goods to and from the South.[69]

With its numerous players, multiple vessels, and extended operations the Texas Adventure epitomizes the modern definitions of criminal conspiracy, organized crime, and racketeering. Though judging past actions through a modern lens can be questionable at best, the concerns of the adventurers' contemporaries were enough to initiate criminal charges by the military and, eventually, a Senate investigation. The failure of both to achieve any disciplinary action may say more about the politics of the age than about the veracity of the evidence. Yet it was also an example of the ability of the powerful to avoid the treatment given to a low-level criminal such as Hoyt, who was originally arrested for trading with the enemy. Sprague's socioeconomic position and concomitant influence effectively prevented any action other than a Senate investigation years later—initiated by Sprague himself—an investigation that finally stated that, 'All the committee can do, under the circumstances, and after having found that there is nothing in the papers implicating Senator Sprague, is to ask, as they now do, that they be discharged from the further consideration of the subject'.[70] Sprague had successfully obfuscated his own involvement through the use of intermediaries. Though Sprague and his associates were not formally a legal corporation, both the secrecy and the influence used to 'fix' the investigation are points of substantiation for Sutherland's belief that white-collar crime is organized crime.[71]

With war the opportunities for profiteering from the tremendous societal changes were enormous. Sprague was but one example of the Civil War profiteering:

> The most important of the nineteenth-century American capitalists acquired their first great fortunes during the war. J. P. Morgan, Philip Armour, Clement Studebaker, John Wanamaker, Cornelius Vanderbilt, and the du Ponts had all been government contractors. Andrew Carnegie got rich speculating in bridge and rail construction while assistant to the Assistant Secretary of War in charge of military transportation.[72]

But in Sprague's case, the difference was arguably treasonous. He chose, as many did, to traffic with the enemy for his personal profit through smuggling. By any definition, he personified the classic white-collar criminal.

WHITE GOLD

The trade in cotton, the foundation of commerce between North and South prior to the hostilities, continued as the war progressed and specie became less available.[73] It had been the backbone of the export trade of the nation prior to the war. By 1860, almost two-thirds of the United States' total exports were cotton.[74] The trade was justified, as many political decisions are, with multiple explanations. Business excuses included protecting commerce from ruin to allowing profiting from the demand of Northern products shipped south; national security grounds included the protection of gold reserves when cotton was used by Northern merchants for foreign purchases in lieu of specie, to minimizing the potential for any European power to justify their own intervention in the conflict in order to maintain their supply of cotton for their own textile trade. Yet what may have been the most mercenary justification was authorizing certain individuals to trade with the South as a form of patronage for individual high officials and flag officers of the military.[75]

This patronage developed from the relationships between the high government officials and the business community that 'created a less critical attitude of government towards businessmen than toward persons of lower socioeconomic class', allowing violations of the law to be ignored.[76] These relationships between governmental officials and business developed for a variety of reasons, according to Sutherland. Many members of both government and business were part of a 'culturally homogeneous' group, coming from the same 'upper strata of society'; those families provided personnel both to government and to business, 'intimate personal' friendships carried across both professions, connections between government officials developed in the business world prior to their governmental service continued, and after their public service these connections assisted in a transition back to employment in their former business community.[77] Those government-business connections enabled the establishment of the patronage and eventually led to a toleration of the contraband cotton trade.

For the Confederate government, the trade allowed the purchase of needed foodstuffs and military supplies both across the lines and across the sea with cotton being used as the collateral for the purchase of military supplies. The historical connections between bankers, merchant houses, and insurers that had developed over the years in the North and in England would, as discussed previously, in some cases continue throughout the war. Besides the merchants shipping cotton through various maritime artifices, a second major source of white-collar crime presented itself: collusion between the opposing sides to the perceived betterment of both.

On July 13, 1861, by an act of Congress, all trade with the states in rebellion was prohibited unless licensed by the president and regulated by the Treasury, which meant, for all practical purposes, Samuel Chase. All goods coming from or going to those states declared in insurrection were subject to forfeiture, as was the vessel or vehicle transporting them.[78] At the start of the war, the problem for Chase was to prevent Northern goods from moving south while at the same time not destroying commerce altogether, thereby upsetting Northern business, particularly in those border areas under the Union flag.[79]

Though the blockade had been established under the president's order of April 19, 1861, with the navy having responsibility, inland trade, including navigable waterways such as the Mississippi and Ohio rivers, was to be addressed jointly by both the Treasury and the army. The Treasury ultimately was responsible for the final disposition of all goods and claims. Chase was slow to put into place extensive regulations, in many cases making decisions based on local conditions, always looking to allow trade under his slowly developing regulations in Union controlled areas. The difficulty was that in allowing trade to these border areas Chase effectively allowed trade with the South. Trying to determine the boundary between belligerents on any given day along hundreds of miles of poorly manned borderland was difficult at the best of times. Goods allowed to enter Kentucky or Missouri, for example, could and were diverted by merchants anywhere to the South, thanks to the network of waterways and railroads connecting the border areas to the Confederacy. Chase, in attempting to placate the merchants, communicated with his agents the objective of confiscation instead of prose-cution—a demonstration of Sutherland's assertion that 'the power relation-ships protect businessmen against critical definitions by government'.[80] As Sutherland remarked, the pressure imposed by these businessmen for special trade privileges led to corrupt government.[81]

Congress, upon being convened by the president in July 1861, gave for-mal authority to Chase to regulate commerce by promulgating rules and regulations to address trade within the border areas and into the South. With agents appointed to implement his directives Chase established and enforced a body of regulations by March of 1862, building a strong political base through patronage that tied all those he appointed to him through personal loyalty.[82] The difficulty was that *any* trade allowed the opportunity for con-traband trade across the frontier. Regulations were constantly modified or added in an attempt to keep trade legal. The use of a permit system identified the cargo and its destination with the intent of proscribing its movement. Yet with the rapid movement of western Union armies, those lands deemed acceptable for trade were at times questionable, since Union forces could not effectively occupy all lands 'held' thereby allowing corrupt merchants to smuggle goods south to the insurrectionists. Memphis, for example, became a hub of illicit traffic. At least one congressman claimed that twenty million to thirty million dollars of supplies transited Memphis bound for the South.[83]

By the fall of 1863, Chase had arranged for trade stores to be created in an attempt to make traders conform to the regulations in secured Confeder-ate lands. Established to supply the wants of families and plantations, they would serve as a conduit to the South, for once supplies were within range of the Southern lines, a porous border could do little to prevent smuggling traffic in both directions: cotton north in exchange for much needed supplies going southward. With the length of the Mississippi opened to trade, the entire river drainage became but a series of cul-de-sacs and waterways for the smuggling traders. A vessel could operate from New Orleans to Mem-phis, clandestinely stopping anywhere convenient along the river to off-load goods or to take on cotton for disposal upriver later in the journey.[84]

Within a year, in an attempt to address this uncontrolled trade, the sec-retary of the Treasury, now W. P. Fessenden, appointed agents to buy cotton directly from the Confederate states. The policy, formally implemented in September of 1864, allowed individuals to sell their cotton at three-fourths of the current New York market price. That same individual then could purchase merchandise totaling up to one-third of the price received, returning the goods to wherever the cotton had been obtained. The law's intent was to establish government control of the cotton traffic, thereby minimizing smuggling while also increasing the national revenue, for all practical purposes, by taxing each purchased bale 25 percent of its New York value.[85]

Yet in its implementation it not only failed to oversee the trade in the military controlled areas, it opened the way for Union merchants and traders to unlimited intercourse with the rebel armies and those who supported them. As written it opened the door for the unscrupulous to penetrate Southern lines and, after purchasing great quantities of cotton, otherwise unmarketable due to the naval blockade, they were guaranteed a market and profit for their goods, selling the bales to Treasury agents for three-fourths of their New York value.[86]

The permit that granted permission for trade in cotton became the catalyst for various frauds allowing contraband cotton to be illegally shipped north. From fraudulently modifying the permits in order to increase the permitted quantity of goods to be shipped north, to enlarging the area of operations permitted to acquire the cotton, whatever could be accomplished to increase profits seems to have been attempted. Some bought the permits from those who had the political patronage to obtain one. Though an 'open' process in name, those with the connections obtained either through political or financial considerations were in a better position to obtain a permit than others.[87] The profit in permitted trade was incredible:

> For an initial $100 in greenbacks, one could buy a 400-lb. bale of cotton in the South. The bale would be worth $500 in greenbacks in the New York market. Since the government paid only three-quarters the current New York price under the terms of the September 1864 regulations, the trader received only $375. The trader could then take goods worth one-third of this amount back to the Confederacy. For $125, the northern trader could purchase 568 pounds of bacon at twenty-two cents per pound. Southerners were willing to pay $6 per pound (in Confederate currency) for bacon. With the $3,408 in Confederate currency, the northern trader could purchase 2,180 pounds of cotton at $1.25 in Confederate currency (subtracting the Confederate discount of 20%, reducing the $3,408 to $2,726.40). Still, the trader would receive over $2,000 in greenbacks after selling the cotton and remitting the one-fourth portion to the government.[88]

The potential profits led to corruption from the highest levels of government to the lowest officials and carried over to both the army and the navy. George Harrington, the assistant secretary of the Treasury from 1861 to mid-1864, was in partnership with the Memphis firm of E. Parkman, Brooks and Company, which held a permit to ship fifteen thousand bales of cotton from the South.[89]

Another rogue involved was a former congressman, Andrew Hamilton. Obtaining a permit through the support of Secretary of State Seward, Hamilton was able to obtain documentation from President Lincoln, similar to what Senator Sprague's associates attempted to obtain, in order to ship cotton out of Texas without molestation by the blockade. When the president's instructions reached Commodore Farragut, Hamilton was able to enlist the support of the secretary of War, Gideon Welles, to have the president's directive rescinded against Seward's wishes.[90]

Treasury agents responsible for issuing the approved permits were lax or corrupt, with some agents actually having received their positions due to the patronage of those very individuals interested in profiting from a fast and loose interpretation of the regulations. This was simply an egregious example of Sutherland's 'power relationship against critical definitions by government'.[91] One agent, Hanson Riley, later admitted under congressional questioning his 'error' in issuing permits that endorsed the shipment of over nine hundred thousand bales of cotton.[92]

The rush for cotton also corrupted the military on two fronts. Rank and file naval officers on the Mississippi decided to travel into the interior and seize cotton wherever it was found, claiming it as a prize of war, and thereby being entitled to a portion of its value as a lawful naval prize. The army was little different with officers seizing and profiting from more than two million dollars in cotton themselves.[93] Though many officers were opposed to the trade and attempted to stop it, recognizing that the trade was supplying the enemy of much needed supplies, one who supported the commerce was General Benjamin Butler. Originally appointed a major general of volunteers at the outbreak of war—the same commission pursued by then Governor Sprague—Butler would, by using his brother Andrew as a 'cut-out' both condone and profit from trade with the belligerents through areas under his control. As a resident of Massachusetts, a stockholder in textile mills, and a future politician who parleyed his skills into a congressional seat after the war and the governorship of Massachusetts twenty years later, all cotton that transited his military district profited him enormously.[94] Butler and his family personified the concept of Sutherland's 'power relationships [that] protect businessmen against critical definitions by government'.[95] As both the government's representative and the businessman that the government was to regulate, Butler epitomized the cross-pollination of white-collar crime between business and politics, effectively corrupting the law, making all the 'definitions' favorable toward its violation to his personal benefit.[96]

Within Butler's military district of the Department of Virginia and North Carolina (encompassing the Norfolk area and northeastern North Carolina counties), Southerners could purchase provisions needed in the South under the approved label of 'family goods', using the profit of Southern cotton transported and sold for funds. These transactions were brokered by local trade stores established under the Treasury's regulations to supply local farmers in the Union held lands with living necessities. As the district commander, Butler had ultimate supervision of these stores and reportedly profited from them.[97]

The corruption and venality pervaded Butler's associates and appointments. Brigadier General George Shepley, having previously served under Butler when he was the military governor in New Orleans, was brought to Virginia where he held the responsibility for issuing permits to move goods across the front. His own adjutant, Captain George Johnson, eventually resigned after being brought up on charges of corruption, yet he then managed one of the trading stores in partnership with a Butler-appointed special provost marshal. Butler's brother-in-law used his association with the general to extort a half share in another trade store and obtained a 40 percent interest in a second one.[98]

By mid-century, though the manufacturing class had come to surpass the merchant capitalists as the nation's financial elite, it was the Northern merchants who were in a symbiotic trade relationship with the Southern planters, New York trading houses moved cotton north and onward to England in exchange for manufactured goods from Britain and the Northern states. Civil war between North and South terminated the trade but exceptions immediately developed, some considered 'acceptable' if not legal, but much of it criminal. The South's objective was to move critical goods such as salt, medical supplies, and military equipment across the line. The business organizations in existence prior to the war continued to serve the South with Northern manufactured goods, including munitions, being smuggled south by Northern business interests via neutral ports or even directly to Southern communities utilizing blockade running vessels, many of which were owned or operated by British interests. Other goods transited Mexico bound for Texas and the greater South with cotton used as currency for payment. Eventually as the North moved into secessionist lands, a corrupt trade in smuggled cotton developed between the South and various Northern military and governmental organizations with certain selected Northern businessmen obtaining, in Sutherland's words, 'special privileges' to profit from the trade.

The Civil War offered many an opportunity to serve their country honorably, but as in all wars, some chose to profit personally by it to achieve economic success that stood as their American Dream. For the South and the Confederate army smuggling was a lifeline that provided needed supplies and was both logical and honorable for men such as Levi White during his service with the Confederate Ordinance Corps. For some Southern farmers, it was at times simply a matter of survival in a time of social disorganization. For others under the Southern banner, such as Charles Stillman and his associates, smuggling served the South while also offering the opportunity to acquire a personal fortune. For the British and other neutral foreign nationals involved in the contraband trade, smuggling was also a way to personal fortune. But for many a Yankee businessman, the profit earned in their trade, at a minimum, was at the expense of their own nation and their claimed allegiance and bordered on treason. These were the respected businessmen to whom Sutherland referred when he first introduced the term 'white-collar crime' in 1939 and whom Merton later described as those who would achieve financial success 'by fair means if possible and by foul means if necessary'.[99] They used their political and professional associates and acquaintances to manipulate and to maneuver around the law. In some cases, they corrupted officials who would otherwise stand in their way to wealth and success. Many avoided the rightful consequences of their actions—General Benjamin Butler and Senator William Sprague being the most flagrant examples known in a business otherwise notorious for reticence and caution in its affairs.[100] They, along with the Northern merchants and manufacturers trading with the South, were one more link in American businesses' continuing white-collar criminality, living by the proposition that 'profits take priority to patriotism'.[101]

NOTES

1. Bruce Catton, *America Goes to War* (Middletown, CT: Wesleyan University Press, 1958, repr. 1986), p. 14.
2. Edwin H. Sutherland, *White Collar Crime: The Uncut Version* (New Haven, CT: Yale University Press, 1983), p. 190.
3. Jim Cullen, *The American Dream: A Short History of an Idea that Shaped a Nation* (New York: Oxford University Press, 2003), pp. 59–69; Sutherland, *White Collar Crime*, pp. 7–8.
4. Keith Bryant and Henry Dethloff, *A History of American Business* (Englewood Cliffs, NJ: Prentice-Hall, 1983), p. 81.
5. Richard D. Goff, *Confederate Supply* (Durham, NC: Duke University Press, 1969), pp. 3–5.
6. Bryant and Dethloff, *A History of American Business*, p. 107.
7. *ibid.*, pp. 105–107.
8. Robert Greenhalgh Albion with the collaboration of Jennie Barnes Pope, *The Rise of New York Port: 1815–1860* (New York, Charles Scribner's Sons, 1939; repr. Boston, MA: Northeastern University,1967), pp. 95–121.
9. William W. Chenault and Robert C. Reinders, 'The Northern-born Community of New Orleans in the 1850s', *Journal of American History*, 51 (1964), 232–247 (pp. 232–233).
10. Edwin Sutherland, *Principles of Criminality*, 4th edn (Philadelphia, PA: J.B. Lippincott, 1947), pp. 6–7.
11. Abraham Lincoln, 'Proclamation,' in Letters Sent, RG 56, NARA, pp. 7–8, as cited in Clinton W. Terry, ' "Let Commerce Follow the Flag": Trade and Loyalty to the Union', *Ohio Valley History*, 1 (2001), 2–14 (p. 6).
12. U.S. Naval War Records Office, *War of the Rebellion: A Compilation of the Official Records of the Union and Confederate Navies* (ORN), 30 vols (Washington, D.C.: Government Printing Office, 1874–1922), ser. 1, XVI, p. 857.
13. Robert Merton, 'Social Structure and Anomie', *American Sociological Review*, 3 (October 1938), 672–682 (pp. 679–682).
14. Goff, *Confederate Supply*, pp. 3–5.
15. Ella Lonn, *Salt as a Factor in the Confederacy* (Tuscaloosa: University of Alabama Press, 1965), pp. 13–18.

16. U.S. War Department, *War of the Rebellion: A Compilation of the Official Records of the Union and Confederate Armies* (ORA), 128 vols (Washington, D.C.: Government Printing Office, 1880–1900), ser. I, XVII, pt. 2, p. 141.
17. ORA, ser. 1, XVII, pt. 2, p. 713; ORA, ser. 4, II, p. 126.
18. William Tecumseh Sherman, *Home Letters of General Sherman*, ed. by M.A. DeWolfe Howe, (New York: Charles Scribner's Sons, 1909), p. 229.
19. Lonn, *Salt*, pp. 161–163.
20. *American Druggist and Chemical Gazette*, 6:173 (1862), as cited in Edward K. Spann, *Gotham at War: New York City, 1860–1865* (Wilmington, DE: Scholarly Resources, 2002), p. 137.
21. Levi S. White, 'Running the Blockade on the Chesapeake Bay', *Baltimore Sun*, December 15, 1907, December 22, 1907, December 29, 1907, January 5, 1908; and Henry Hollyday, 'Running the Blockade.' *Confederate Veteran* 29: 3 (March 1921): 93–96, as cited in Eric Mills, *Chesapeake Bay in the Civil War* (Centreville, MD: Tidewater, 1996), pp. 159–164.
22. Stephen. R. Wise, *Lifeline of the Confederacy: Blockade Running during the Civil War* (Columbia: University of South Carolina Press, 1988), p. 7.
23. *ibid.*, p. 47.
24. Eric J. Graham, *Clydebuilt: The Blockade Runners, Cruisers and Armoured Rams of the American Civil War* (Edinburgh: Birlinn, 2006); Wise, *Lifeline of the Confederacy*, p. 107.
25. Wise, *Lifeline of the Confederacy*, pp. 150 and 161.
26. *ibid.*, p. 71.
27. *ibid.*, p. 111.
28. *ibid.*, pp. 71–72; ORN, ser. 1, XVII, pp. 299–300.
29. Wise, *Lifeline of the Confederacy*, pp. 158–161.
30. *ibid.*, p. 72.
31. *ibid.*, p. 107.
32. Sutherland, *White Collar Crime*, p. 191.
33. Wise, *Lifeline of the Confederacy*, pp. 63–66.
34. Robert Carse, *Blockade: The Civil War at Sea* (New York: Rinehart, 1958), p.19.
35. Albion, *The Rise of New York Port*, p. 105.
36. Chenault, 'The Northern-born Community', p. 233.
37. Richard V. Francaviglia, *From Sail to Steam: Four Centuries of Texas Maritime History, 1500–1900* (Austin: University of Texas, 1998), p. 128.
38. Spann, *Gotham at War*, p. 6; *New York Times*, January 8, 1861, p. 2.
39. Spann, *Gotham at War*, pp. 6–11 and 31.
40. Mills, *Chesapeake Bay*, p. 161.
41. Sutherland, *White Collar Crime*, pp. 190–191.
42. Stuart L. Bernath, *Squall Across the Atlantic: American Civil War Prize Cases and Diplomacy* (Berkeley: University of California, 1970), p. 5–11; Spann, *Gotham at War*, p. 136.
43. House of Representatives, Report from the Committee on Public Expenditures, New York Custom-House, 38th Cong.,1st sess., Report No. 111, p. 8.
44. Kenneth J. Blume, 'The Mid-Atlantic Arena: The United States, the Confederacy, and the British West Indies, 1861–1865', (unpublished doctoral dissertation, State University of New York at Binghamton, 1984), pp. 203–204.
45. Charles Perry, 'Clandestine Commerce: Yankee Blockade Running', *Journal of Confederate History*, 4 (1989), 89–111 (pp.102–103).
46. Wise, *Lifeline of the Confederacy*, pp. 191–192; ORN ser. 1, II, p. 293.
47. Ludwell H. Johnson, 'Commerce between Northeastern Ports and the Confederacy, 1861–1865', *Journal of American History*, 54 (1967), 30–42 (pp. 36–37).
48. *ibid.*, pp. 37–38.
49. ORN, ser. 1, IX, pp. 176–178.
50. Johnson, 'Commerce between Northeastern Ports', pp. 30–42 and 35–36.

51. ORN, ser. 1, XVII, pp. 101 and 109–111; ORN ser. 1, XVIII, p. 66.
52. ORN, ser. 1, XVII, pp. 101 and 403.
53. House of Representatives, Report from the Committee on Public Expenditures, New York Custom-House, 38th Cong., 1st sess., Report No. 111, p. 7.
54. Sutherland, *White Collar Crime*, pp. 246–250.
55. House of Representatives, Report from the Committee on Public Expenditures, New York Custom-House, 38th Cong.,1st sess., Report No. 111; House of Representatives, Report from the Committee on Public Expenditures, New York Custom-House, 38th Cong., 2nd sess., Report No. 25; James. W. Daddysman, *The Matamoros Trade: Confederate Commerce, Diplomacy and Intrigue* (Cranbury, NJ: University of Delaware Press, 1984), pp. 151–178; L. Tuffley Ellis, 'Maritime Commerce on the Far Western Gulf, 1861–1865', *Southwestern Historical Quarterly*, 77 (1973), 167–226; Marilyn McAdams Sibley, 'Charles Stillman: A Case Study of Entrepreneurship on the Rio Grande, 1861–1865', *Southwestern Historical Quarterly*, 77 (1973), 227–240.
56. *New York Times*, March 29, 1860, p. 1; April 5, 1860, p. 4; April 18, 1861, p. 4; February 10, 1862, p. 2; March 6, 1863, p. 5; November 4, 1873, p. 1.
57. Senate Executive Document No. 10, Part 3, 41st Cong., 3rd sess., p. 5.
58. *ibid.*, p. 3; Senate Report No. 377, 41st Cong., 3rd sess., p. 1.
59. Senate Executive Document No. 10, Part 3, 41st Cong., 3rd sess., pp. 3–5, 7–8, 19–20, 23–24, 26–29, 36, 38–39, 42–44, 46–47.
60. Senate Report No. 377, 41st Cong., 3rd sess., pp. 3–4.
61. Senate Executive Document No. 10, Part 3, 41st Cong., 3rd sess., pp. 6, 9–10, 20–21, 24, 27, 30, 38–39, 44; Wise, *Lifeline of the Confederacy*, p. 297.
62. Senate Executive Document No. 10, Part 3, 41st Cong., 3rd sess., pp. 21, 24, 39, 49, 53–56, 60–71, 78–80.
63. *ibid.*, pp. 6–7, 9–10, 14, 21, 24–25, 31, 76.
64. *ibid.*, pp. 7, 10–11, 15–16, 21–22, 24, 30–31, 39, 50, 57, 57–58, 64–66, 72–73, 76, 78–80.
65. *ibid.*, pp. 20, 22, 24, 31–32, 40, 58, 81–87, 89–97.
66. *ibid.*, pp. 24, 31–32, 37–39, 45.
67. *ibid.*, pp. 7, 10–11, 32, 57–58, 71.
68. *ibid.*, pp. 2–26, 29–52, 56–57, 72–75.
69. *ibid.*, pp. 47–48; Senate Report No. 377, 41st Cong., 3rd sess., p. 15.
70. Senate Report No. 377, 41st Cong., 3rd sess., p. 18.
71. Sutherland, *White Collar Crime*, pp. 227–238.
72. Richard F. Haufman, *The War Profiteers* (Indianapolis, IN: Bobbs-Merrill, 1970), p. 9.
73. Goff, *Confederate Supply*, p. 44.
74. Total Exports: North, 'Balance of Payments,' *loc. cit.*, Table I and Table B-1, Appendix B, Cotton Exports: U.S. Congress, House Miscellaneous Documents No. 49, part 2, 48th Cong., 1st sess. (1864), Tables 2 and 7, as cited in Douglass C. North, *The Economic Growth of the United States, 1790–1860* (New York: W.W. Norton, 1966), Appendix I, p. 233.
75. *Congressional Globe*, 38th Cong., 2nd sess. , p. 1351; Ludwell H. Johnson, 'Contraband Trade during the Last Year of the Civil War', *Mississippi Valley Historical Review*, 49 (1963), 635–652 (p. 635).
76. Sutherland, *White Collar Crime*, p. 251.
77. *ibid.*, pp. 251–255.
78. Act of July 13, 1861, 12 *Stat.* 255, c. 3.
79. Terry, ' "Let Commerce Follow the Flag" ', pp. 2–14.
80. E. Merton Coulter, 'Commercial Intercourse with the Confederacy in the Mississippi Valley, 1861–1865', *Mississippi Valley Historical Review*, 5 (1919), 377–395; Senate Bill 1, 37th Cong., 1st sess. (July 6, 1861); Senate Report No. 108, Part 3, 37th Cong., 3rd sess.; Sutherland, *White Collar Crime*, p. 252.

81. Sutherland, *White Collar Crime*, p. 93.
82. Terry, ' "Let Commerce Follow the Flag" ', pp. 6–7.
83. ORA, ser. 1, VIII, pp. 584–585; ser. 1, XIII, pp. 698–700; Senate Report No. 108, 37th Cong., 3rd sess., U.S. Congress, *Congressional Globe*, 28th Cong., 1st sess., 4:3324; Ludwell H. Johnson, 'Northern Profit and Profiteers: The Cotton Rings of 1864–1865', *Civil War History*, 12 (1966), 101–115.
84. ORA, ser. 1, XXI, pt. 3, p. 361; ser. 1, XXXII, pt. 1, pp. 514–515; ser. 1, XXXIX, pt. 2, pp. 27–28 and 30–31.
85. *Congressional Globe*, 38th Cong., 2nd sess., Appendix, p. 30; Johnson, 'Contraband Trade', pp. 637–638.
86. *Congressional Globe*, 38th Cong., 2nd sess., p. 1350; Coulter, 'Commercial Intercourse', pp. 388–390.
87. *Congressional Globe*, 38th Cong., 2nd sess., p. 1350; Coulter, 'Commercial Intercourse', pp. 377–395; Johnson, 'Northern Profit and Profiteers', pp. 102–115; David G. Surdam, 'Traders or Traitors: Northern Cotton Trading During the Civil War', *Business and Economic History*, 28, (1999), 302–312.
88. House Report No. 24, 38th Cong., 2nd sess., as cited in Surdam, 'Traders or Traitors', p. 302.
89. Johnson, 'Northern Profit and Profiteers', p. 103.
90. ORN, ser. 1, 21, pp. 643–645 and 706–710; Johnson, 'Northern Profit and Profiteers', pp. 108–110.
91. Sutherland, *White Collar Crime*, p. 252.
92. *Congressional Globe*, 38th Cong., 2nd sess., p. 1351; 38th Cong., 1st sess., p. 2823; Surdam, 'Traders or Traitors', p. 305.
93. *Congressional Globe*, 37th Cong., 3rd sess., pp. 1330–1335, 1428; 38th Cong., 1st sess., pp. 2821–2822; 2nd sess., pp. 1349–1356; ORA ser.1, XXIV, pt. 3, p. 538.
94. Thomas Graham Belden and Marva Robins Belden, *So Fell the Angels* (Boston, MA: Little and Brown, 1956), p. 45; U.S. Congress, *Congressional Globe*, 37th Cong., 3rd sess., p. 1334; ORA ser. 1, XXIV, part 3, p. 538; Johnson, 'Contraband Trade', p. 641.
95. Sutherland, *White Collar Crime*, p. 252.
96. *ibid.*, pp. 8–9.
97. Johnson, 'Contraband Trade', pp. 641–642; Surdam, 'Traders or Traitors', p. 308.
98. Johnson, 'Contraband Trade', pp. 643–644; Surdam, 'Traders or Traitors', pp. 302–312; ORA, Ser. 1, XXXVI, pt. 3, p. 266.
99. Robert K. Merton, *Social Theory and Social Structure* (New York: The Free Press, 1968), p. 223.
100. Edwin H. Sutherland, 'White-collar Criminality', *American Sociological Review*, 5 (1940), 1–12 (p. 1).
101. Sutherland, *White Collar Crime*, p. 190.

4   Filibustering and Revolutionaries

When Edwin Sutherland presented his premise of white-collar crime and the criminals who committed it, one group of violations discussed were war crimes. He specifically mentioned violations of embargo and neutrality laws, believing that understanding war crimes revealed a preference for profit over patriotism.[1] These types of violations go back to the earliest administrations with the nation dealing with its first embargo violations in 1807 under the government of Jefferson. Yet prior to the embargo legislation, the fledgling republic's first president, George Washington, had issued a proclamation in an attempt to address international neutrality issues as early as 1793.[2] This proclamation was built on the principle that a neutral state was bound to refrain from interfering in a war between two powers when both of which were at peace with that neutral state. In attempting to prevent citizens of the United States from aiding in the hostilities, it would focus on the export of goods from the United States versus the importation of goods.[3] Though charged and prosecuted under the neutrality statutes, the violations were simply another form of smuggling—the illicit import or export of goods.[4]

These ongoing violations of neutrality laws over the coming century were brought about by a continuing political situation where an 'excess of definitions favorable to violation of law' always seemed to exist over 'definitions unfavorable to violation of law'.[5] The first and foremost definition was the neutrality law itself. Weak, it continually allowed numerous opportunities to skirt its requirements by even the most unsophisticated of persons. Even when enforcement was attempted, the forces arrayed against the violators were limited. Customs activity concentrated on revenue enhancement, with the limited number of revenue marine vessels originally directed toward inbound smuggling now focused on a sundry list of maritime functions. With the marshals serving the administrative needs of the courts as their enforcement arm and the military only used in an ad hoc manner, what few successes that were achieved were an accomplishment in themselves. But the greatest 'definition favorable to violation of law' for the filibusters , those individuals involved in private military actions attempting to overthrow a friendly government, was the support of a large portion of the population. Various groups came together to form a constituency supporting filibustering movements over the next century. Business interests sought new markets, Southern interests attempted to extend slavery during the first half of the century, and many others saw the filibusters as a mailed arm used to extend democracy. Individuals who joined believed that their self-interest, specifically their financial self-interest, promoted the national interest. Few, if any, saw their actions as war crimes.

With the Constitution of the United States prohibiting any tax or duty on goods exported from any state, the idea of smuggling in America is generally recognized as the movement of goods across the country's border or frontier and into the nation's commerce in violation of the law.[6] The goods themselves may be illegal—certain drugs for instance, or the smugglers may be avoiding taxes and duties by clandestinely landing the goods, which themselves are not otherwise contraband. Yet smuggling also includes the illegal export of goods from a country, either after having been totally banned from export or though legal to ship foreign, having a prohibitively high rate of duty. Some entrepreneurs chose to circumvent the exorbitant rates by exporting the goods illegally, as in England when the Crown initiated a duty on the export of wool in 1275, eventually leading to a surge in frauds against the revenue.[7] For England's former colony, it would instead be about banning the exportation of war materials.

For the United States the issue of neutrality led to the passage of a series of proclamations, regulations, resolutions, and legislation during the nation's first 150 years that incorporated the concept of illegal exportation of goods. The first Neutrality Act, passed by Congress in 1794 after President Washington had issued two previous executive proclamations, was in response to European conflicts and was an attempt by the United States to both avoid entanglements with the belligerent powers and to profit from them. Instigated by the activities of the minister of France, M. Genet, who had planned to attack British vessels by utilizing privateers outfitted in American ports, the legislation (made permanent by the Act of April 24, 1800) was intended to prohibit U.S. citizens from accepting commissions to serve a foreign prince or state, from enlisting or hiring others to enlist in the service of a foreign prince or state, from outfitting or arming a vessel to be used by a foreign prince or state in war against a prince or state at peace with the United States, from increasing the force of any ship of war in service to the same, and from initiating a military expedition from the United States against a prince or state at peace with the United States. Intent to export arms or inappropriately outfitted or equipped vessels in violation of the Neutrality Act would subject the vessel to seizure and the malefactor to imprisonment and/or fines. The Act of June 14, 1797, had earlier extended the neutrality law to those who committed enumerated acts 'without the limits of' the United States and also extended coverage to include acts against U.S. citizens or property.[8]

With 'profits being the *raison d'être* of privateers' and their investors being primarily merchants and shipowners, the government was addressing one of the earliest forms of white-collar crime.[9] But the neutrality laws also had the potential to snare more than a merchant investing in a privateer. William Blount, one of Sutherland's respected men serving as a senator from the newly established state of Tennessee, was impeached for just such a violation. But the Senate, after having expelled Blount, chose not to address the accusations, claiming they lacked jurisdiction in the matter and setting a precedent for failing to deal with one of its own. In the years after the Civil War, Senator William Sprague of Delaware would benefit from a similar reticence. Senator Blount had suffered financially from extensive western land speculations and believed that British control of Spanish and French territories would strength his position. He had been accused of being involved in a plot to incite the Cherokee and Creek nations in support of Britain against both Spanish Florida holdings and French Louisiana lands after a letter was discovered in his handwriting, alluding to the intrigue.[10]

With Napoleon's invasion of Spain in 1808, the Spanish colonies of South and Central America saw an opportunity to challenge their colonial rulers and would have the sympathies of Americans in their struggle for independence. Along with that sympathy, some also saw an opportunity for personal fame and fortune.[11] A new American Dream, one founded in the concept of revolution and independence from European domination, came to include the ideology of Manifest Destiny as a justification for individual and national aggrandizement. Many American citizens, congressmen, and presidential administrations viewed the objectives of these efforts positively. In attempting to fulfill its international obligations of neutrality, however, the government of the United States tried to utilize the neutrality laws as a tool to control the ambitions of various parties, both foreign and domestic, from overtly aiding the numerous attempts at independence being supported from American soil.[12]

On February 3, 1806, the vessel *Leander* departed New York in a filibustering attempt to instigate a Venezuelan revolution. The attempt was organized by Francisco de Miranda with the support of Colonel William S. Smith, surveyor of the port of New York and Samuel Ogden, the owner of the *Leander*.[13] Along with the previously mentioned conspirator Senator Blount, Smith and Ogden may be two of the earliest examples in the new republic of Sutherland's white-collar criminals considered 'respected business and professional men'.[14] Smith, appointed as the surveyor of the port of New York by John Adams in 1800, exemplified the tendency to select war veterans for critical government positions in the early years of the nation. Having fought in twenty-two engagements and served on the staff of both Generals Lafayette and Washington, he was appointed the U.S. Marshal for New York prior to his customs appointment.[15] Ogden, a merchant, was the owner of several vessels operating out of New York. Miranda traveled to Santo Domingo and, having acquired two schooners with approximately two hundred men in service, sailed south only to be engaged by two ships of the Spanish fleet. The schooners along with the sixty men on board, including at least thirty-four Americans, were captured while Miranda was able to flee in the *Leander*. Though Miranda avoided trial, his two American supporters, Smith and Ogden, were indicted within two months and faced trial in July 1806 for violating the Neutrality Act by supporting the filibustering effort, including providing the means to achieve Miranda's revolution. Ogden's indictment specifically referenced the vessel '*Leander*, one hundred fifty men, thirty cannon, five hundred muskets, four thousand pikes, thirty tons of cannon balls, one hundred swords, and one hundred fifty quarter casks of gun-powder' for the expedition.[16] Eventually both were found 'not guilty', but the adventure cost Smith his commission as surveyor of customs.[17]

By 1817, perceived weaknesses in the earlier neutrality law, which failed to allow preventative measures to be instituted against filibusters, led to legislation that would require armed vessels to give bond and be subject to detention by the collectors of the customs if they suspected that the vessel was in violation. The Act of April 20, 1818, codified the previous neutrality laws and repealed all former acts giving the nation one consistent statute that governed neutrality for the next 120 years.[18]

Texas brought forth the next major wave of filibustering with the over-throw of Mexican rule north of the Rio Grande. So many Americans joined the independence movement instigated by American colonists and resident Mexicans unhappy with the government of Santa Anna that within the first three months of 1836, three-quarters of the rebel army consisted of fili-busters from the United States who had arrived after the first battle of the revolution near Gonzales. Little effective action was taken by the Jackson administration in curtailing this critical military support to the Texians, and within a dozen years Texas would enter the Union.[19]

With the Canadian Rebellion of 1837 drawing American sympathy, once again the neutrality laws were found wanting and the administra-tion of President Van Buren requested a revision of the law that extended, albeit for only two years, its authority to detain any vessel, arms, ammu-nition, or vehicle about to cross the border for military expeditions. This both enlarged the definition of seizeable vessels beyond those only built for warlike purposes and included, for the first time vehicles used to transport goods across the frontier. Sympathizers both smuggled arms and ammuni-tion to the rebels and offered personal support. Rensselaer Van Rensselaer, for example, led a party of Americans in support of the rebellion, eventually occupying Navy Island, located within Canadian waters on the Niagara. Though effectively isolated by loyalist Canadians, the Canadian winter, and the preventive actions taken by U.S. authorities, various other attempts would be made to enter Canada over the next four years, with numerous military and civil actions being taken by both governments to suppress the activities. The Revenue Cutter Service's *Erie* cruised the Niagara River to prevent filibusters from reinforcing Navy Island, along with threatening the confiscation of any vessels leased to the filibusters. During November of 1838, for example, a chartered sloop was seized by customs officers, as was another vessel by a U.S. marshal, both with military assistance. There were numerous continuing skirmishes between filibusters and Canadian loyalists, with some filibusters hoping for a war between the United States and Britain that would achieve their ends. The conflict and consequent skirmishes were only terminated upon the signing of the Webster-Ashburton Treaty between the United States and Great Britain.[20]

The Revenue Cutter Service, using vessels such as the *Erie*, served as the primary maritime preventive force for the nation throughout the nineteenth century. Called variously the Revenue Service, the Revenue Marine, the Revenue Marine Service, the Revenue Cutter Service, and, eventually in 1915, the U.S. Coast Guard, its first vessels, a fleet of ten cutters placed into service in 1791, were originally conceived as a deterrent to maritime smuggling into the fledgling nation. With the duties on imported goods the primary source of financing for the new nation, and with its merchant's historical tendency of flaunting the navigation laws of Britain during colonial times, the nation's first secretary of the Treasury, Alexander Hamilton, proposed that a system of deterrence be developed similar to what was in use by the Crown. Originally ten cutters were built and stationed at the major ports and operated, except during a short period time in the mid-1800s, under the direction of the collector of customs.[21]

During the Revenue Cutter Service's early years, the prevention of smuggling was its original legislated responsibility, although other maritime duties coalesced with that primary duty. The enforcement of the nation's embargo, navigation, and piracy laws extended to the Cutter Service's personnel, as did the enforcement of its neutrality laws used to address filibustering. To accomplish these responsibilities, which continued to grow throughout the century, the service had only a limited number of men and cutters. In 1844, for example, the Revenue Marine identified 493 men in service, of which 80 carried commissions, 45 were petty officers, and 323 served as seamen. Another 30 were assigned as stewards while 15 did duty as cooks among a fleet of fifteen vessels responsible for the entire Atlantic seaboard, the Gulf, and the Great Lakes. By 1881, those numbers only increased to 930 officers and men operating thirty-six vessels while the operational area would expand on the Pacific coast north to the territory of Alaska.[22]

Holding their commissions at the will of the president and with the administrations recognizing the importance of their responsibilities to the financial integrity and security of the nation, the custom collectors originally were selected for their influence and standing in their respective communities. Many of the early eighteenth-century appointees both to the collector positions and to the subsidiary positions under the collector, such as masters of the revenue cutters, were also Revolutionary War veterans. By manning these critical offices with personnel loyal to the government in general and the sitting administration in particular, an expectation for decisions to be made in favor of any administrative directive or intent could be reasonably expected by Washington. The influence and power of the local collector was further strengthened with almost one thousand staff positions nationwide being filled by the various collectors in 1801. In a symbiotic relationship, those with the influence were selected as collectors, thereby obtaining the power to select and hire local staff, reinforcing their local prestige and influence at least until the next national election.[23] But this also had the disadvantage of further reinforcing 'the initial cultural homogeneity, the close personal relationships, and the power relationships [that] protect businessmen against critical definitions by government' and offering the unacknowledged opportunity for white-collar crime.[24]

By 1857, though almost three thousand persons were employed in the collection of customs, one-third in the New York district, few positions were dedicated to the prevention of smuggling, including filibustering attempts. Besides the appointed positions of collector, surveyor, and naval officer, occupations included inspectors, messengers, watchmen, clerks, storekeepers, porters, appraisers, gaugers, measurers, aids, boatmen, bargemen, laborers, and packers, along with various aids, assistants, and deputies. All were created in support of the collection of revenue—customs duties were the principal receipts of the nation's treasury—or were used to fulfill the numerous collateral duties assigned by various administrations. From first collecting various statistics related to commerce, navigation, fisheries, and manufacturing to documenting and controlling shipping, enforcing quarantine and steamboat safety laws, and protecting the rights of seamen, the duties of the collector and his personnel only increased as the nation grew and commerce became integral, and defining, to the nation. These personnel served in coastal administrative districts scattered from Passamaquoddy, Maine, in the Northeast, down the Atlantic seaboard and extending across the Gulf of Mexico to the Mexican land border as far as Paso del Norte (present day El Paso, Texas), then picking up the Pacific coast from San Diego to Puget Sound, Washington Territory, while interior districts ran from New Orleans north through the Mississippi valley to Minnesota and eastward along the Ohio and the Great Lakes. Over twelve thousand miles of coastline, nine thousand miles of island shoreline, and eleven thousand miles of rivers measured to the head of tide were under their responsibility. Yet, outside of a maritime port of entry, the preventative force for the nation was primarily limited to the small fleet of revenue cutters augmented at times by the U.S. military.[25]

The U.S. marshals, and their various deputies responsible for serving the federal courts by the execution of various court directives, also led the attempt to address filibustering. Besides handling the administrative work of the federal courts, including serving warrants, subpoenas, seizure papers, and other court orders, they also answered to the president who may have appointed them and at whose will they served. Established under the

Judiciary Act of 1789, though they became the nation's primary enforcement arm in the nineteenth century, the marshals were also burdened with numerous administrative and ancillary duties. These responsibilities included federal court disbursements, the national census, registering of enemy aliens, enforcing militia service, prisoner custody and security, distributing federal proclamations, and the disposal of seized vessels and goods. Their enforcement duties were limited to federal statutes and encompassed the pursuit of fugitives, including the pursuit and return of fugitive slaves, enforcement of counterfeiting and neutrality laws, and the capture and arrest of African slavers. When required, the authority of the civil government could also be supported by military force, a situation that occurred on numerous occasions when dealing with filibustering during the first one hundred years of the republic.[26]

With the marshals organized administratively across the United States, one marshal appointed for every federal court district, the president had at hand a de facto but effective civilian arm to represent the federal government on a local level. When filibusters initiated their exploits, in many cases it was the marshals, working in conjunction with the district attorneys (later known as the U.S. attorneys) who initiated legal action in the name of the government. Utilizing what was already at hand, various administrations and the Congress turned to the marshals across the nation as they turned to customs in the seaports to address political concerns as they developed. Besides directly attacking the filibusters by preemptively enforcing the neutrality law provisions, the marshals also addressed the issue in a reactive manner. For example, when the 'Patriots' of the Canadian Rebellion returned to the United States, the marshals pursued them across the Northern states. Having successfully arrested one of their leaders, others were under continual pressure—pressure that helped prevent an effective resurgence of the movement.[27]

MANIFEST DESTINY

John L. O'Sullivan, a New York journalist writing in 1845, coined the term Manifest Destiny, first in arguing for the annexation of Texas and later in the same article for annexation along the northern border in the U.S. dispute over Oregon with Britain. O'Sullivan claimed that America had the right to acquire lands across the width of the continent:

> [Other nations] have undertaken to intrude themselves into it between us and the proper parties to the case, in a spirit of hostile interference against us, for the avowed object of thwarting our policy and hampering our power, limiting our greatness and checking the fulfillment of our manifest destiny to overspread the continent allotted by Providence for the free development of our yearly multiplying millions.[28]

In the coming years, Manifest Destiny would become the slogan for all who would justify expansionist policies or plans, though that expansion had been going forth since the conception of the nation itself. As American economic expansion spread from the Atlantic seaboard south to the Caribbean, west around the Cape to the Pacific and East Asia, as well as across the plains and into the Rockies and beyond, many accepted the idea as simply the fulfillment of the democratic ideal.[29] It was an ideological tent that could be all encompassing, welcoming those who supported the extension of slavery to those who wanted to realize an extension of republican principles, from those who looked for new markets for goods and services to those who were interested in an expanded Anglo-Saxon hegemony. With technological development assisting from steam trains to telegraphs, a modern press promulgating the ideas across a community, and an unstable European power finding it difficult to maintain a colonial empire, many in the United States came to support, if not outright participate in, the filibustering attempts, especially in the South and in the burgeoning urban centers.[30] It would also offer the motivation for numerous entrepreneurs to find justifications and 'definitions' in favor of white-collar crimes committed for the cause, whichever cause it might be; once again, the political and business interests intersected.

CUBA

Narciso Lopez, a former Spanish field marshal and the son of a Venezuelan land owner, became a rallying point for those interested in achieving Cuban independence. Though initially attempting to find an American commander to lead a military force, turning first to Jefferson Davis and then to Robert E. Lee, Lopez eventually led the army himself, utilizing veterans of the Mexican-American War as subalterns. Befriended by John L. O'Sullivan, who then served as Lopez's business manager and public relations representative, Lopez used O'Sullivan to provide a bridge for Lopez to develop support for his cause in the United States.[31] In 1849, with approximately five hundred recruits gathered at Round Island, Mississippi, awaiting embarkation to Cuba, the U.S. Navy was dispatched to prevent their departure. Three vessels—the steamer *New Orleans*, the *Florida*, and the *Sea Gull*—were also seized by New York authorities under the orders of the U.S. attorney. It would be another year before Lopez was successful in actually landing a force of over five hundred on Cuban soil only to be rebuffed within forty-eight hours by a superior Spanish force, suffering over sixty casualties in the attempt. Another fifty-four crewmen and filibusters were jailed by Spanish authorities after the capture of two of the filibusters' vessels.[32]

When Lopez's force returned to the United States, landing at Key West, Florida, their vessel the *Creole*, was eventually seized by customs. The *Creole* had been purchased earlier for sixteen thousand dollars for use in the filibustering attempt by former senator and co-conspirator John Henderson. Lopez himself was later indicted, along with nine officers of the invading militia and other prominent supporters of the expedition, including Governor John A. Quitman. Quitman, a judge from the highest state court and a general of the militia of the state of Mississippi, resigned his office while under indictment. After a series of federal trials in New Orleans, long a hotbed for filibustering, led to hung juries, the U.S. attorney dropped the charges against the defendants.[33]

A year later in April 1851, the steam vessel *Cleopatra* was to transport approximately four hundred recruits on Lopez's next attempt, but the *Cleopatra* itself was discovered by the U.S. marshal at a New York dock and detained after the discovery of twenty-four kegs of gun powder and other military supplies. Three of Lopez's co-conspirators, including John L. O'Sullivan and the captain of the *Cleopatra*, who had formerly served as the skipper of the *Creole* seized the previous year in Key West, were indicted by the U.S. attorney, though the vessel was eventually released back to O'Sullivan who sold her. Lopez again succeeded in departing the United States, in August, from New Orleans via Key West. After landing approximately four hundred recruits, the packet *Pampero* returned to Florida for reinforcements and supplies only to be hunted down and seized by a revenue cutter under the direction of the collector of customs in Jacksonville, Florida. The U.S. attorney for the Northern District of Florida followed up by successfully initiating forfeiture procedures against the *Pampero* under the Neutrality Act. Lopez and his army would fail with many who survived the battles being taken prisoner and with some, as Lopez was, executed.[34]

By 1853, with a new administration in the White House that countenanced territorial expansion, Quitman was offered the leadership of another movement to make Cuba independent, with some believing that Cuban independence would follow the Texas model, eventually leading to annexation with the United States. His services would also lead to a one million dollar settlement for Quitman upon its success. Quitman's own American Dream awaited but a short sail across the Straits of Florida. Attempting to avoid the same mistakes Lopez's haste had created, Quitman spent time obtaining funds and the necessary numbers of personnel needed for the expedition. One co-conspirator who provided Quitman with financial resources was the New York banker and shipping line luminary John Law, owner of the U.S. Mail Steamship Company.[35] In mid-1854, Associate Justice John Campbell commenced an investigation of Quitman and his associates, through the federal grand jury, eventually requiring Quitman and two others to post a bond as a guarantee of their conduct or face arrest. In due course all three did, but the investigation delayed any immediate attempt at launching the mission. Yet by January 1855, Quitman had three steam vessels contracted to move up to four thousand filibusters and was again preparing to launch his invasion.[36] One of those vessels, the *Massachusetts*, would be seized off

New Jersey with munitions and war material for eventual use in Cuba. It took the direct intercession of the president to prevent Quitman from continuing his efforts, though the knowledge that the Spanish government in Cuba was well aware of his plans and had arrested co-conspirators on the island had to have only sustained Quitman's decision to finally resign from the expedition.[37]

Within five years, the nation was on the brink of war, eventually eliminating any demand for extending slavery and providing a closer and more immediate alternative to men looking for glory and fame. National expansion extended westward across the continent with the Homestead Act of 1862 offering the opportunity for inexpensive land and the Pacific Railroad Act of 1862 developing the Western railroads. The two acts both opened the lands to easy access and mitigated the need for an isthmus transit route, a continuing justification for filibustering attempts in Central America.[38]

Though over the intervening years numerous insurgents would continue to attempt to overthrow the government, not until 1895 would the Cuban insurrectionists create a climate once again able to command extensive support of potential American filibusters. Yet its form would be one of supplying munitions and material as much as men to the island insurrectionists. Federal officials would be hard pressed to enforce the Neutrality Laws, either against Cuban filibusters or gun runners, but would have some successes.

Revenue cutters seized half a dozen vessels from Tampa to Savannah over the following two years, along with various cargoes of weapons, munitions, and sundry supplies, but even their successes in stopping the gun-running were limited, at best. In June of 1897, the *McLane* seized the tug *Dauntless* while carrying men and munitions, but all charges were dismissed and by November the federal government had her under surveillance again, suspecting that the *Dauntless* had just returned to Key West after landing munitions in Cuba. From August of 1897 until March of 1898, the collector for the customs district of Key West, which encompassed the sub-ports of Punta Gorda, Boca Grande, and Punta Rassa on the west coast of Florida as well as the eastern coastal communities of Palm Beach and Miami, coordinated the enforcement efforts with numerous United States and foreign officials in an attempt to suppress filibustering to Cuba. Yet in that eight month period, no vessels identified in correspondence were seized nor were any individuals apprehended in south Florida.[39]

The difficulties of coordinating an effective interdictive effort within the district is reflected in a three month snapshot of the daily record of communication and intelligence traffic of the customs officials in Key West, Florida, in 1897:

August 6—Treasury report of munitions and provisions being removed from Key West to another unidentified key nearby for shipment to

Cuba; report of an unnamed schooner having left with provisions for the same key.

August 17—Report from the Spanish consul of a shipment of war supplies from NY to the east coast of Florida.

August 20—Treasury report that the tug *Alexander Jones* was in hiding and was to carry an expedition and the tug *Dauntless* was to join the *Donna T. Briggs* to take an expedition.

August 30—Information received that a Cuban expedition sailed from Charlotte Harbor the 28th on an unknown vessel.

September 13—Treasury information received regarding the filibustering movements of the pilot boat *Sommers W. Smith*.

September 20—Report forwarded that approximately 14 men landed by small boat from a steamer, supposedly the *Sommers W. Smith* but only letters and papers among seven valises and three canvas bags seized from a carriage.

October 2—Treasury information regarding an expedition against Greater Republic of Central America (encompassing Honduras, Nicaragua and El Salvador) received.

October 9—Information received from the Spanish consul about an expedition being fitted out in the area of Key West.

October 9—Telegram from the US attorney regarding information about an expedition departing from someplace between Wright Key and Bahia Honda and that it had be reported that the schooner *Dellia* had left Key West—a later report was forwarded on the 22nd that no indications of an expedition forming in their neighborhood was found.

October 12—Information received from the U.S. attorney reporting that an expedition was forming and that the tug *Alexander Jarvis* disappeared.

October 13—Information received that the tug *Monarch* had been seen and was suspected of being used for the transportation of an expedition.

October 13—Information was forwarded that there had been no chance of preventing the tugs *Mary Rhus* and *A.F. Denney* from leaving Punta Gorda on an expedition.[40]

Within six months, the nation was at war with Spain and within nine months American troops had landed in Cuba, effectively ending filibustering expeditions to the island. The failure to successfully prevent filibustering in south Florida was not for lack of trying. Yet any local success by the government against the smuggling of military materials and filibustering attempts was with minimal enforcement assets that were generally limited to a couple of revenue cutters and any transient naval vessel, to communications restricted to dispatches by vessel or telegraph cables, to a vaguely written neutrality law being enforced, and to a segment of the population supportive of the filibustering efforts that was a microcosm of the greater national narrative.[41]

WILLIAM WALKER AND NICARAGUA

During the years prior to the Civil War, numerous filibustering expeditions were formed both to support Texas self-determination prior to its actual independence and to separate other Mexican states from the central government. Whether to the Yucatan, Baja, or Sonora in support of a revolutionary or simply as a presumptuous El Norte invader, the attempts were generally a failure. The major exception was William Walker. Born in Tennessee, trained in medicine in Pennsylvania and Europe, and having read the law in Nashville, Walker rejected both professions for journalism. He eventually sailed to California in 1850 and wrote for the *San Francisco Herald*. At times intemperate, he ended up wounded at least once in a duel over his choice of verbiage. Within the year, Walker had returned to law, but by 1853, he became involved in his first filibustering adventure. Traveling to Mexico with the idea of developing a colony, he was denied permission to enter the interior but determined to take the state of Sonora by force of arms. After returning to San Francisco, Walker and his associates raised funds to charter the brig *Arrow* and to purchase the necessary arms and material for an expedition. The local commander of the army eventually seized the *Arrow* as it was being loaded. The following day, Walker's legal expertise came into play when he first obtained an order from a state court directing the U.S. marshal to release the vessel to the local sheriff. When the army commander refused, citing the instructions given him by the president to stop filibusters, the local state court demanded that the commander show cause as to why he should not be held in contempt of court. At the same time, Walker sued the commander for damages totaling thirty thousand dollars. In due course, a deal was struck releasing the *Arrow* with the state court dropping all charges against the army commander. In the interim Walker shipped on board the *Caroline* with arms and forty-five men for Sonora while a second vessel, the *Anita*, later supported the expedition with another one hundred fifty men, also clearing San Francisco but with no impediments from federal officials.[42] As a lawyer, Walker simply manipulated the letter of the law, to circumvent its spirit and, as Sutherland remarked of white-collar criminals, regarded the enforcement of the law as reprehensible rather than its violation.[43]

Walker's Republic of Sonora, formally declared as the Republic of Lower California, suffered desertion, rebellion, and pressure from Mexican citizens to the point that he retreated north seven months later, surrendering to U.S. troops at the border south of San Diego. Of the approximately two hundred original filibusters, the remnants of his army totaled thirty-three. Walker was tried the following October with one of his associates having been found guilty and a second pleading guilty to neutrality law violations. Judge Ogden Hoffman of the Federal District Court of the Northern District of California sentenced the two determined guilty to fines of fifteen hundred dollars while Walker successfully defended himself, a jury coming in with a 'not guilty' verdict within eight minutes, seemly accepting, as Sutherland suggested, that 'the businessman does not fit the stereotype of criminal'.[44]

By the end of the year, Walker's notoriety led to him being offered an opportunity to support an indigenous revolution in Nicaragua. By the spring of 1855, he had once again successfully departed the United States with little federal hindrance, having marketed his latest venture as a colonization enterprise, an expedient that skirted the ramifications of the neutrality laws. By November, Walker controlled the Nicaraguan government and had the newly appointed president appoint him as commander of the army. Recruiting 'emigrants' to his cause, the administration of Franklin Pierce attempted to prevent potential filibusters from supporting Walker; in December the vessel *Northern Light* was denied clearance for three days only to be released with few arrests as most of the filibusters were traveling as ticket holding passengers on a commercial vessel of the Accessory Transit Company, under the control of Cornelius Garrison and Charles Morgan, former associates of 'Commodore' Cornelius Vanderbilt. Vanderbilt had previously established a franchise for the transport of passengers and cargo across Nicaragua and after reasserting control over the company in 1856 Vanderbilt continued to cooperate with Walker, who provided political stability and legal security for Vanderbilt's isthmus business interests by transporting filibusters and material on his vessels until Walker arranged for the franchise to be stripped from the 'commodore'. Over two thousand men traveled south and joined Walker's army.[45]

In April, the steamer *Oriziba* was boarded by federal officials searching for filibusters, of which few were identified, reportedly from information received from Vanderbilt's agents, and passed to the federal attorney as part of Vanderbilt's response to the loss of his franchise. Morgan and Garrison's vessels included the steamers the *Texas*, the *Tennessee*, and the *Sierra Nevada*, all used to transport filibusters and supplies to Walker's army. In January the *Tennessee* was boarded and some associates of Walker found on board were arrested on federal warrants; the vessel departed the next day after some on-board repairs were completed. At least one newspaper reported that thirty-five hundred dollars' worth of supplies, along with muskets and ammunition had been smuggled aboard prior to departure. Whether these muskets were a portion of those supplied by George Law, another influential shipping entrepreneur, to Walker in 1856 is open to conjecture.[46]

By May 1857, Walker had returned to the United States, having been driven out of Nicaragua by a coalition of troops from the surrounding nations. Ever the optimist, he continued his filibustering attempts to return to Nicaragua for the next three years. By July, a shipping line had been created to give credence to the proposition that filibusters en route to Nicaragua were simply emigrants; they were not shipping out on vessels engaged in filibustering in violation of the neutrality laws, but were affording themselves legal transportation as would any commercial traveler. By November, the government had issued an arrest warrant against Walker and had detained the *Fashion*, a vessel of the newly created shipping line, only to release it after failing to obtain any evidence of its filibustering intent. Departing New Orleans, she sailed for Mobile where Walker boarded, having been released earlier on bond. Though inspected yet again, she was allowed to clear with approximately one hundred fifty troops and provisions on board. Slipping past an American war ship, Walker was able to land his filibusters, but they were eventually taken into naval custody and returned to the United States. Walker was allowed to travel via the *Northern Light* to New York where he surrendered to the U.S. marshal. Shortly after Walker's departure on the *Fashion*, one of his alleged recruiters was arrested in Charlestown. Walker was again put on trial in New Orleans in May, but a hung jury precluded any further action by the federal district attorney.[47]

Mobile was again the port of embarkation in November of 1858 when Walker attempted to transport three hundred to four hundred filibusters to Nicaragua on the *Alice Tainter* only to be denied clearance by customs officials. Walker was once again under grand jury investigation but, again, avoided indictment. A month later, the schooner *Susan* successfully slipped out from under the revenue cutter *McClelland* in the night only to wreck on a reef off Guatemala. The beached filibusters would be returned to Mobile courtesy of the British navy. Walker had remained stateside to coordinate further support for his attempt to return to Nicaragua.[48]

By October, he was prepared to head south with the steamer *Philadelphia*. The *Philadelphia* had departed New York bound for New Orleans where approximately two hundred filibusters awaited her. She then applied for clearance, but the New Orleans collector of customs denied her papers; while customs searched the vessel, crew members disposed of munitions over the side. Three of the reputed leaders of the filibusters awaiting departure were arrested but later released when no indictment was forthcoming. It was months before Walker made his final voyage to Central America and, ultimately, died at the hands of a Honduran execution squad on September 12, 1860.[49] Within three months, South Carolina would secede from the Union, and the nation's self-serving interest in filibustering and Manifest Destiny would suddenly be overshadowed by the clash between national sovereignty and slavery. For potential filibusters, glory could be found on domestic battlefields. The riches to be acquired by 'unscrupulous American business entrepreneurs' later labeled as 'robber barons' in Nicaraguan transit intrigues would now be gained in war-time profiteering schemes.[50]

William Walker was not the sole individual in the mid-nineteenth century who violated the neutrality laws of the United States by smuggling arms and munitions south of the border with his filibusters. Three and a half years after Walker's failed expedition, Henry Crabb, also an attorney and an associate of Walker, led approximately ninety filibusters to their deaths in Sonora, either killed in combat or executed by Mexican troops with the bodies reportedly left for the hogs, sparing one under-aged boy.[51]

Jose Maria Jesus Carbajal (also spelled Caravajal or Carabajal) attempted to establish Tamaulipas as an independent state, promising reduced tariffs for border merchants in an attempt to appeal to their economic interests. In September 1851, after obtaining arms and munitions from merchants, one believed to be Charles Stillman, who would benefit from the reduced tariffs, Carbajal crossed the border with a mixed force of 170 Mexicans and filibustering Americans and captured the town of Camargo. Advancing on Matamoros (a border town inland from where the Rio Grande River enters the Gulf of Mexico) with a force of approximately 400 men—the army having been strengthened by more Americans, including some former Texas Rangers led by Captain John 'Rip' Ford and a couple of dozen deserters from the local U.S. Army barracks—Carbajal placed the town under siege but eventually had to retreat under the threat of Mexican reinforcements. He tried again in February 1852 with 244 men but failed once more only to be arrested by the U.S. Army, along with eleven of his men. Released on bail, it was another year before Carbajal was able to mount another expedition of eighty men, which was little more than a brigand's raid that led to a ransom payment of two thousand dollars (after a demand of thirty thousand dollars could not be met) for the release of the alcalde and another inhabitant of Reynosa. Arrested a second time, he was finally brought to trial the following year. As was traditional with filibusters, he was acquitted.[52]

Throughout the rest of the nineteenth century, numerous others followed the siren call of glory and fame only to be disappointed, yet even in the twentieth century some still responded to the anachronism of filibustering. Seven individuals, including an owner of the *Los Angeles Times*, Harry Chandler, were indicted in 1915 and tried in Southern California for neutrality violations after they attempted to overthrow the government of Baja California. The evidence showed that Baltazar Aviles, former governor of Baja California and supporter of Pancho Villa, was attempting to form a military force to reestablish himself in his previous position after having been replaced by a Carranza associate in 1914. Evidence also suggested that Chandler's extensive California and Mexico ranch, managed by a co-indicted conspirator, was to be the rallying point for the filibusters. The government also introduced testimony and a check that implied that Harry Chandler had offered financial support to the rebellion. The defense attorneys were able to delay the trial more than two years, eventually convincing the presiding judge to deliver a directed verdict of not guilty. The attorneys claimed that the indictment was faulty, as there could be no conspiracy to enter the military services of the populace of Lower California because the people of that country were not legally recognized. The defense had introduced an earlier message to Congress from President Wilson, which indicated that Mexico had no government and that if armed conflict between the two nations required the introduction of American soldiers, it was to be initiated only to help the people establish a government in Mexico. This proffer permitted the judge to dismiss the case under legal grounds that would prevent any further trial against the defendants, effectively providing, in Sutherland's words, 'differential implementation of the law'.[53]

Filibustering in the nineteenth century was an extension of Manifest Destiny, itself a personification for some of the American Dream. Adventure, glory, and wealth were all offered to the young unemployed males looking for their chance at opportunity. A national culture glorified filibustering. Politicians, newspapers, periodicals, and plays reinforced an expansionist narrative and fulfilled one of Sutherland's definitions of social disorganization—'the organization within a society of groups which are in conflict with reference to specified practices'—in this case the laws, regulations, and rules of the federal government.[54] Even novels such as Richard Harding Davis' *Soldiers of Fortune* became best sellers constituting a sub-genre labeled 'imperial fiction'. A former managing editor of *Harper's Weekly*, Davis published *Soldiers* in 1897 after a visit to Cuba in the company of Frederic Remington, returning again during the Spanish-American War in the company of Teddy Roosevelt and his Rough Riders, the First United States Volunteer Calvary. His novel and newspaper stories contributed to the nation's belligerent attitude toward its southern neighbors. With the military having been used to support and sustain American business interests overseas on numerous previous occasions, it took little effort to believe that a private venture would not also be condoned, if not outright supported, by various administrations. Whether native born or immigrant, filibusters found many in business or politics motivated and supportive of these illegal ventures. Whether it was business trying to open new markets for their products, Southern elites trying to extend the dominance of slavery, or expansionist zeal in extending representative democracy and capitalism throughout the Caribbean basin, all would work at circumventing the smuggling and neutrality laws of the nation to achieve their version of the American Dream.

An acceptance of an entrepreneurial worldview where the pursuit of individual self-interest promoted national interest was inherent within the entire filibustering movement, even to the extent of disregarding the laws of the land in its pursuit. No filibustering expedition could even remotely succeed without an effective organization of conspirators planning, organizing, and leading the movement while also circumventing the law. No soldier could join, no firearm could be bought, and no ship could sail without the organized criminal activity of the Walkers, the Lopezes, the Crabbs, and their political and financial backers, such as George Law, 'Commodore' Vanderbilt, and

Harry Chandler. These were Sutherland's respectable businessmen committing crimes in the course of their occupations. Without the collusion and corruption of various governmental officials, many attempts would have been delayed if not altogether prevented from launching. If white-collar crime can also be defined as crimes committed by persons against the organizations for which they work, those officials complacent in stopping these expeditions and who failed to fulfill their governmental responsibilities were as guilty as any customs inspector or collector involved in graft or bribe-taking. The organized criminal activity involved in each expedition that conspired to smuggle munitions and troops out of the United States was little different than the organized criminal activity involved in smuggling alcohol and drugs into the United States years later.[55]

NOTES

1. Edwin H. Sutherland, *White Collar Crime: The Uncut Version* (New Haven, CT: Yale University Press, 1983), pp. 174–191.
2. U.S. Congress, American State Papers, Foreign Relations, 1, pp. 140–141.
3. Charles G. Fenwick, *The Neutrality Laws of the United States* (Washington, D.C.: Carnegie Endowment for International Peace, 1913), p. 13.
4. Alan L. Karras, *Smuggling: Contraband and Corruption in World History* (Lanham, MD: Rowman and Littlefield, 2010), p. 49. Current U.S. law reinforces the concept that smuggling incorporates exportation as well as importation violations with 18 USC 545 titled, Smuggling Goods into the United States, and 18 USC 554 titled, Smuggling Goods from the United States. During the late twentieth century smugglers trafficking in narcotics, though charged under various narcotics statutes, might not necessarily even be indicted for the act of smuggling under 18 USC 545. This prosecution strategy, intentionally or not, prevented a jury from choosing to convict on the lesser charge (18 USC 545 at the time only carried a maximum sentence of five years imprisonment) in lieu of convicting under one or more narcotics charges, which carried the probability of a greater prison sentence; the penalty for conviction under 21 USC 952, Importation of Controlled Substances, and 21 USC 953, Exportation of Controlled Substances was, in many cases, 'imprisonment of not less than 10 years and not more than life' for each offense. If previously convicted for a similar drug offense, a violator was facing a minimum twenty year sentence. See 21 USC 960, Prohibited Acts A.
5. Edwin H. Sutherland, *The Principles of Criminology*, 4 edn (Chicago: J.B. Lippincott, 1947), p. 6.
6. U.S. Constitution, Art.1, Sec. 9, Clause 5.
7. Henry Atton and Henry Hurst Holland, *The King's Customs, An Account of Maritime Revenue & Contraband, Traffic in England, Scotland, and Ireland, from the Earliest Times to the Year 1800,* 2 vols (London: John Murray, 1908; repr. New York: Augustus M. Kelley, 1967) I, pp. 6–8, 27–31; Graham Smith, *King's Cutters: The Revenue Service and the War against Smuggling* (London: Conway Maritime Press, 1983), p. 9; Neville Williams, *Contraband Cargoes: Seven Centuries of Smuggling* (North Haven, CT: Shoe String Press, 1961).
8. American State Papers, For. Rel., I, pp. 140–141; 1 *Stat.* 381, c. 50 (1794); 1 *Stat.* 520, c. 1 (1797); 1 *Stat.* 54, c. 35 (1800).

9. Robert Greenhalgh Albion and Jennie Barnes Pope, *Sea Lanes in Wartime: The American Experience, 1775–1942* (New York: W.W. Norton, 1942), pp. 23–24.

10. N. Lowell Brown, *High Crimes and Misdemeanors in Presidential Impeachment* (New York, Palgrave Macmillan, 2010), pp. 36–39; *Senate Journal*, 5th Cong., 1st sess., July 7, 17978; 5th Cong., 1st sess., July 8, 17978; 5th Cong. 3rd sess., January 14, 1799; *House Journal*, 5th Cong., 3rd sess., January 14, 1799.

11. Robert E. May, *Manifest Destiny's Underworld: Filibustering in Antebellum America* (Chapel Hill: University of North Carolina Press, 2002), pp. 5–6.

12. Fenwick, *The Neutrality Laws of the United States*, p. 32.

13. Thomas Lloyd, *The Trials of William S. Smith and Samuel G. Ogden, for Misdemeanours, Had in the Circuit Court of the United States for the New York District, in July 1806* (New York: Riley, 1807), pp. viii, 101.

14. Sutherland, *White Collar Crime*, p. 7.

15. U.S. Customs Service, *A Biographical Directory of the U.S. Customs Service, 1771–1989* (Washington, D.C.:U.S. Customs Service, 1985).

16. Lloyd, *The Trials of William S. Smith and Samuel G. Ogden*, pp. viii, 101.

17. Charles H. Brown, *Agents of Manifest Destiny: The Lives and Times of the Filibusters* (Chapel Hill: University of North Carolina, 1980), pp. 3–6; Fenwick, *The Neutrality Laws of the United States*, pp. 32–33; Henry Ingersoll, 'Diary and Letters of Henry Ingersoll, Prisoner of Carthagena, 1806–1809', *American Historical Review*, 3 (1898), 674–702; Lloyd, *The Trials of William S. Smith and Samuel G. Ogden*, pp. 242, 287.

18. 3 *Stat.* 447, c. 88 (1818), eventually known as the *Revised Statutes*, Sections 5281–5291.

19. American State Papers, Military Affairs, 6, pp. 416–427; May, *Manifest Destiny's Underworld*, pp. 8–10.

20. *Senate Journal*, 27th Cong., 3rd sess., August 11, 1842; *Daily Ohio Statesmen*, January 1, 1838, p. 3, January 9, 1838, p. 3, January 23, 1838, p. 3, January 25, 1838, p. 3; May, *Manifest Destiny's Underworld*, pp.10–13; Fenwick, *The Neutrality Laws of the United States*, pp. 41–45; Irving King, *The Coast Guard Under Sail: The U.S. Revenue Cutter Service, 1789–1865* (Annapolis, MD: Naval Institute Press, 1989), pp. 97–98; Robert May, 'Manifest Destiny's Filibusters', in *Manifest Destiny and Empire: American Antebellum Expansionism*, ed. by Sam Haynes and Christopher Morris (College Station: Texas A&M University, 1997), 146–179.

21. 1 *Stat.* 145 (1789); Atton and Holland, *The King's Customs*, I, pp. 356–357; Stephen H. Evans, *The United States Coast Guard, 1790–1915: A Definitive History* (Annapolis, MD: U.S. Naval Institute, 1949), pp. 3–5; King, *The Coast Guard Under Sail*, pp. 2–6, 112; Carl E. Prince and Mollie Keller, *The U.S. Customs Service: A Bicentennial History* (Washington, D.C.: U.S. Customs Service, 1989), pp. 35–36.

22. Evans, *The United States Coast Guard*, p. 7; King, *The Coast Guard Under Sail*, pp. 35–52, 63–78, 114; Irving H. King, *The Coast Guard Expands, 1865–1915* (Annapolis, MD: Naval Institute Press, 1996), p. 246.

23. Evans, *The United States Coast Guard*, pp. 9–12, 27; King, *The Coast Guard Under Sail*, pp. 7–9; Prince and Keller, *The U.S. Customs Service*, pp. 36–39.

24. Sutherland, *White Collar Crime*, pp. 250–251.

25. Senate, Executive Document No. 1*Report of the Secretary of the Treasury on the State of the Finances, for the Year Ending June 30, 1857*, 35th Cong., 1st sess. ; U.S. Census Office, *The Seventh Census of the United States: 1850* (Washington, D.C.: Robert Armstrong, 1853), p. xxx; May, *Manifest Destiny's Underworld*, p. 125; Laurence F. Schmeckebier, *The Customs Service:*

Its History, Activities, and Organization (Baltimore, MD: Johns Hopkins Press, 1924), pp. 1–20.

26. Frederick S. Calhoun, *The Lawmen: United States Marshals and Their Deputies, 1789–1989* (Washington, D.C.: Smithsonian Institution, 1989), pp. 15–63, 77–93; May, *Manifest Destiny's Underworld*, p. 125.

27. Calhoun, *The Lawmen*, pp. 63–67; Graham Allison and Philip Zelikow, *Essence of Decision: Explaining the Cuban Missile Crisis*, 2nd edn (New York: Longman, 1999), pp. 174–175.

28. John Louis O'Sullivan, 'Annexation', *United States Magazine and Democratic Review*, 17 (July and August, 1845), 5–10.

29. For example, see 'Review of the Past Week', *Hartford Daily Courant*, September 26, 1851, 'The Revolution in Northern Mexico—Its Origin and Object—Another Cuban Invasion', *New York Daily News*, October 24, 1851, 'The Central American Question—What Walker May Do', *New York Daily News*, January 1, 1856, p. 4; and 'Aid for Walker and the Filibusters', *New York Herald*, December 21, 1856, p. 1.

30. Brown, *Agents of Manifest Destiny*, pp. 40–41; Robert W. Johannsen, 'The Meaning of Manifest Destiny', in *Manifest Destiny and Empire: American Antebellum Expansionism*, ed. by Sam W. Haynes and Christopher Morris (College Station: Texas A&M University, 1997). 7–20; Robert E. May, 'Manifest Destiny's Filibusters', in Haynes and Morris, *Manifest Destiny and Empire*, pp. 146–179.

31. Tom Chaffin, *Fatal Glory: Narciso Lopez and the First Clandestine U.S. War against Cuba* (Charlottesville: University Press of Virginia, 1996), pp. 52–57.

32. Brown, *Agents of Manifest Destiny*, pp. 47–51, 62–67; Chaffin, *Fatal Glory*, p. 89; *Hartford Daily Courant*, June 1, 1850, p. 2.

33. Brown, *Agents of Manifest Destiny*, pp. 67–70; *Hartford Daily Courant*, August 28, 1851, p. 2.

34. Brown, *Agents of Manifest Destiny*, pp. 72–80; May, *Manifest Destiny's Underworld*, p. 135; *Sun*, October 8, 1851, p. 1.

35. Chaffin, *Fatal Glory*, p. 25.

36. Brown, *Agents of Manifest Destiny*, pp. 70, 118–119, 129–130, 253.

37. *ibid.*, pp. 256–257; Johannsen, 'The Meaning of Manifest Destiny', pp. 156–157; May, *Manifest Destiny's Underworld*, p. 136.

38. U.S. Congress, *Congressional Globe*, Senate, 37th Cong., 2nd sess. (1862), p. 1951; Brown, *Agents of Manifest Destiny*, p. 462; 12 *Stat.* 392 (1862); 12 *Stat.* 489 (1862).

39. King, *The Coast Guard Expands*, pp. 109–110.

40. U.S. Customs Service, *Neutrality Confidential* (Washington, D.C.: U.S. Customs Service, 1988), pp. 1–18.

41. May, *Manifest Destiny's Underworld*, p. 137.

42. Brown, *Agents of Manifest Destiny*, pp. 174–197; *Chicago Daily Tribune*, December 23, 1853, p. 2; May, *Manifest Destiny's Underworld*, pp. 158–159; *New York Daily Times,* November 14, 1855, p. 4; *Times-Picayune*, published as the *Daily Picayune*, October 22, 1850, p. 2.

43. Sutherland, *White Collar Crime*, pp. 231–232.

44. Brown, *Agents of Manifest Destiny*, pp. 194–217; Christian G. Fritz, *Federal Justice in California: The Court of Ogden Hoffman, 1851–1891* (Lincoln: University of Nebraska Press, 1991), pp. 112–122; *Hartford Daily Courant*, November 15, 1854, p. 2; May, *Manifest Destiny's Underworld*, pp. 154–155; *New York Daily Times*, March 13, 1854, p. 2, June 9, 1854, p. 1; Sutherland, *White Collar Crime*, p. 232.

45. Brown, *Agents of Manifest Destiny*, pp. 237–243, 267–270, 316–317; May, *Manifest Destiny's Underworld*, p.149; *New York Herald*, November 29, 1856, p. 1.

46. Brown, *Agents of Manifest Destiny*, pp. 341, 366, 388; May, *Manifest's Destiny's Underworld*, p. 174; *New York Herald*, January 29, 1857, p. 1, January 30, 1857, p. 1.
47. Brown, *Agents of Manifest Destiny*, pp. 413–419, 422, 427; *Hartford Daily Courant*, November 12, 1857, p. 3; May, *Manifest Destiny's Underworld*, pp. 136, 141–142; *New York Times*, November 13, 1857, p. 4, December 28, 1857, p. 1; *Times-Picayune*, published as the *Daily Picayune*, May 28, 1857, p. 5.
48. Brown, *Agents of Manifest Destiny*, pp. 429–32; May, *Manifest Destiny's Underworld*, p. 136; *New York Herald*, November 28, 1858, p. 1.
49. Brown, *Agents of Manifest Destiny*, pp. 441–442; May, *Manifest Destiny's Underworld*, p. 137. *New York Herald*, October 4, 1860, p. 1; *New York Times*, August 22, 1860, p. 4, August 27, 1860, p. 8.
50. Howard Abadinsky, *Organized Crime*, 9th edn (Belmont, CA: Wadsworth, 2010), p. 41; Brown, *Agents of Manifest Destiny*, pp. 462–464.
51. Brown, *Agents of Manifest Destiny*, p. 409n; J. Evetts Haley, *Jeff Milton: A Good Man with a Gun* (Norman: University of Oklahoma Press, 1948), p. 180; May, *Manifest Destiny's Underworld*, p. 191; Diana Lindsay, ed., 'Henry A. Crabb, Filibuster, and the *San Diego Herald*', *Journal of San Diego History*, 19 (1973), 34–42.
52. Brown, *Agents of Manifest Destiny*, pp. 150–157; *Hartford Daily Courant*, October 4, 1851, p. 2, January 5, 1852, p. 2, March 20, 1852, p.2, April 13, 1853, p. 2, January 18, 1854, p.2; May, *Manifest Destiny's Underworld*, pp. 36–38; 'Comision Pesquisadora de la Frontera del Norte: Report to the President,' *U.S.-Mexico Borderlands: Historical and Contemporary Perspectives*, ed. by Oscar J. Martinez (Wilmington, DE: Scholarly Resources,1996), 58–61; *New York Daily Times*, October 30, 1851, p. 4.
53. Lowell L. Blaisdell, 'Harry Chandler and Mexican Border Intrigue, 1914–1917', *Pacific Historical Review*, 35 (1966), 385–393; *Los Angeles Times*, May 15, 1917, p. II2, May 16, 1917, p. II1, May 17, 1917, p. II2, May 18, 1917, p. II1, May 19, 1917, p. II5, May 22, 1917, p. II2, May 23, 1917, p. II2, May 24, 1917, p. II10, May 25, 1917, p. II2, May 26, 1917, p. II3, May 29, 1917, p. II2; Oscar J. Martinez, *Troublesome Border* (Tucson: University of Arizona Press, 1988), p. 49; Sutherland, *White Collar Crime*, pp. 53–54.
54. Sutherland, *White Collar Crime*, p. 255.
55. Richard Harding Davis, *Soldiers of Fortune*, ed. by Brady Harrison (Peterborough, Ontario, Canada: Broadview Press, 1897, repr. 2006); May, 'Manifest Destiny's Filibusters', pp. 146–179; Steven F. Messner and Richard Rosenfeld, *Crime and the American Dream*, 4th edn (Belmont, CA: Thomson Wadsworth, 2007), pp. 6–7, 28; Prince and Keller, *The U.S. Customs Service*, pp. 146–156.

5 The Mexican Revolution, 1910–1920

By the dawn of the twentieth century, America already had a long and entrenched history of smuggling as a form of white-collar crime. The immediate precursors to American smuggling as an instance of white-collar criminality were the eighteenth-century merchants who directly profited from the contraband their ships imported into the colonies. The likes of John Hancock and his uncle Thomas exemplified the white-collar criminals of the colonial era and established the prototype of a reputable class of individuals involved in crimes supportive of their business interests, specifically the smuggling of contraband to benefit the bottom line of their business ledgers. At the beginning of the nineteenth century, the entrepreneurial descendants of these colonial merchants turned again to white-collar crime and smuggled, at first, to survive the draconian regulations of a government attempting to avoid entanglements in the conflict between two of the major military powers of modern Western civilization. Yet within only a few years, after the nascent nation had become enmeshed again in war against its former colonial master, some of these same mercantilists profited by trading with the new nation's enemy, putting profit above patriotism and the law, trafficking both across the northern land border and across the seas.

That same notion of profit above patriotism again came into play for many during the Civil War with Northern merchants trafficking in munitions and much needed supplies to various Confederate representatives. Cotton, the 'white gold' of the South, was also a major catalyst of white-collar crime. The profit of smuggling cotton bales across the border to the markets of New York and onward was enough to not only attract civilian speculators but also to corrupt government and military personnel of the highest rank and status. From General Butler to Senator Sprague, the opportunity to profit was paramount to their respective duties to the Union cause.

Throughout the century many filibusters looked for an opportunity for success and wealth, smuggling weapons out of the United States to achieve the fulfillment of what some believed was the nation's Manifest Destiny. Supported by the respected individuals who conspired with the leaders of the various filibustering groups in circumventing the neutrality laws of the Republic, the likes of 'Commodore' Vanderbilt and others served their own financial interests and hoped to profit in a variety of ways. In some cases, if not directly supported by the government, various administrations over the years acquiesced to the conspiracies by simply ignoring their actions as these filibustering attempts were in line with their own predilections and were supported by large segments of the populous.

By 1910, a new opportunity for illegitimate profit materialized on the southern border of the nation but instead of being initiated by filibusters invading from the north, it was created by the unstable conditions and social disorganization of America's contiguous southern neighbor, Mexico. Along the borderlands of the two nations, in that area of '[i]isolation, weak institutions, lax administration, and a different economic orientation', the trafficking of munitions to the revolutionists of Mexico by American business and professional men would be the latest iteration of white-collar smuggling.[1]

The end of the Mexican-American War in 1848 with the annexation of the northern half of Mexico through conquest epitomized the concept of Manifest Destiny, with some expansionists of President James Polk's administration believing that all of Mexico should be seized. Yet even while the White House accepted the Treaty of Guadalupe Hidalgo and the later Gadsden Treaty, the United States' second longest land border was a continuous source of friction for the two nations in the coming years.[2]

After the Civil War and through the 1880s, smuggling across the border with Mexico would be of limited consequence to the federal government. Energy was instead expended addressing conflicts with numerous Native American tribes along the artificial borderlines that, in many cases, bisected historical tribal lands. With limited military personnel to cover the border—only about 1,900 army regulars scattered the length of the line in 1877—it was years before some semblance of national control was established. Hostile Indian nations, cattle rustling, and bandit raids were always a higher priority, at times almost serving as a catalyst for leading the country back into war with Mexico. Though customs ports of entry were eventually found the entire length of the line, limited effort was dedicated to addressing smugglers transiting the border between them. By the turn of the century, approximately 150 customs officers were responsible for the entire Mexican-American frontier, with most officers' responsibilities centered primarily on revenue collection. For the nine hundred miles from Presidio, Texas, to the Nogales area of Arizona, only eleven customs mounted inspectors, also known as 'line riders', were responsible for the prevention of smuggling outside the ports in 1887. By 1909, that number had increased to only fourteen line riders for almost seven hundred miles of river from south of Laredo north toward El Paso, for example. Contraband included smuggled mescal, a distilled liquor from Mexico, and cattle infected with ticks being run north around the ports to avoid inspection. Through the ports, cigars, lace, and ornamented needlework were subject to illegal importation to avoid duty payments by tourists. In San Diego, the proclivity of women to conceal contraband on their person when returning to the United States from Tijuana led to recommending the hiring of customs' first female inspector in 1906. But it was not until the start of the Mexican Revolution that major trafficking rose to the level of organized criminal activity and of white-collar crime found with the early filibusters of the nineteenth century. That traffic was again in armaments and material in support of the insurgent efforts.[3]

In 1876, Porfirio Diaz overthrew the government of Sebastian Lerdo de Tejada and later was elected president of the Republic of Mexico. Lerdo and his former minister of war, General Mariano Escobedo, escaped to the United States and immediately attempted to develop a counter-revolution against the new government. Within months of Diaz assuming power, Lerdistos crossed the border only to be repelled by the Porfiriato forces. Continuing organizational efforts in Texas led to the military internment of Escobedo and several aides for neutrality violations. With formal recognition of the Diaz government by the United States and the capture of Escobedo himself after re-entering Mexico in 1878 any threat to Diaz from the Lerdistos had passed.[4] After years of political control under the Diaz dictatorship, various outbreaks of revolutionary zeal blossomed in Mexico. One was former journalist Catarino Garza's rebellion on the Texas-Mexico border that led to over one hundred indictments in 1892 for neutrality and smuggling violations and Garza's exile and eventual death three years later while fighting in Colombia.[5]

Two brothers, Ricardo and Enrique Flores Magon, along with others, also served as catalysts for revolution. Having escaped persecution by the Porfiriato by traveling north to the United States, following in the tradition of previous insurrectionists, including Diaz himself, Ricardo Flores Magon organized the *Partido Liberal Mexicano* (PLM). The brothers' activities in the United States in support of their insurrection led to the arrest of Ricardo's associates in October 1906 in El Paso for neutrality violations and he subsequently became a fugitive. Other associates in St. Louis were also arrested with Ricardo Flores Magon finally apprehended in Los Angeles in August 1907, eventually serving prison time for neutrality violations. Though the Liberal Party survived, continuing in its attempts to institute a revolution over the next few years, many of its members joined the Madero cause. As with many of the Cuban filibustering attempts, the United States assisted the targeted government by enforcing the neutrality laws against the insurrectionists, obtaining and utilizing intelligence from Mexico related to the activities of the revolutionary movements.[6]

By 1909, investigations of war material shipments south to Mexico were underway by American law enforcement. Reports of numerous shipments of guns and ammunition concealed in piano cases or masked as machinery had been received, as had a report of firearms being stolen from a south Texas ranch. 'Gun running was going on by the wholesale' with ranchers selling cattle to obtain funds to purchase firearms that were then shipped across the border to be hidden in the mountains pending the start of the revolution.[7]

Porfirio Diaz ran for reelection once again in 1910. With Francisco Madero challenging his continued presidency and having now controlled Mexico for over thirty years, Diaz had the popular Madero confined until he had successfully secured his eighth term. Madero, shortly after being released, traveled to San Antonio, Texas, and organized an insurrection. Though under surveillance by the Secret Service and other law enforcement agents, Madero and two brothers managed to evade them and depart for the border. Armed groups were reported joining Madero with customs mounted inspectors finding insurrectionists bivouacked south of the Rio Grande. Customs mounted inspectors also crossed into Mexico at least twice to obtain information on the movements and strength of the revolutionists. Madero eventually returned to San Antonio and traveled onward undetected. In preparation of Pascual Orozco's attack against Portifirist troops in Ciudad Juarez in February 1911, Madero then returned to Texas and moved to El Paso, crossing over to follow his military commander's retreat south after learning that an arrest warrant had been issued against him.[8]

While Madero was attempting to build an effective military force south of the Rio Grande, Ricardo and Enrique Flores Magon launched their own initiative in Baja California using numerous foreign nationals as troops in their military actions. At least half were American adventurers with one contemporary source claiming only 10 percent of their troops were Mexican nationals. Seizing Mexicali in late January with fewer than two dozen men, their force grew within weeks to over two hundred who had crossed the border south. By May, the town of Tijuana (with a population of less than one thousand) fell into the hands of the Magonistas, giving them control of the entire Mexican-California border. Though American troop strength was increased to 1,700 personnel in an attempt to address the movement of volunteers in violation of the neutrality laws, as well as the smuggling of firearms and munitions into Mexico, success was minimal with soldiers of fortune and armaments being successfully moved south. One published report identified Los Angeles, via the town of Holtville in Imperial County, California, as the source of four thousand rounds of ammunition and a case of rifles for Magonistas fighting in Mexicali. The ammunition was being 'smuggled across the line under the very noses of the United States soldiers on patrol' with another case of arms and five cases of ammunition concealed in another Imperial County town, Heber, that had been shipped from San Francisco and were waiting shipment south (if they had not already been transported across the border).[9]

The difficulty the government found itself in was the very nature of tracking. When goods were smuggled north into the United States, line riders located the tracks of individuals, animals, wagons, or motorized vehicles along the border or at known trafficking locations in the interior just north of the line and then forecasted the smugglers' probable direction and destination. Either by leapfrogging forward along the presumed route toward its ultimate destination or telephoning or wiring ahead, the smugglers could be intercepted. Yet when trying to 'cut sign' and locate southbound tracks of gunrunners or insurrectionists, the opportunity to either jump forward or wire ahead was limited by the same border that generally prevented the incursion of government agents into Mexico. When the tracks were located it was usually too late to apprehend the smugglers as they had already crossed the border. Even attempting to locate a suspect shipment of guns and ammunition was problematic as numerous railroad stops were available for off-loading firearms disguised as machinery, baggage, or other legitimate goods while in rail transit. With so many in the border areas supportive of the insurrectionists' objective, the activities of military troops and government agents were easily reported to the independence movement.[10]

By June, the Magon movement was becoming disorganized with some troops pledging their allegiance to Madero after the fall of Ciudad Juarez to the Maderista forces the previous month and the development of a political split between the two revolutionary leaders. On June 22, a force of almost seven hundred men attacked the Magonista positions holding Tijuana, forcing them to retreat to the United States after suffering thirty-one dead. One hundred five men made it across the line and then surrendered to the army. Ricardo and Enrique Flores Magon, along with two others, were convicted the following year of violating the neutrality laws and sentenced to twenty-three months of federal custody. Within two years of release, Ricardo's socialist-anarchist writings put him back in custody and eventually he was tried twice and sentenced in the final case to twenty-one years in prison, dying in Leavenworth Federal Penitentiary in Kansas in 1922.[11]

Reports of munitions smuggling continued, with large sales of ammunition taking place in local mercantiles. Federal agents monitored stores of munitions for potential movement south. The Treasury Department attempted to have the manifests of all ships offloading cargo at Galveston, Texas, examined for any arms or ammunition with the local customs personnel at the final border destination of the munitions notified to try to identify the final consignee. Two legitimate firms in El Paso were responsible for approximately half of the munitions that transited the port of Galveston, Shelton Payne Arms Company and Krakauer, Zork and Moye, both doing business in seeming compliance with the law and both cooperative with law enforcement regarding the domestic shipments. Krakauer assets exceeded $1.1 million, making it a major mercantile firm along the Mexican border. A third firm identified in Laredo was the A. Duetz and Brothers Hardware Company. In a three-month period, customs documented almost one hundred cases of firearms with five to twenty-five rifles a case and almost seven hundred cases of ammunition with one thousand to ten thousand rounds per case through one port alone. A fourth store, the Young Brothers Hardware Company in Shafter received twenty-one thousand rounds of ammunition from San Antonio in the first two months of 1911 and intended to sell the munitions to the insurrectionists. In the tradition of early American commerce, however, the actual sale of the ammunition was not considered in violation of either the smuggling statutes or the neutrality laws. No violation could be substantiated until the ammunition was either used to outfit an expedition or army against Mexico on U.S. territory or an attempt was actually made to smuggle the goods across the border without passing through the port of entry. Though the local collector of customs attempted to obtain an authorization to seize the munitions, it was denied. All were selling their goods to the insurrectionists, but all did so seemingly within the loose confines of the neutrality laws. Krakauer, Zork and Moye, as well as Shelton-Payne were eventually indicted for smuggling and neutrality violations, but the cases against both firms collapsed. If an indictment could even be obtained, a local jury still had to render a guilty verdict. A local judge could, if he felt so justified, overturn a guilty verdict, direct an acquittal, or even dismiss a case prior to a trial. The neutrality laws historically had been evaded easily in the nineteenth century and as the twentieth century opened, there was little difference in effect.[12] The representatives of these companies were classic examples of white-collar criminals committing a white-collar crime.[13] Unlike the revolutionists who were running guns as patriots, the white-collar criminals associated with these mercantile companies were conspiring to run guns simply for profit.

Madero's brother, Gustavo, traveled to New York to arrange the purchase of two Gatling guns, a quantity of Mauser rifles, and ammunition from the firm of Francis Bannerman and Son. Though the Gatlings stayed in New York, the Mausers and the ammunition, captured during the Spanish-American War and stored in the interim in New York, were shipped to El Paso. Shelburne G. Hopkins of Hopkins and Hopkins, a law firm and an example of Sutherland's 'professional men', was employed by Madero and had an extensive background in international law, engaging an ex-Secret Service agent to move the shipment south. Though disguising a small portion of the munitions as furniture, he was arrested upon arrival in El Paso and the munitions were seized. With the law precluding forfeiture as there was no evidence of either a neutrality or a smuggling violation, the munitions were later released to the Shelton Payne Arms Company. The rest of the Bannerman purchases, on advice of Madero's attorneys, were shipped in small lots three times a week to Shelton Payne. They were then moved into the community where half-a-dozen local homes stored them until they were smuggled across the border. Shelton Payne also previously had received from a business associate of the Madero family two thousand Mauser rifles and six hundred thousand rounds of ammunition that had followed a similar shipping procedure, being stored in Brooklyn, New York, and sent in small lots to El Paso.[14]

Even a Civil War relic was considered a viable weapon in the Maderistas' battle against the Diaz forces in the north. A brass, muzzle-loading cannon on display in the City Hall Plaza of El Paso was found to be serviceable and in April 1911, was hooked to a car, stolen, and hidden in a hay barn pending shipment southward. While waiting for an auspicious moment to move it across the river, black powder was ordered from Shelton Payne and twelve-pound shot was made at a local foundry, as were casings for the canisters at a tin shop. Three farm wagons were used to move the cannon, a ton of its ammunition, a Colt machine gun with ten thousand rounds of ammunition, and two hundred rifles with two hundred thousand rounds of ammunition in one shipment. The wagons traveled thirty-five miles below El Paso to a passable ford across the Rio Grande, camouflaged as ranch supplies to move past the Army National Guard troops that patrolled the roads around El Paso. Used by Villareal at Ojinaga and Camargo, the cannon was returned to El Paso and the City Hall Plaza by the grateful insurrectionists after the revolution.[15]

As the situation in Mexico deteriorated, more army troops were brought into play in an attempt to bolster the limited effectiveness of federal law enforcement. In some smuggling incidents, the manpower inherent in an army unit would be required to interdict a smuggling operation in progress; in January 1911, a group of over one hundred Maderistas unloaded cases of munitions from freight cars of the Southern Pacific Railroad, using more than two hundred mules and burros to move the contraband across the Rio Grande. Later that month, soldiers found a cache of weapons including seven hundred guns and three thousand cartridges north of Eagle Pass, Texas. In February an army patrol assisted by a customs mounted inspector arrested a small party of insurrectionists for neutrality and smuggling violations in west Texas. Steadily increasing the American military presence as the revolution progressed, President Taft mobilized approximately twenty thousand troops and naval personnel overnight on March 6, 1911, originally claiming the movement of troops to the border area was only for maneuvers and training. Shortly afterward Taft admitted that he was attempting to stop munitions and personnel from going into Mexico in support of the insurrectionists and, if needed, to protect American interests and lives in Mexico. The U.S. ambassador to Mexico, Henry Lane Wilson, estimated that one billion dollars had been invested south of the Rio Grande, and the *New York Times* reported that seventy-five thousand American citizens resided there, ten thousand in Mexico City alone. The mobilization also offered an opportunity to show support for the Diaz government without unduly antagonizing any future government as the justification was simply the enforcement of the U.S. neutrality and smuggling laws. This addressed the concerns of the Diaz administration, which had complained on numerous occasions of the lax enforcement of the law against insurrectionists. Yet few of the 20,000 troops would ever serve on the border. With over 10,000 being assigned to San Antonio, almost 4,000 in Galveston, and another 1,500 in San Diego, those actually riding the line never exceeded 3,500 troops. For the rest, it served as a training exercise.[16]

Besides the numerous federal agency employees involved in attempting to address smuggling and neutrality violations—U.S. customs agents, treasury agents from the Secret Service, Bureau of Investigation agents (later known as the Federal Bureau of Investigation), postal inspectors, U.S. Marshals, U.S. attorneys, State Department representatives, soldiers, and the judiciary—state enforcement officers were also brought into the battle against smuggling. The governor of Texas sent National Guard troops to the Texas border to limit the spillover of Mexican conflicts into Texas. In cooperation with President Taft, the Texas Rangers were given authority to enforce federal neutrality laws while the federal government in exchange agreed to assist in funding an expansion of the Ranger force. With numerous federal agencies addressing the border problem from their own organizational perspectives, a dubious new layer of politics was added to the mix, at times leading to conflicting enforcement directions and objectives.[17]

By April 1911, Madero forces were again ready to attack Ciudad Juarez and to demand the surrender of the federal garrison. The garrison refused to do so, and negotiations between the Diaz government and Madero were initiated while an armistice suspending military activities was accepted by both armies. Madero forces were allowed to import food and medical supplies through the port of entry and could visit El Paso via a footbridge. During the night ammunition was also passed over to the Maderistas by smugglers. The negotiations eventually were unsuccessful, and after two days of battle, Madero's forces captured the city. This created a situation in which the insurrectionists held the port of entry and, under the neutrality and smuggling laws, were legally authorized to import all arms and ammunition appropriately manifested. Twice before at Ojinaga and at Agua Prieta, rebel forces had held a port of entry but had been denied access to munitions from north of the line. With the capture of Ciudad Juarez by Madero's military commanded by Pancho Villa and Pascual Orozco, the administration finally determined that neutrality laws did not proscribe the export of weapons or ammunition through a port of entry and that they had no legitimate grounds to deny the Madero military the arms they required. By the end of May this became a moot point as Porfirio Diaz resigned his presidency and Madero was later elected to the same office.[18]

Within three months of Madero becoming president, General Orozco rebelled against Madero and occupied Ciudad Juarez, making El Paso the port of entry for rebel arms yet again. In an attempt to restrict the shipment of arms from the United States the Joint Resolution of March 14, 1912, was promulgated by Congress:

> *Resolved by the Senate and House of Representatives of the United States of America in Congress assembled*, That the joint resolution to prohibit the export of coal or other material used in war from any seaport of the United States, approved April twenty-second, eighteen hundred and ninety-eight, be and hereby is, amended to read as follows:
>
> That whenever the President shall find that in any American country conditions of domestic violence exist which are promoted by the use of arms or munitions of war procured from the United States, and

shall make proclamation thereof, it shall be unlawful to export except under such limitations and exceptions as the President shall prescribe any arms or munitions of war from any place in the United States to such country until otherwise ordered by the President or by Congress.

Sec. 2. That any shipment of material hereby declared unlawful after such a proclamation shall be punishable by fine not exceeding ten thousand dollars, or imprisonment not exceeding two years, or both.[19]

The president then immediately issued the proclamation required, declaring that conditions in Mexico qualified under the joint resolution. Though the resolution and proclamation could not address border smuggling, they did have the ability to prevent otherwise legitimate arms from being shipped into Mexico to rebel forces holding any border port of entry, such as at Juarez. Of course further restrictions only increased illegal trafficking in firearms and other military contraband. The Orozquistas ordered their munitions through a dealer such as Krakauer by previously placing money on account with the dealer and then presenting an order in code for a specific quantity of ammunition to be drawn on account. Though the purchase process was simple, the actual transportation was often of concern. Runners were employed to carry small quantities of ammunition on their person while they walked or rode across the border to Ciudad Juarez, at times wearing clothing with pockets sewn on the inside to carry a larger quantity of cartridges. Other shipments were smuggled across the line near Columbus, New Mexico; one shipment purchased from dealers in Albuquerque was shipped by Express to Deming and then freighted by wagon to Columbus to be smuggled across.[20]

In many cases, the information and intelligence for effective enforcement against Orozco's forces was developed in conjunction with Mexican government agents. Allowed to operate freely in the United States, the Maderistas would provide surveillance of munitions shipments and even confronted some owners of their potential violation of U.S. law. In at least one case, the Maderistas frightened an owner into abandoning his own property. Working hand-in-glove with federal agents, they also employed the Thiel Detective Agency to obtain intelligence on Orozquista activity both in the United States and in northern Mexico.[21]

By early 1913, Madero was ousted by Victoriano Huerta, but within eighteen months Huerta was himself in exile, replaced by Venustiano Carranza. The embargo, lifted in January of 1914 in an attempt by the Wilson administration to provide support to the enemies of Huerta, was reestablished when Carranza condemned the U.S. invasion of Vera Cruz. As with other laws related to neutrality, loopholes also developed; it was determined that the new embargo only covered the land border. When Carranza captured the port of Tampico, he immediately arranged for arms shipments from the United States to clear through the local customhouse, in some cases transiting a third country, with few impediments placed in his way by the administration. Meanwhile, Huerta was blocked from obtaining munitions by the American control of the port of Vera Cruz. In spite of the embargo smuggling persisted across the entire border as unrest continued.[22]

The Albert Steinfeld and Company, Albert Steinfeld himself, and an associate were indicted in 1913 for attempting to export twenty thousand cartridges from Tucson to Sonora. Steinfeld, a major merchant and banker who also was involved in the copper mining industry, effectively squashed the case with the federal district judge for Arizona dismissing the charges. The Phelps-Dodge Mercantile Company in Bisbee, Arizona, part of the Phelps, Dodge copper empire, and the Douglas Hardware Company of Douglas, Arizona, an associated business, along with the managers of the two companies, were also indicted in federal court for violating the neutrality laws related to the shipment of war munitions. That indictment charged the companies with shipping 140,000 cartridges from Douglas to Bisbee with the ultimate destination being Sonora, Mexico. The ammunition, manufactured by the Winchester Arms Company, was destined for the Constitutionalists fighting to overthrow Huerta. With extensive copper and railroad holdings in Sonora, Walter Douglas, president of Phelps-Dodge, was more than interested in cooperating with the local governmental authorities and preventing the compromise of his mining businesses.[23]

Federal District Judge William Sawtelle, recently appointed the first district judge for the newly admitted state of Arizona by President Woodrow Wilson, dismissed all charges against the defendants in both cases (as he did the Krakauer, Zork and Moye and the Shelton-Payne cases), writing that, in part, the indictment was faulty because mere intent did not constitute a violation of the neutrality law without an actual shipment being made from a definite point in the United States to a definite point in Mexico. Though the destination identified in the indictment indicated the state of Sonora, simply identifying a large geographical area, although within the forbidden territory as specified in law, did not fulfill the requirement of being a *specific point* within that forbidden territory. To quote Judge Sawtelle:

> I do not consider the mere shipping of munitions of war from one point in the United States of America to another point in the United States of America an offense under the joint resolution of Congress above referred to, and I do not consider the mere intent to ship goods from a point within the United States of America into the United States of Mexico an offense, unless the intent is coupled with an actual shipment made from a definite point in the United States of America to a definite point in the United States of Mexico.[24]

The Department of Justice chose not to appeal the decision. Cleveland E. Dodge, a vice president of Phelps-Dodge and close friend and Princeton classmate of President Wilson, had reportedly donated fifty-six thousand dollars to the president's recent election campaign.[25] The political, legal, and business interests seemed to have intersected once again, much to the benefit of Phelps-Dodge.

When the district attorney earlier notified the Department of Justice that the grand jury might also indict the Winchester Arms Company, one of the sources of the munitions, the Justice Department informed him that they were 'very doubtful as to the propriety [of] indicting Winchester Arms Company or any of its officers' claiming that the 'company has for some time voluntarily furnished this department with information [. . .] as to shipments [of] arms and ammunition to States on Mexican border'.[26] No indictment was forthcoming. The Winchester Arms Company was affiliated with the Remington Arms and Ammunition Company with Marcellus Hartley Dodge, a nephew of Cleveland Dodge, being one of its directors.[27] Sutherland's statement that 'white collar criminals are relatively immune because of the class bias of the courts and the power of their class to influence the implementation and administration of the law' is evidenced by the lack of effective action taken against the gun merchants of the Southwest during the years of the Mexican Revolution.[28]

Over the next half-a-dozen years, the ongoing Mexican Revolution led to tremendous instability along the U.S.-Mexican border with raids, cattle rustling, invasions—both southbound and northbound—continued smuggling, and various junta attempts at overthrowing whatever Mexican government was currently in power. Texas continued as the entrepot for junta hopefuls attempting to overthrow the Carranza government. Both Huerta and Orozco were arrested on neutrality violations and died within the year, Orozco shot while being pursued by law enforcement and the military, and Huerta of natural causes.[29]

In the coming years, smuggling led to the arrest of Carranza's consul in New York, technology entered the picture with automobiles transporting concealed munitions across the line, and surreptitious vessels were, once again, employed. American destroyers intercepted a schooner off the California coast bound for Mexico and seized several thousand rounds of ammunition en route to Villistas. The munitions had been brought aboard the schooner by fishing boats, and after being intercepted, the captain first tried to destroy the schooner only to beach the vessel in an attempt to escape (smuggling tactics that were to be seen again within the decade by rumrunners smuggling off both coasts). In 1919, one estimate placed the quantity of smuggling between $17 million and $20 million a year; $14 million worth of goods from the United States with $4 million to $6 million being arms and ammunition to Carranza, Villa, and others. Cars were smuggled south to avoid Mexican duties and narcotics, silks, and jewelry were some of the contraband northbound.[30]

Various attempts at revolutionary action to overthrow the Diaz government of Mexico created a condition of social disorganization along the length of the Mexican-American border. Madero replaced Diaz, only to be ousted by Huerta, who was followed by Carranza. That very instability allowed the borderlands area to create its own rules, whatever the central governments may have demanded. With American-owned mines and railroads south of the line and much needed munitions available north from various merchants, accommodation was beneficial for many in the border area. Corporations and the individuals behind them benefited financially from the upheavals of the Mexican Revolution and the '[i]solation, weak institutions, lax administration, and a different economic orientation' in the borderlands allowed them to manipulate the situation to their benefit, little recognizing or complying with the laws of the nation that protected them from similar turmoil.[31] While the revolutionists were fighting and smuggling for a patriotic cause, the war crimes of Phelps-Dodge, Shelton Payne, and their ilk were simply the latest link of white-collar, organized criminality less than a generation prior to the foremost era of smuggling in America. Their ultimate motive for assisting gunrunners was little different from those future rumrunners—profit, first and foremost—achieving the American Dream of economic success whatever the cost, fair means or foul.

NOTES

1. Oscar J. Martinez, *Troublesome Border* (Tucson: University of Arizona Press, 1988), p. 2.
2. *Senate Executive Journal*, 30th Cong., 1st sess., March 9, 1848, April 25, 1854; Martinez, *Troublesome Border*, pp. 11–21.
3. Jim Brown with additional material by Rand Careaga, *Riding the Line: The United States Customs Service in San Diego, 1885–1930: A Documentary History* (Washington, D.C.: U.S. Customs Service, 1991), pp. 15, 59, 70; Michael Dennis Carman, *United States Customs and the Madero Revolution* (El Paso, TX: University Of El Paso Press, 1976), pp. 5–7, 12, 18, 23; Robert D. Gregg, *The Influence of Border Troubles on Relations between the United States and Mexico, 1876–1910* (Baltimore, MD: Johns Hopkins Press, 1937), pp. 11–14; J. Evetts Haley, *Jeff Milton: A Good Man with a Gun* (Norman: University of Oklahoma Press, 1948), pp. 165, 172–174.
4. Gregg, *The Influence of Border Troubles*, pp. 23–27, 59–60; Frank A. Knapp, 'A Note on General Escobedo in Texas', *Southwestern Historical Quarterly*, 55 (1952), 394–401; *New York Times*, December 8, 1876, p. 5.
5. *Dallas Morning News*, January 16, 1892, p. 1, November 15, 1892, p. 1, December 2, 1892, p. 1, December 16, 1892, p. 6, March 23, 1895, p. 8; Elliott Young, *Catarino Garza's Revolution on the Texas-Mexico Border* (Durham, NC: Duke University, 2004). pp. 177–179.
6. Charles C. Cumberland, 'Precursors of the Mexican Revolution of 1910', *Hispanic American Historical Review*, 22 (1942), 344–356; Linda B. Hall and Don M. Coerver, *Revolution on the Border: The United States and Mexico, 1910–1920* (Albuquerque: University of New Mexico, 1988), pp. 17–18; *Los Angeles Times*, August 25, 1907, p. 15.
7. Ira Jefferson Bush, *Gringo Doctor* (Caldwell, ID: Caxton Printers, 1939), p. 157; Carman, *United States Customs and the Madero Revolution*, pp. 14–15.

8. Carman, *United States Customs and the Madero Revolution*, pp. 15–22, 27–30; *New York Times*, June 27, 1910, p. 1.
9. Lowell L. Blaisdell, 'Was It Revolution or Filibustering? The Mystery of the Flores Magon Revolt in Baja California', *Pacific Historical Review*, 23 (1954), 147–164; Peter Gerhard, 'The Socialist Invasion of Baja California, 1911', *Pacific Historical Review*, 15 (1946), 295–304; *Los Angeles Times*, April 23, 1911, p. I4.
10. Carman, *United States Customs and the Madero Revolution*, pp. 23–24.
11. Gerhard, 'The Socialist Invasion', pp. 295–304; Martinez, *Troublesome Border*, pp. 47–48; *Los Angeles Times*, June 26, 1912, p. II8, July 5, 1912, p. III1, February 19, 1916, p. II1, July 7, 1916, p. II1, July 23, 1916, p. II8, July 18, 1918, p. II1, July 20, 1918, p. II1, November 27, 1922, p. I1.
12. Carman, *United States Customs and the Madero Revolution*, pp. 20–21, 26–27, 50–51, 55; Charles H. Harris, III, and Louis R. Sadler, 'The Underside of the Mexican Revolution: El Paso, 1912', *Americas*, 39 (1982), 69–83; *New York Times*, December 3, 1913, p. 2.
13. Edwin H. Sutherland, *White Collar Crime: The Uncut Version* (New Haven, CT: Yale University Press, 1983), p. 7.
14. Bush, *Gringo Doctor*, pp. 180–181; Carman, *United States Customs and the Madero Revolution*, pp. 55–56.
15. Bush, *Gringo Doctor*, pp. 181–188; Carman, *United States Customs and the Madero Revolution*, pp. 56–57.
16. Carman, *United States Customs and the Madero Revolution*, pp. 32–49; *New York Times*, January 26, 1911, p. 6, January 27, 1911, p. 1, March 8, 1911, p. 1, March 9, 1911, p. 1, March 10, 1911, p. 1.
17. Hall and Coerver, *Revolution on the Border*, pp. 20–21.
18. Bush, *Gringo Doctor*, pp. 194, 202; Carman, *United States Customs and the Madero Revolution*, pp. 60–74; *New York Times*, April 27, 1911, p.1, May 11, 1911, p. 1, May 26, 1911, p. 1.
19. Resolution of March 14, 1912, No. 10, 37 *Stat.* 630.
20. Charles G. Fenwick, *The Neutrality Laws of the United States* (Washington, D.C.: Carnegie Endowment for International Peace, 1913), pp. 57–58; Harris, 'The Underside of the Mexican Revolution', pp. 69–83.
21. Carman, *United States Customs and the Madero Revolution*, pp. 60–74; Harris, 'The Underside of the Mexican Revolution', pp. 69–83; *New York Times*, March 30, 1912, p. 3.
22. Robert E. Hannigan, *The New World Power: American Foreign Policy, 1898–1917* (Philadelphia: University of Pennsylvania Press, 2002), pp. 172–175; *New York Times*, December 3, 1913, p. 2, February 4, 1914, p. 2, May 16, 1914, p. 2.
23. *Los Angeles Times*, December 3, 1913, p. 12; *New York Times*, December 5, 1913, p. 2, December 11, 1913, p. 2, July 3, 1914, p. 1.
24. *United States v. Phelps-Dodge Mercantile Co. et al.*, 209 F 910.
25. *Chicago Daily Tribune*, November 3, 1915, p.8; John S. Goff, 'The Organization of the Federal District Court in Arizona, 1912–1913', *American Journal of Legal History*, 8 (1964), 172–179; J.D. Rosenblum, *Copper Crucible: How the Arizona Miner's Strike of 1983 Recast Labor-Management Relations in America*, 2nd edn (Ithaca, NY: Cornell University Press, 1988), pp. 16–29; *United States v. Phelps-Dodge Mercantile Co. et al.*, 209 Fed. 910; *United States v. Steinfeld & Co., et al.*, 209 Fed. 904.
26. *New York Times*, September 9, 1916, p. 20.

27. *Chicago Daily Tribune*, October 23, 1915, p. 5; *New York Times*, January 16, 1916, Magazine, p. SM1, September 9, 1916, p. 20.
28. Sutherland, *White Collar Crime*, p. 34.
29. Hall, *Revolution on the Border*, pp. 25–26; *Los Angeles Times*, September 29, 1915, p. I1, March 22, 1916, p. 15; *New York Times*, June 19, 1916, p. 2.
30. *Atlanta Constitution*, March 9, 1916, p. 3; *Los Angeles Times*, April 11, 1917, p. I1; *New York Times*, June 19, 1916, p. 2, January 4, 1917, p. 10, September 7, 1919, p. 25; *San Francisco Chronicle*, April 11, 1917, p. 1.
31. Martinez, *Troublesome Border*, p. 2.

6 Prohibition—Part 1

For American white-collar criminality, the opportunities for smuggling tended to be contingent on a specific governmental action instigated by contemporary political circumstances and conflicts, war seemingly the primary cause. President Jefferson's attempt to prevent the American merchant fleet from antagonizing stronger foreign states was but one case in point. The ensuing war with Britain was simply an archetype of the development of profit-making techniques during later conflicts. In both cases, the restrictions that created the opportunity for commercial profit from smuggling were short-lived, ending with peace and the reestablishment of commerce between the formerly belligerent powers.

The same catalyst existed during the Civil War, with hostilities offering a repetition of the smuggling opportunities through trade with the enemy previously found during the War of 1812. Four generations later, conflict again offered profitable prospects for gunrunners during the Mexican Revolution when business interests supplied various participants with needed munitions to achieve their personal and political ambitions, at times in contravention of U.S. interests and law. Filibusters were simply another iteration of this political conflict, as were the laws in place to address the various administrations' concerns for the political consequences of these quasi-military adventures—even when they fit a specific administration's own objectives. Attempting to achieve a 'free and democratic' Cuba without creating an international imbroglio was but one illustration.

Yet the greatest era of smuggling in American history involving the entire spectrum of its citizens was yet to come. Created from a social movement that developed over the history of the American Republic, it endured nationally for thirteen years, challenged an aspect of American culture, extended federal government into local communities to an unprecedented level, corrupted a nation's attitude toward law, and created a new organized version of American crime while also profiting many a white-collar criminal. It was the golden age of smuggling: it was the years of American Prohibition.

Since the founding of the original settlements along the Atlantic seaboard of North America, alcohol has been part of the warp and weft of the U.S. narrative. Used for solace and trade, it eventually led to the worst crime spree in American history and to the development of what is thought of as contemporary organized crime, differentiating it and defining it from its earlier lineage only through its reincarnation in later criminal ventures.

In 1620, besides carrying the Pilgrims to the New World, the *Mayflower* was also manifested with a quantity of beer and aquavitae for the Plymouth Company. When the Massachusetts Bay Company was established almost ten years later, the *Arabella* was ballasted with approximately ten thousand gallons of beer along with malt and aquavitae. Eventually, fruit trees planted in the colony provided domestic fruit cider for the immigrants.[1] As the population grew, so did the demand for alcohol; the town of Boston had forty-nine taverns by 1702, eventually increasing license holders to 155 a generation later. The surrounding communities experienced similar growth.[2] However, James Oglethorpe, the founder (in 1732) of the colony of Georgia, believed that alcohol usage impeded the work of those laborers who had settled there and that alcohol had become a detriment to the development of the colony. He arranged for the prohibition of rum within the colony via the English Parliament. Much to his chagrin, those who sought their spirits could easily cross the Savannah River to obtain the contraband or they could await entrepreneurs from the Carolinas to smuggle it across the river to market. With the law being ignored by so many, it was repealed by 1749.[3]

Rates of consumption were considered high in America with over three gallons per capita consumed annually prior to the Revolution. Drinking encompassed all aspects of colonial society, from ceremonies and social gatherings such as marriages and dances, to business arrangements and public assemblies, including elections and militia musters. Alcohol, for all intents, was the social lubricant of the community. Water quality was sometimes considered questionable, and whiskey often served as a substitute.[4] Leading figures in the colonies—and some future revolutionaries—were involved intimately in the distilling, distributing, and retailing of alcohol. Importers and wholesalers included Robert Morris of Philadelphia, Peter Livingston of New York, and the Brown family of Providence, while George Washington himself was a distiller. Retailers included Thomas Chittenden of Vermont, James Garrard of Kentucky, and Samuel Frances of New York.[5] 'Whiskey was truly the spirits of independence'.[6] Whiskey also became crucial to the economy of the new nation by tying the new settlements of the West to the Atlantic seaboard. Served as both a marketable, portable commodity converted from a perishable bulk product and as a form of currency in a specie-strapped country, whiskey helped bind the new territories to the founding states, aiding in the creation of a national economy.[7]

With the rapid expansion of the country at the beginning of the nineteenth century along with the growth of manufacturing and urban communities, a sense of anomie developed for some within certain trades heavily impacted by the changes. That discord led to the use of alcohol as an elixir to relieve their disquiet. Craftsmen threatened by the changes as well as those whose livelihood kept them isolated or constantly on the move, such as stage drivers, boatmen, and canal builders were all likely candidates to justify heavy drinking. A culture of individualism and masculinity supported their drinking habits, and consumption climbed to five gallons per capita in the new nation. The professions were not exempt. Doctors and the clergy—as well as those in college—were also noted for their above average rates of consumption.[8]

Yet by the mid-1800s, the middle class was reacting to the excessive consumption through the temperance movement. Whether responding to domestic solitary binge drinking, defending nativist values over a growing immigrant population of Germans and Irish who considered drinking as culturally acceptable if not a 'symbol of ethnic loyalty',[9] or confronting the problems of industrialization that led corporate owners toward temperance for their workers, the middle class became the 'moral stewards' in the vanguard of an era of social reform.[10] Churches and religious meetinghouses became bases for the temperance movement with the Quakers having outlawed drinking at various functions during the late eighteenth century, to be followed by the Presbyterian and Methodist churches, which joined the temperance movement in the early 1800s.[11]

By 1851, the governor of the state of Maine signed into law a ban on the sale of alcohol within the state, initiating the first state-wide prohibition. While also providing for the destruction of any liquor confiscated, the ban did not prevent the citizens of Maine from importing liquor for their own consumption from the neighboring states where sales were considered legal, auguring the eventual smuggling of alcohol from Canada. Yet other states followed with their own prohibitionary laws: Massachusetts, Vermont, Rhode Island, and the territory of Minnesota in 1852; Michigan in 1853; and Connecticut in 1854, with more to follow.[12]

The temperance movement would continue to grow and eventually change its objectives from a preference for the moderate use of non-distilled beverages to one of total abstinence. From attacking the licenses of taverns and supporting voluntary abstinence, the movement came to recognize that adopting a legislative mandate would achieve its objectives even against those who opposed abstinence. The temperance movement evolved into the prohibition movement. Consumption eventually dropped to the lowest levels in the history of the nation through the movement's efforts.[13]

Though dealing with setbacks approaching the Civil War, judicial review overturning some state statutes, and other states repealing their previous prohibition legislation if not simply ignoring the law, the movement continued its assault with the assistance of progressive reformers and modern industrialists. For reformers, the local saloons were breeding grounds of public drunkenness, political corruption, and crime, including prostitution and gambling. The Catholic Church campaigned against alcohol as a moral danger, having recognized its negative effects through the churches' social work. For the tycoons of American capitalism, drunkenness of skilled and unskilled workers directly impacted the bottom line. John D. Rockefeller, Henry Ford, William Randolph Hearst, and Andrew Carnegie were all prohibitionists and powerful allies of the temperance movement. Though legislative action slowed during the Civil War, Kansas and North Dakota would pass prohibition legislation in the decades following the war.[14]

By the time the United States entered the First World War, more than a dozen states had some form of prohibition, but legislative battles led to various state and local differences. Some states had statewide prohibition, but many others allowed some form of local option. Some allowed importation for personal use, others allowed homemade wine. As with many movements with a moral agenda, the crusade, now led by the Anti-Saloon League, addressed their concerns across numerous venues. If minimizing tavern licenses locally did not achieve the objective, reformers partnered with state legislatures of whatever party that agreed to support abstinence. If the state proved ineffective, the national government was targeted. In 1913, for example, Congress passed the Webb-Kenyon Act, making it illegal to transport liquor from a state that allowed alcohol to one that prohibited it, justifying its jurisdiction under the interstate commerce clause of the Constitution. Though a previous law, the Wilson Act of 1890, had allowed states to regulate importation, based on subsequent court decisions the law did not grant the states the authority to prohibit importation.[15]

With the change in strategy, a major opportunity presented itself at the start of the World War. The European conflict offered the opportunity to make abstinence a patriotic act in support of the nation's war effort. The Sheppard Act was passed in March 1917, prohibiting the sale, manufacture, or importation of liquor into the District of Columbia—the district that encompassed the nation's capital and was under direct federal control—and went into effect the following November. Other laws leading incrementally toward prohibition continued to be passed during the congressional session, with the Lever Food and Fuel Control Act having the greatest impact.[16] The objective, as the formal title of the legislation stated, was to 'provide further for the national security and defense by encouraging the production, conserving the supply, and controlling the distribution of food products and fuel'; the bill also gave the prohibitionists a powerful weapon to further their interests: patriotism.[17] Outlawing the use of foods—in particular grain—in the manufacture of distilled spirits the law, along with the later War Prohibition Act forbidding the manufacturing of beer and wine, became a successful tool to challenge the loyalty of those that distilled or brewed them. Especially effective against German brewers in America, one of the major foils against the temperance movement, the series of wartime legal initiatives gave momentum to a permanent national prohibition—the Eighteenth Amendment to the Constitution of the United States. Originally submitted in July 1917, the amendment passed Congress in December and the first state ratified it the following month. One year later, Nebraska became the thirty-sixth state to do so, meeting the constitutional requirement for implementation of the amendment. On January 20, 1920, the Eighteenth Amendment went into effect, outlawing 'the manufacture, sale, or transportation of intoxicating liquors within, the importation thereof into, or the exportation thereof from the United States and all territory subject to the jurisdiction thereof for beverage purposes'.[18]

With the Eighteenth Amendment giving both the federal government and the states concurrent jurisdiction to enforce Prohibition, Congress followed up the amendment with the Volstead Act, formally known as the National Prohibition Act, one of many laws to enable the enforcement of Prohibition. The act defined what was considered an illegal alcoholic beverage, regulated the trade in non-beverage alcohol, and continued wartime prohibitions until the Eighteenth Amendment went into effect. It also empowered the commissioner of Internal Revenue to investigate violations of the federal law. With the passage of the Volstead Act, Congress had given teeth to Prohibition. National prohibition had effectively been achieved, if not yet in substance, at least in law.[19] The stage was also set for white-collar criminality: otherwise legitimate businessmen in the distillery and brewery industries in Canada directly profited from conspiring to violate the same law.

DETROIT

There were three major sources of illicit liquor during Prohibition: smuggling, diversion of industrial and medicinal alcohol, and illicit manufacturing by distilling, brewing, or producing wine. At the implementation of Prohibition, smuggling offered the easiest method to obtain quality liquor, and communities along the Mexican and Canadian borders showed a 'noticeable increased activity', yet it was believed that there would be a 'steady decline in violations.'[20] The optimism of the prohibitionists seemed to have carried over to the bureaucracy.[21]

With the enactment of the Volstead Act, the major responsibilities for enforcement of Prohibition fell, against the wishes of the department, under the secretary of the Treasury. With the Bureau of Internal Revenue under the Treasury and with Congress believing that Internal Revenue already had the expertise in investigating liquor tax violations (skills believed similar to enforcing Prohibition), the Prohibition Unit of the IRS was instituted. With customs and the Coast Guard already part of the organizational structure of the Treasury—the Coast Guard having been returned to the control of the Treasury from the navy at the end of World War I—all three major forms of illicit liquor violations came under the jurisdiction of the Treasury. Yet with the war winding down, the agency was in no position to enforce the new federal law.[22]

While the Prohibition Unit was being established—with officers having little if any enforcement experience—the Coast Guard's priorities (operating from the Bering Sea to the North Atlantic) were focused on its traditional missions, including rescue and salvage, ice patrols and winter cruising, anchorage and harbor monitoring, fishery protection, and the enforcement of various navigation and safety laws, with the workload exceeding previous levels. Customs, first and foremost a revenue-oriented organization, was focused on collecting duty. As traditional customs work volume increased (merchandise entries climbed by 20 percent from 1919 to 1920, for example), a number of employees involved in Prohibition enforcement were returned to their more customary duties in an attempt to address a manpower shortage aggravated by a shrinking workforce in comparison to pre-war staffing levels. Duties unrelated to customs' primary function but nonetheless considered a priority included the licensing, admeasuring, entering, and clearing of vessels; crew discharge; and public health-related responsibilities, as well as statistical compilation of merchandise transiting the border. With almost nineteen thousand miles of land and marine border to protect and over forty-four thousand vessels entering the United States subject to customs inspection yearly, the total strength in 1920 between the agencies was 10,927 personnel: 4,294 in the Coast Guard with the rest serving under customs. The newly established Prohibition Unit had another 948 field agents nationwide. Within a year there were a third less. As late as 1925, when General Lincoln C. Andrews was appointed assistant secretary of the Treasury, Andrews claimed that he had only 170 customs patrolmen for all the land borders of the United States and 110 prohibition enforcement agents.[23]

Some communities along the American-Canadian border served as precursors to the problems of Prohibition enforcement months prior to the enactment of the Volstead Act. In 1916, Michigan chose to outlaw alcoholic beverages within the state effective May 1, 1918. Detroit, the state's largest city and fourth largest in the United States, was considered a wet city, as were most urban environs. As such it had a large population that was only too willing to flaunt the new laws. Originally running alcohol from wet Ohio north to the city, after Ohio went dry in May of 1919 another venue closer to home became the method of choice for numerous rumrunners prior to national prohibition.[24]

Detroit was originally established as a military outpost that served as a commercial portal to the interior of northern America first used by the French and later by the British. Located on the narrowest part of the approximately thirty mile long strait ('strait' being a translation of *detroit* from French) connecting the upper Great Lakes country deep within the continent to the lower Great Lakes—linking Lake Huron to Lake Erie via Lake St. Claire— and the St. Lawrence waterway and eventually the Atlantic, the settlement controlled passage into the interior and served as a French base for the fur trade with the indigenous population. After the French ceded their Canadian holdings to Britain (with the exception of the islands of St. Pierre and Miquelon in the North Atlantic off the coast of Newfoundland) after the Seven Years' War and Britain ultimately ceded much of North America to the newly-formed United States after the American Revolution, the strait eventually became a gateway for contraband into the United States during Prohibition.[25]

Agreeing to the American compromise of establishing the boundary between the United States and Canada through the middle of the Great Lakes and down the center of the Detroit River, Detroit was separated from Canada by a waterway approximately one mile wide. The south bank (Canadian side) of the river was then developed by the British after formally turning over Detroit to the Americans in 1796. Heralding the future Canadian-American trade liaison, the new settlement exported forty-three thousand gallons of liquor across the strait to Detroit in the following year.[26]

As early as April 1918, the river started to carry organized smuggling traffic when three local shipyard workers pooled their savings, traveled to Montreal, and bought twenty-five cases of whiskey. By using a small row boat, these blue-collar entrepreneurs transported their alcohol across the river into the United States, circumventing inspection by either country. After two more journeys to Montreal and with the addition of a fourth partner, the syndicate was soon purchasing thousand-case loads.[27]

The reason for driving to Montreal was that the province of Ontario had its own prohibition laws in effect that precluded the purchase of liquor locally. That was soon to change. Though Ontario continued to outlaw the local purchase of alcohol, the law allowed residents to import liquor from another province for personal consumption. Of greater importance, however, the manufacture and export of liquor was a federal, not provincial, matter. In January 1920, when the United States was initiating national prohibition, the Dominion of Canada's wartime prohibition concluded. Though many provinces, including Ontario, continued prohibition under provincial laws, distilleries and breweries were operated under Dominion regulations and therefore were allowed to produce a commercial product for export. With Ontario bordering the states of New York, Pennsylvania, Ohio, Michigan, and Minnesota, the province became a key source of America's liquor. It was not long before modern entrepreneurs took advantage of a golden opportunity. 'As the prohibitionists watched, almost helplessly, the worst happened: In the next ten years, along the shores of the Detroit River, the prohibition dream became an American nightmare'.[28]

Personal and smalltime smuggling quickly developed with passengers traveling across the river by ferry, using numerous methods of concealment in a game of cat and mouse with the customs inspectors. Working Canadian women traveled to Detroit on the daily ferries to their clerical jobs while carrying liquor on their person or in lunchboxes, playing on the inspectors' paternal familiarity with them. Babies were used as props and bottles were concealed in the babies' carriages (a crying baby could always be used to distract the inspectors at the appropriate time, if required). If a baby was unavailable, simulating a pregnancy could offer the same opportunity for concealment. Girdles, corsets, and custom-made garments with numerous pockets to conceal bottles were worn though simply cinching a pants belt to tightly hold a bottle in the waistband could be effective at times. Even small quantities of farm produce carried by hand were used to conceal contraband. In one case, a smuggler had a basket of eggs that had been individually filled with alcohol after being emptied of their more mundane contents. After accidently bumping the basket into a taxi, the smell of whiskey from the broken eggs permeated the air so much so that the smuggler quickly abandoned his produce and 'beat it' to avoid arrest.[29]

The use of vehicles offered the opportunity to move greater quantities. The techniques developed for moving whiskey surreptitiously from Ohio to Detroit at the start of Michigan's state prohibition were quickly adapted. Cars were modified with false compartments or had tanks built underneath the bodies. Some had fuel tanks replaced with ones that were compartmentalized to carry alcohol in one area while the fuel was segmented in another section. Rear seats were removed with cases of liquor replacing them. Spare tires carried whiskey in lieu of air. Whatever could be modified or replaced to conceal and transport alcohol was considered.[30]

Trains manifested with international cargo were obvious targets for concealment. Moving from Windsor to Detroit via the Michigan Central Railroad Tunnel or the various railroad ferries, loads bound for the United States with Canadian goods such as hay or machinery were used to conceal cases of whiskey and beer, which were removed shortly upon entry to the United States but prior to a customs inspection. Other cars were manifested for Mexico only to be diverted and unloaded in stateside freight yards when convenient. Cargos loaded in Buffalo, New York, were shipped directly across Canada to Detroit in lieu of the longer domestic route around the southern shores of Lake Erie, sealed by customs prior to their departure from the United States. While transiting Canada, the seals were broken and the legitimate cargo replaced with contraband, the doors being resealed with a stolen or counterfeit customs seal. Upon reentry to the United States, the cargo was passed on unopened as the inspected seal was found intact. Customs and shipping documents were either forged or illegally obtained. Though small quantities could be moved by train under the Detroit River by anyone with knowledge of the rail system, the cost to load a boxcar was prohibitive for all but the best financed syndicates. Investigations eventually determined that more than one brewery in Canada was directly profiting from these frauds. It was not until 1925 that criminal sanctions of imprisonment came into play in an attempt to minimize violations.[31]

Innovation in transportation applied as much to smuggling as it did to more prosaic commercial ventures during the Prohibition era. Besides trains, trucks, and cars, airplanes came into use, having been effectively developed during the recent World War. Even with the limitations in capacity, operating range, and functional hours, more than one smuggler attempted to use them to fly over the river and over any border security. Ralph Capone, brother and partner of Al Capone—labeled Chicago's 'most notorious gangster' by the news media—ran an organization moving liquor south across the border, operating numerous aircraft, which included a Ford Tri-Motor in the fleet.[32] The Capones worked with Blaise Diesbourg, a Canadian trafficker who also exported Canadian alcohol to other major organizations such as the Purple Gang of Detroit. At one point, Diesbourg was loading a plane a day, twenty-five cases per aircraft, alternating landing sites by using farmers' fields on the Canadian side to minimize exposure to Ontario law enforcement.[33]

Planes would also be used in their original role of 'battlefield' surveillance and observation. John Elliot, Ben Kerr's associate and fellow rumrunner, was a pilot and owner of a float plane that was suspected of being used for counter-surveillance further east over Lake Ontario.[34] The Coast Guard, six years into Prohibition, eventually acquired seaplanes for observation of the northeastern Atlantic seaboard.[35]

Aviation in the 1920s was considered a glamorous adventure thanks to its hazardous history. Popular movies lionized aviators' exploits during the World War, best exemplified by Howard Hughes' *Hell's Angels*. Newspapers and magazines glorified their escapades as well.[36] The delivery of air mail was compared to the dangers and excitement of the western frontier's Pony Express, while aircraft speed records and long distance flights were the grist of newspaper editors. With the use of aircraft in smuggling, that same adulation carried over to the new smugglers of the air.[37]

During the winter, smugglers drove loads of contraband liquor across the frozen river or Lake St. Claire just northeast of Detroit, sometimes using expendable junk autos to cross the ice. When short stretches of open water became an obstacle, the jalopies or trucks were driven across a makeshift bridge of boards up to eighteen feet long stacked upon each other to continue onward to the States. Deliveries were also made on the ice when cars coming from Michigan met midway to transfer the liquor. In one case twenty-two cars picked up four hundred cases that were waiting on the ice, immediately returning to the United States.[38] At times sleds were dragged behind vehicles to spread the weight across a larger area of the lake's surface and prevent the vehicle from breaking through and sinking in the lake or river. At other times picturesque ice boats were drafted and, thanks to their speed, could easily outrun pursuing vehicles. Some smugglers simply put sled runners on boats and towed one or more of them across the frozen waterways; if suddenly pursued, they cut the load loose and drove away.[39]

Vessels, however, were the backbone of Detroit smuggling, first and foremost. Boats of all descriptions were put to use, from rowboats, canoes, and duckboats, to tug boats and even a converted oceangoing World War minesweeper. The schooner *Shark*, a former personal yacht, carried fourteen hundred cases of beer on a single trip across Lake Erie. Speedboats were eventually used, with many being built specifically for the rum running trade, some of the fastest utilizing twin aircraft Liberty engines for propulsion. The former minesweeper, the *Vedas*, brought loads from Montreal to Windsor, Ontario. At times the *Vedas* ran a load straight over to the United States, while at other times it served as a mothership, anchoring just outside the territorial waters of the United States where it awaited stateside boats to pick up the contraband and then deliver it directly to the United States. The steamer *City of Dresden*, after being refitted with new engines, was put back into service as a smuggler. *The Maude*, an eighteen-ton tug, was capable of moving eight hundred cases a trip. From a few cases in a rowboat to four hundred, eight hundred, or more cases of whiskey in larger craft, the loss of any vessel was simply the cost of doing business, easily addressed out of the profits.[40]

Liquor smuggling started slowly as Canadian customs officials believed exporting alcohol to the United States was unlawful; the actual legal status was questionable, at best. Canadian sellers would signal passing boats and haggle over prices, loading from concealed stores. Both men and women pooled their resources to fund their smuggling ventures. Done primarily under cover of darkness, small amateurs operating with small loads dominated the business in the early stages. Yet even for small-scale operations, profits were exceptional. The Detroit police commissioner claimed that he knew of 'more than fifty Detroiters who made more than $100,000 each in the first six months of Prohibition transporting across the Detroit River'.[41] With whiskey being bought as low as $30 to $35 a case and sold as high as $175 to $180 stateside, a crew moving 2,500 cases each month earned in excess of $25,000, leaving the vessel owner turning a profit exceeding $10,000.[42] More than one Canadian bought a farm or business from the profits and most families along the Detroit had someone associated with the business in one manner or another.[43]

Communities on both sides of the river, upstream and downstream of Detroit, were involved in the trafficking, either profiting from it or plundered by it. The blue-collar town of Ecorse, located south of Detroit, quickly became a 'hub of commerce' in the trade. It had a maritime community ready to profit from the opportunity of Prohibition, the docks for off-loading, and a police force that all but ignored the prohibition laws, making only two arrests in all of 1923 under them. On at least two occasions, crowds of citizens prevented Treasury agents from seizing goods and transporting arrestees from the area. The town of Hamtramck, under orders of Governor Alex Groesbeck of Michigan, was taken over by the Michigan State Police and the mayor eventually convicted for prohibition violations. Other communities faced similar problems.[44]

The Gold Coast of Lake St. Claire just north of Detroit had its own distinctive problems. A wealthy area bordering the lake and having numerous boat docks for the various estates and summerhouses, many a rumrunner off-loaded his goods at these convenient, private facilities. Eventually as Prohibition enforcement developed, agents encountered the privileged of these communities. Failing to show a level of deference to wealth, more than one encounter between the two led to an untoward incident, including inappropriate shootings.[45]

While many involved in this contraband trade were amateurs or, eventually, gangsters and their confederates, it was the distillers, financial backers, corrupt government officials and other associates who qualified as the white-collar criminals of Sutherland's writings. Operating legitimate distilleries, breweries, and export companies, they were involved intimately in the trafficking of contraband into the United States. Trafficking was integral to their business plan, and they conspired with whoever was needed on both sides of the border to achieve their bottom line. This was their version of the American Dream, whatever side of the border they lived on. As one New Zealander remarked after mistakenly identifying a Canadian as American, 'Same piece of real estate'.[46] If the Michigan waterfront was the entry point for the contraband liquor, Windsor and the adjacent communities in Ontario were the sources. Almost one million cases of liquor were shipped to Windsor and the surrounding area during the first seven months of Prohibition, effectively increasing the local per capita consumption rate ten times above its pre-war average. With the high profits available from resale to smugglers, little was actually consumed locally. Some estimated that up to a quarter of the population along the Detroit River was involved in the export trade. Local court fines for smuggling violations totaled almost $250,000 that year. More than one Canadian mansion was built across from Detroit, paid for with the proceeds of rum running.[47]

Some individuals became extremely successful in the export business. Blaise Diesbourg moved cases of liquor purchased at the numerous export docks and shipped them across the river year-round by boat, car, or plane. Using a truck in the winter carrying four hundred cases, for example, he arranged to deliver the load onto the ice where it was re-loaded onto twenty-two autos that continued the journey to the U.S. shore. As mentioned earlier he also coordinated the use of aircraft for the Capone organization.[48] Harry Low, another major Canadian rumrunner, used speedboats, building a network to move beer and whiskey. Low bought the WWI minesweeper, the *Vedas*, and, at times, put it to use as a mothership along the boundary-line waters of Lake Erie while traveling between Montreal and Windsor. Rumrunners from the United States rendezvoused with the *Vedas*, offloading the liquor to the American vessels, which would then make a direct run into the United States and, by never landing on Canadian soil, minimized their exposure to law enforcement. He was the founder of one brewery and established an export firm with one of his partners associated with a second brewery. While serving as the managing director of the Carling Export Brewing and Malting Company, Low attempted to bribe a Michigan Central Railway employee to assist in getting carloads of beer into the United States by concealing them as box cars in transit through Canada in bond. Though unsuccessful, there was evidence of numerous successful loads using similar methods.[49] Jim Cooper became a middleman for Hiram

Walker and Sons distillery by establishing Dominion Distillery Products, which purchased directly from Hiram Walker only to then sell the whiskey to smugglers. When he died in 1931, Cooper's estate was valued at almost five hundred thousand dollars, not including his home, a forty-room mansion in his wife's name that cost over two hundred thousand dollars to construct when completed in 1925 for Cooper.[50] Low and Cooper epitomized the white-collar criminal that profited from Prohibition: otherwise respectable businessmen violating the law in course of their occupations, be it through the use of bribery or conspiring with others to smuggle alcohol across the border.

An Ontario court decision would break open the Canadian export trade and all but flood Detroit in quality liquor. In an attempt to avoid legal action and to comply with customs requirements, liquor purchased in Ontario for export was manifested for delivery to a location other than the United States, such as Mexico or various Caribbean nations. But in July of 1921, importation of liquor from another province into Ontario was made illegal. One of the breweries, the British-American Brewing Company, challenged the seizure of a shipment of beer to Wyandotte, Michigan. The Canadian magistrate hearing the case, W. E. Gundy, upheld the brewery's argument that the brewery operated under Dominion charter; the province had no authority to prohibit the exportation of its product to any country, whether legal or not within that consigned destination. Manipulating the law, the brewer effectively circumvented Canadian enforcement, reinforcing Sutherland's concept of a white-collar criminals' self-image: '[e]ven when they violate the law, they do not conceive of themselves as criminals'[51] and that they maintain their 'public status' by 'public adherence to the law'.[52] With that decision, the question of legally exporting alcohol from Canada to the United States was settled, at least from a Canadian perspective. The decision also opened the brewing, distilling, and exportation business to serious organization and finance. The Essex Export Company, Ltd., was the first of many Canadian alcohol-related businesses to be established within days of the magistrate's ruling, opening the opportunity for white-collar crime versus simply 'ordinary' blue-collar street crime.[53] The political, legal, and business interests had again intersected, this time to the benefit of the Canadian liquor industry.

Enforcement activities were slow to start. It was believed that the forces already in existence, including the local police, customs inspectors, and state enforcement agencies, could deal with any scofflaws, yet it did not take long for most to realize that the tools at hand were insufficient to address the demand for imported liquor. Eventually the Detroit Police Department, the Michigan State Police, the Immigration Service's Border Patrol, the Customs Patrol, and the U.S. Coast Guard began working the river in an uncoordinated attempt at preventing rum running. The Detroit Police Department successfully seized the vessel *Tennessee II*, reputedly the fastest boat on the river, in the fall of 1920 while it was off-loading. The vessel was drafted into the service of the slow-to-develop 'Prohibition Navy', the moniker given to the hodgepodge of vessels eventually serving law enforcement's effort at interdicting smuggling across the Detroit and its associated bodies of water. The following spring, two new vessels joined the police department's fleet. It was another year before the Michigan State Police put their own vessel on the water, built for the mission; another followed a year later and four more followed two years hence.[54] Though primarily a federal problem, limited funding was appropriated to address the federal enforcement of the new law. Lack of funding led to limited manpower, poor training, and inadequate equipment. For years the Customs Patrol only operated seized vessels for lack of appropriations to purchase marine craft. Understaffed, even by 1927, though authorized for forty-two personnel, only twenty-four slots were filled with only three boats operational.[55] It took the Coast Guard four years to obtain the appropriations needed to build a national interdiction fleet by reconditioning twenty-five destroyers (transferred from the navy), each approximately three hundred feet long, to do patrol duty off the Atlantic coast, and by building 203 seventy-five-foot patrol boats for coastal and inland waters along with 30 thirty-five-footers and 73 thirty-six-footers capable of speeds as high as twenty-four miles per hour. Eventually the Coast Guard would build 33 thirty-four-foot speedboats able to travel thirty to thirty-four mph (those equipped with Liberty engines) besides utilizing various seized vessels to deal with the rumrunners' faster smuggling vessels in the Detroit and other Great Lakes areas of operation. It was not until 1926 that all federal vessels in the Detroit area were under one unified command, the politically appointed collector of customs.[56]

Organized smuggling organizations, coming into play by 1923, developed their own maritime force, one of the most famous being the Little Jewish Navy associated with the Purple Gang, which served as a supplier for Capone in Chicago. Operating about a dozen speedboats, they used force of numbers to chase away any enforcement attempts until law enforcement eventually obtained larger vessels, along with the armaments that went with them. John Wozniak of Ecorse, Michigan, the commandant of another smuggling force known as 'Peajacket's Navy', employed two dozen seamen to move alcohol across the river. These organizations were not limited to the Detroit River. All along Lake Erie and Lake Ontario, various organizations moved liquor south to the United States.[57]

The quantity of alcohol being moved across the border only increased with the Gundy decision. In 1924, the value of liquor entering the United States across both its northern and southern borders was estimated at approximately forty million dollars.[58] Over forty thousand cases of Canadian whiskey transited the Detroit area alone during one week in May 1927.[59] For the year April 1, 1927, to March 31, 1928, 3,101,820 gallons of Canadian beer and whiskey, along with 268,694 gallons of foreign beer, whiskey, and wine, were exported from Windsor alone, totaling over $20 million.[60] An estimated 75 percent of all smuggled liquor was moving across from Ontario to Michigan and less than 5 percent was being apprehended.[61] The success of these smuggling ventures was, in no small part, thanks to the government of the Dominion of Canada. By 1928, the Canadian government was making thirty million dollars in annual taxes on exported liquor with liquor taxes providing up to a one-fifth of all Dominion and provincial revenue.[62]

In attempting to address the flood of liquor, in Michigan alone over one hundred thousand arrests were made for liquor law infractions during Prohibition.[63] Within six months of Prohibition being enacted, over ten thousand apprehensions were made by federal prohibition officers nationally.[64] Convictions in federal courts nationwide rose from 17,962 in the first full fiscal year after the implementation of Prohibition to 37,018 in the fiscal year ending June 20, 1926. By 1930, the number rose to 54,085.[65] One Border Patrol agent working north of Detroit arrested over two hundred persons between 1927 and 1933.[66] Vessels were impounded but, as those arrested would return to the business, so too would their boats. Boats were seized three or four times in one year, each time being forfeited only to return to the trade after being bought at auction, liberated from storage, or returned by the courts. During operations in 1928 and 1929, the government seized 366 boats in the Detroit area only to have all but one stolen.[67]

As stated earlier, the first smugglers tended to be local 'mom and pop' operations, but as with many industries, these independents were overshadowed by the growth of a few major organizations. Groups developed that focused on export and shipping from Canada. Members of the Pascuzzi Combine were a classic example of white-collar crime: legitimate distillery and brewery businesses supplied the contraband in partnership with smugglers, American distributers, and retailers of alcohol, with financial links to both the Riverside Brewery and the Amherstburg Distillery in Ontario. The Combine was indicted in 1929 after a nine-month-long investigation, as were associates of what was known as the Miller Combine. Between the two groups, forty-two individuals were implicated in moving liquor across the border and on to New York and Chicago, among other cities. Detroit's Purple Gang was another involved in bootlegging, high-jacking, and rum running through the Little Jewish Navy.[68]

Enforcement had the potential to be a dangerous business for all sides, police, rumrunners, and civilians alike. By April 1929, fifty-five U.S. officers were killed enforcing prohibition laws. One hundred thirty-five civilians were killed by government agents during the same period with unknown numbers of rumrunners killed by accidents or by associates in the profession.[69] Ben Kerr, a long-time rumrunner, died as he tried to cross Lake Ontario in the dead of winter, attempting to avoid law enforcement. His partially disabled boat was lost, the hull split by ice, with hypothermia killing both Kerr and his crewman.[70] One hijacker, known as the Gray Ghost for the coloring of both his wardrobe and his boat, had a propensity for robbing smugglers who were en route to Canada with funds for the purchase of contraband. He was found murdered on the streets of Detroit.[71] Other hijackers were suspected of donning customs patrol officer uniforms to assist in stopping rumrunners, only aggravating the potential for an aggressive response by rumrunners when later stopped by legitimate authorities in similar uniforms.[72] Civilians were also dragged into the conflict, at times unknowingly.[73] In 1925, two sons of the vice president of Fisher Body Company, along with the son of the president of a catering company, were fired on after they failed to stop when challenged on the waterway.[74] A sixty-five-year-old postal carrier was shot in the back while fishing in a skiff the following year. A year later an innocent boater and his eleven-year-old daughter were killed after being rammed by a federal boat, which then departed without assisting the victims.[75]

The continuing entrepreneurship of law enforcement in personally profiting from the trade contributed to the problems of enforcing Prohibition, including preventing the smuggling of liquor into the United States. This graft was simply an extension of white-collar crime as defined by Sutherland.[76] The captain of the Harbor Division of the Detroit Police Department used police boats to run loads and directed officers to offload the cargo, payment being made with a portion of the goods. The captain seemed to have little hesitation in storing at least one of the shipments in his own quarters in the police station house.[77] In numerous communities, including Trenton and Lincoln Park, portions of the police department, if not the entire staff, assisted the rumrunners.[78] Coast Guard crews were also compromised, the financial incentives even greater than for a cop or a customs officer. An enlisted guardsman was paid thirty-six dollars a month, less than the profit from the sale of just one case of Scotch whiskey brought across the Detroit. One cutter out of Monroe, Michigan, relinquished a seized cargo of liquor to a second smuggling vessel in the presence of the original smuggler. Within the first six years of Prohibition, 750 Coast Guard employees were discharged from the service for misconduct and another 550 were charged in the following two years for various offenses associated with Prohibition corruption.[79] The Customs Patrol was little different with twenty arrested in December 1928. Even after cleaning up the service the following year, 60 of the 150 patrol inspectors resigned in 1930 alone, with more patrolmen being indicted. More than two million dollars in graft was claimed to have been paid in 1928 to allow smugglers to land contraband liquor.[80]

But it was the distillers, the brewers, and those associated with them that exemplified Sutherland's white-collar criminal more than any other group of organized smugglers on either side of the border. Some of the greatest and grandest names in the future Canadian liquor industry built empires thanks to the opportunities presented by Prohibition in the United States. Again, they personified the white-collar criminal by being respectable businessmen who violated the smuggling laws in the course of their occupation, as the traders of Jefferson's administration, the opportunists of the Civil War and Mexican Revolution, and the filibusters of the previous one hundred years had themselves done. Though Detroit was the obvious geographical frontline of this war on liquor, with a number of distilleries and breweries located within a couple of miles of the U.S. border, other areas also came into play, including the northern Great Plains/Prairie border and the northern New York/New England areas. The most infamous, however, were the maritime commerce lanes, some of which were the historical trading routes used by earlier generations of smugglers during previous conflicts. These would be utilized again by a new generation of white-collar criminals.

NOTES

1. Dean Albertson, 'Puritan Liquor in the Planting of New England', *New England Quarterly*, 23 (1950), 477–490; Andrew Barr, *Drink: A Social History of America* (New York: Carroll and Graf, 1999), p. 33; Mark Edward Lender and James Kirby Martin, *Drinking in America: A History* (New York: The Free Press, 1982), pp. 2–3.
2. Henry Bamford Parkes, 'Morals and Law Enforcement in Colonial New England', *New England Quarterly*, 5 (1932), 431–452.
3. Barr, *Drink: A Social History*, pp. 39–41.
4. *ibid.*, pp. 205–206; W. J. Rorabaugh, *Alcoholic Republic: An American Tradition* (New York: Oxford University Press, 1979), pp. 7–8, 19–20, 95–98.
5. Rorabaugh, *Alcoholic Republic*, pp. 48–49.
6. *ibid.*, p. 92.
7. *ibid.*, pp. 74, 81–86, 91–92.
8. Lender and Martin, *Drinking in America*, pp. 47–48; Rorabaugh, *Alcoholic Republic*, pp. 125–146.
9. Lender and Martin, *Drinking in America*, p. 60.
10. *ibid.*, p. 65.
11. *ibid.*, pp. 64–68; Rorabaugh, *Alcoholic Republic*, pp. 37–38, 188–189.
12. Lender and Martin, *Drinking in America*, pp. 42, 84; Barr, *Drink: A Social History*, p. 177.
13. Lender and Martin, *Drinking in America*, pp. 71–72, 84.
14. *ibid.*, pp. 85, 92–93, 102–114; Kenneth M. Murchison, *Federal Criminal Law Doctrines: The Forgotten Influence of National Prohibition* (Durham, NC: Duke University, 1994), pp. 4–5.
15. Sean Dennis Cashman, *Prohibition: The Lie of the Land* (New York: Free Press, 1981), pp. 6–10; Lender & Martin, *Drinking in America*, pp. 111–112; Webb-Kenyon Act, 37 *Stat.* 699 (1913); Wilson Act, 26 *Stat.* 313 (1890).
16. Lever Act, 40 *Stat.* 276 (1917); Reed Amendment, 39 *Stat.* 1058, 1069 (1917).
17. Lever Act, 40 *Stat.* 276 (1917).
18. Cashman, *Prohibition: The Lie of the Land*, pp. 10–25; Eighteenth Amendment, U.S. Constitution.
19. National Commission on Law Observance and Enforcement, *Report on the Enforcement of Prohibition Laws of the United States* (Washington, D.C.: Government Printing Office, 1931); Volstead Act, 41 *Stat.* 305 (1919).
20. *Annual Report of the Secretary of the Treasury on the State of the Finances for the Fiscal Year Ended June 30, 1919, with Appendices* (Washington, D.C.: Government Printing Office, 1920), p. 163.
21. National Commission on Law Observance and Enforcement, *Report on the Enforcement of the Prohibition Laws of the United States*, pp. 22–35.

22. *Annual Report of the Secretary of the Treasury on the State of the Finances for the Fiscal Year Ended June 30, 1919*, pp. 502–503; National Commission on Law Observance and Enforcement, *Report on the Enforcement of the Prohibition Laws of the United States*, pp. 10–13.

23. *Annual Report of the Secretary of the Treasury on the State of the Finances for the Fiscal Year Ended June 30, 1920, with Appendices* (Washington, D.C.: Government Printing Office, 1921), pp. 604–605, 644–651, 689–701; National Commission on Law Observance and Enforcement, *Report on the Enforcement of the Prohibition Laws of the United States*, p. 14.

24. Larry Engelmann, Intemperance: *The Lost War against Liquor* (New York: The Free Press, 1979), pp. 22–47; U.S. Bureau of the Census, *Fourteenth Census of the United States Population: Number and Distribution of Inhabitants, Summary of Results* (Washington, D.C.: Government Printing Office, 1921), p. 76.

25. Melvin G. Holli, 'The Founding of Detroit by Cadillac', *Michigan Historical Review*, 27 (2001), 129–136.

26. Albert B. Corey, *Canadian-American Relations along the Detroit River* (Detroit, MI: Wayne State University Press, 1957), pp. 1–5; Holli, 'The Founding of Detroit by Cadillac', pp. 129–136; D. W. Meinig, *The Shaping of America: A Geographical Perspective on 500 Years of History, Volume 1, Atlantic America, 1492–1800* (New Haven, CT: Yale University Press, 1986), pp. 267–270, 323–332.

27. Engelmann, *Intemperance: The Lost War against Liquor*, p. 75.

28. Engelmann, *Intemperance: The Lost War against Liquor*, pp. 70–72.

29. 'The Eggs Were Loaded', *New York Times*, May 17, 1920, p. 23C; H. Gervais, *The Rumrunners: A Prohibition Scrapbook* (Scarborough, Ontario, Canada: Firefly, 1980), p. 45; Janet Langlois, 'Smuggling Across the Windsor-Detroit Border: Folk Art, Sexual Difference and Cultural Identity', *Canadian Folklore*, 13 (1991), 23–34; Philip P. Mason, *Rumrunning and the Roaring Twenties: Prohibition on the Michigan-Ontario Waterway* (Detroit, MI: Wayne State University, 1995), p. 45; 'Rum-Running Typists', *New York Times*, June 25, 1922, p. XX3.

30. Gervais, *The Rumrunners*, p. 118; Mason, *Rumrunning and the Roaring Twenties*, p. 44; 'Rum Flood Pouring in from Canada', *Oregonian*, February 21, 1921, p. 3.

31. 'Canuck Rum Runners Go After Record when They Find Troops Are Patrolling American Line', *Macon Daily Telegraph*, August 14, 1921, p. 6; Cashman, *Prohibition: The Lie of the Land*, pp. 31–32; Engelmann, *Intemperance: The Lost War against Liquor*, pp. 86–87; Royal Commission on Customs and Excise, *Interim Reports (Nos.1 to 10)* (Ottawa, Ontario, Canada: F. A. Acland, 1928), pp. 75–76, 81, 83; James C. Young, 'Border Battle on Rum Grows in Intensity', *New York Times*, May 22, 1927, p. XX5.

32. 'Deserved Rewards', *Chicago Daily Tribune*, August 11, 1932, p. 10; 'Capone Loses Fight To Bar "Confession"', *New York Times*, October 9, 1931, p. 3.

33. 'Bootlegging Airplanes', *Literary Digest*, July 22, 1922, p. 24; 'The Bootlegger's Bad Ways and Big Profits', *Literary Digest*, December 30, 1922, pp. 31–34; Engelmann, *Intemperance: The Lost War against Liquor*, pp. 84–86; Gervais, *The Rumrunners*, pp. 27–29, 41–42.

34. Edward Butts, *Outlaws of the Lakes* (Toronto: Lynx Images, 2004), p. 160.

35. Eric S. Ensign, *Intelligence in the Rum War at Sea, 1920–1933* (Washington, D.C.: Joint Military Intelligence College, 2001), pp. 34–36.

36. *Hell's Angels*, dir. by Howard Hughes (The Caddo Company, 1930).

37. Engelmann, *Intemperance: The Lost War against Liquor*, p. 86; 'Five Miles a Minute at Venice', *Literary Digest*, October 8, 1927, p. 13; 'A New

World's-Record Speedster', *Literary Digest*, September 29, 1923, pp. 56–58; 'The Spirit of the Old "Pony Express" Now Carries' the Air Mail', *Literary Digest*, October, 9, 1920, pp. 76–82.

38. Gervais, *The Rumrunners*, pp. 29–31.
39. Engelmann, *Intemperance: The Lost War against Liquor*, pp. 88–91; Mason, *Rumrunning and the Roaring Twenties*, pp. 42–43.
40. Engelmann, *Intemperance: The Lost War against Liquor*, p. 77; Gervais, *The Rumrunners*, pp. 23–31, 42–44, 76; National Commission on Law Observance and Enforcement, *Report on the Enforcement of the Prohibition Laws of the United States*, p. 24; *Windsor Star*, January 31, 1953, as quoted in Gervais, *The Rumrunners*, pp. 52–55; James C. Young, 'Border Battle on Rum Row Grows in Intensity', *New York Times*, May 22, 1927, p. XX5.
41. Engelmann, *Intemperance: The Lost War against Liquor*, p. 77.
42. *ibid.*, p. 77; Gervais, *The Rumrunners*, p. 52.
43. Engelmann, *Intemperance: The Lost War against Liquor*, pp. 70–77; Gervais, *The Rumrunners*, pp. 40–41, 52; Mason, *Rumrunning and the Roaring Twenties*, p. 41.
44. Engelmann, *Intemperance: The Lost War against Liquor*, pp. 105–111, 157–158.
45. *ibid.*, pp. 97–104.
46. Cited in David Dyment, *Doing the Continental: A New Canadian-American Relationship* (Toronto: Dundurn, 2010), p. 15.
47. *ibid.*, pp. 71–72.
48. Gervais, *The Rumrunners*, pp. 23–31.
49. Gervais, *The Rumrunners*, pp. 75–79; Royal Commission on Customs and Excise, *Interim Reports (Nos. 1 to 10)*, pp. 61–62.
50. Gervais, *The Rumrunners*, pp. 91–97; Royal Commission on Customs and Excise, *Interim Reports (Nos. 1 to 10)*, pp. 74–77.
51. Edwin H. Sutherland, *White Collar Crime: The Uncut Version* (New Haven, CT: Yale University Press, 1983), p. 230
52. *ibid.*, p. 232.
53. Engelmann, *Intemperance: The Lost War against Liquor*, pp. 72–75.
54. *ibid.*, pp. 78–79.
55. *ibid.*, pp. 79–82.
56. Donald L. Canney, *U.S. Coast Guard and Revenue Cutters, 1790–1935* (Annapolis, MD: Naval Institute Press, 1995), pp. 85–91, 104–105; Engelmann, *Intemperance: The Lost War against Liquor*, pp. 82–83; National Commission on Law Observance and Enforcement, *Report on the Enforcement of the Prohibition Laws of the United States*, p. 19; Malcolm F. Willoughby, *Rum War at Sea* (Washington, D.C.: Government Printing Office, 1964), pp. 87–90.
57. 'Curb Tightened on Canadian Liquor', *New York Times*, June 4, 1927, p. 19; Engelmann, *Intemperance: The Lost War against Liquor*, pp. 92, 97; Gervais, *The Rumrunners*, p. 24: Paul R. Kavieff, *The Purple Gang: Organized Crime in Detroit, 1910–1945* (Ft. Lee, NJ: Barricade Books, 2000), pp. 31, 110–111; James C. Young, 'Nightly Rises the Tide of Border Rum', *New York Times*, June 5, 1927, p. SM3.
58. Senate, Subcommittee of the Committee of the Judiciary, *National Prohibition Hearings,* 69th Cong., 1st sess., April 5–24, 1926, p. 17.
59. 'Curb Tightened on Canadian Liquor', *New York Times*, June 4, 1927, p. 19.
60. *Detroit News*, May 6, 1928, as cited in Mason, *Rumrunning and the Roaring Twenties*, p. 144.
61. Mason, *Rumrunning and the Roaring Twenties*, p. 144.

62. Engelmann, *Intemperance: The Lost War against Liquor*, pp. 77–78.
63. *ibid.*, p. 159; Mason, *Rumrunning and the Roaring Twenties*, p. 112.
64. National Commission on Law Observance and Enforcement, *Report on the Enforcement of the Prohibition Laws of the United States*, p. 13.
65. *ibid.*, pp. 13–14.
66. Mason, *Rumrunning and the Roaring Twenties*, p. 108.
67. Engelmann, *Intemperance: The Lost War against Liquor*, p.114; Mason, *Rumrunning and the Roaring Twenties*, pp.108–109, 144; National Commission on Law Observance and Enforcement, *Report on the Enforcement of the Prohibition Laws of the United States*, pp. 13–14, 143.
68. Engelmann, *Intemperance: The Lost War against Liquor*, pp. 97, 145; Kavieff, *The Purple Gang*, p. 110; 'Two Big Rum Rings Indicted in Detroit', *New York Times*, October 19, 1929, p. 2.
69. '190 Deaths in Raids Under Prohibition; Search Curb Issued', *New York Times*, April 6, 1929, p. 1.
70. C.W. Hunt, *Booze, Boats and Billions: Smuggling Liquid Gold!* (Toronto: McClelland and Stewart, 1988), pp. 280–283, and *Whisky and Ice: The Saga of Ben Kerr, Canada's Most Daring Rumrunner* (Toronto: Dundurn Press, 1995), pp. 179–182.
71. Engelmann, *Intemperance: The Lost War against Liquor*, pp. 94–95.
72. *ibid.*, p. 99; 'Hi-jackers Wear Federal Uniforms', *New York Times*, July 4, 1929, p. 5.
73. 'Stimson Studying Rum-running Clash', *New York Times*, June 22, 1929, p. 1.
74. Engelmann, *Intemperance: The Lost War against Liquor*, pp. 99–100.
75. U.S. Congress, *Congressional Record*, vol. 71, pt. 3 (June 17, 1929), p. 2992, as reported in Mason, *Rumrunning and the Roaring Twenties*, pp. 109, 166 n.8; National Commission on Law Observance and Enforcement, *Report on the Enforcement of the Prohibition Laws of the United States*, p. 38.
76. Sutherland, *White Collar Crime*, pp. 8–9.
77. Engelmann, *Intemperance: The Lost War against Liquor*, p. 118.
78. 'Detroit Police Target of Federal Inquiry', *New York Times*, April 18, 1929, p. 4; Engelmann, *Intemperance: The Lost War against Liquor*, pp. 105–111.
79. Irving King, 'U.S. Coast Guard in the Rum War', (Typescript, 1993), Dossin Great Lakes Museum Library, E-18, as cited in Mason, *Rumrunning and the Roaring Twenties*, p. 107; National Commission on Law Observance and Enforcement, *Report on the Enforcement of the Prohibition Laws of the United States*, p. 19.
80. 'New Liquor Treaty Sought with Canada, *New York Times*, December 1, 1928, p. 13; 'Says Federal Agents Bossed Rum-runners', *New York Times*, March 22, 1929, p. 8; 'Ten Held in Detroit in Grafting Case', *New York Times*, November 27, 1930, p. 7.

7 Prohibition—Part 2

THE GREAT PLAINS

West of Detroit, the forty-ninth parallel became the contested Canadian-American boundary in lieu of the Detroit River and its associated waters. The borderline between Canada and the United States across the prairie is dominated by almost nine hundred miles of an artificial land division that offers no natural geographical barriers between the two countries. In other areas of the United States, natural barriers required smugglers to transfer cargo from a vessel to a vehicle or to transit remote, hostile terrain creating a point of weakness and an opportunity for exposure and apprehension. To smuggling traffic, the geography along the forty-ninth parallel offered no such threat. By simply driving a high-speed auto over the border and into the United States via a back road or across a farmer's field, the rumrunner limited his exposure to law enforcement along the frontier in the early years of Prohibition.[1]

The autos used by the smugglers tended toward the larger, more powerful vehicles, which had both the interior space to carry numerous cases of whiskey and the power to carry heavy loads on back roads or over mountain trails. With rear seats removed, heavy duty springs installed, and possibly a metal plate covering the rear of the gas tank to prevent pursuing law enforcement from puncturing it with gun fire, the Buicks, Packards, Cadillacs, Hudson Super-Sixes, and Marmons of the era ran south, sometimes with a pilot car ahead to determine if some county sheriff or federal agent had established a check point. In many cases their loads eventually traveled as far as the western cities of Denver and Salt Lake City and the major metropolitan areas of the Midwest, including Omaha, Des Moines, Tulsa, and Chicago.[2]

As in the Detroit area, Canada allowed 'export houses' to be established in numerous towns across the plains and along the U.S. border, many eventually serving the American trade instead of simply being warehouses for inter-province shipment. For example, in the small town of Govenlock, Saskatchewan, located fifty miles north of Havre, Montana, at least three export houses operated in support of the rumrunners. Fifty miles north in

Maple Creek, another export house could be found competing with those of Govenlock. Rumrunners arrived during the day, loading up and departing under cover of darkness bound for the United States. Seventy-two bottles of 12 percent beer (marketed as a 'barrel' and actually composed of three burlap sacks each holding twenty-four bottles) sold wholesale for twenty dollars and returned a stateside retail price of seventy dollars. Distilled beverages wholesaled from thirty-two to thirty-six dollars for a twelve-bottle case of Scotch and retailed for seventy dollars. With mark-ups such as these, one run could easily return a profit of one thousand dollars for a two- to three-day trip. In comparison, the annual wage of those federal agents attempting to apprehend the rumrunners was approximately two thousand dollars.[3]

Besides autos, pack horses were used further west through the mountains. With five to six cases on each mount and eighteen to twenty horses per trip, the packer could make six hundred dollars for the use of his outfit. The rumrunner would have arranged a load to be waiting north of the border, then driven his car through customs clean, only to meet up with the pack animals at a prearranged location far south of any border checkpoints.[4]

In circumventing the various prohibition laws of the Dominion and of the individual provinces, one family developed a liquor empire during Prohibition that carried on into the late twentieth century—the Bronfman family. The family personified the idea that organized crime existed prior to the modern versions of the racketeer and the 'mob'. Their case was a classic example of Sutherland's white-collar crime. The Bronfmans bridged an earlier lineage of smuggling, fraud, and trading in illegal goods and services to the modern notion of organized crime. They were both the antecedent of modern stereotyped organized crime and its real embodiment.

In the early 1900s, the Bronfman family was in the hospitality trade, operating four hotels in three provinces. With war time prohibition, the hotels, previously subsidized by customer traffic in their bars, were in serious financial distress. Sam Bronfman obtained a license in Montreal to import and sell liquor retail. Following in the footsteps (or snowshoes) of the Hudson's Bay Company, he also established a mail order business, exporting liquor from Quebec across provincial lines under Dominion law. He established warehouses in Ontario and Saskatchewan to supply neighboring provinces. When the government closed down mail order operations, the family obtained a Saskatchewan wholesale druggist's license and shipped medicinal whiskey to retail drugstores throughout the province. The family returned to mail order business when Canadian laws again allowed it, opening numerous 'export houses' where liquor was stored and then sold to neighboring provinces; the Kenora, Ontario, facility served the Winnipeg, Manitoba, area, for example. The family's unpaid tax bill from the business, dating back to 1917 but not resolved until 1921, totaled approximately two hundred thousand dollars.[5]

Establishing approximately twenty export houses in Saskatchewan alone, the Bronfmans were a dominant player in supplying the rumrunners on the prairie. Competing against the likes of the Hudson's Bay Company empire, the Bronfmans still managed to control almost a third of all export houses in the province. The Bienfait warehouse, selling a variety of brands to American rumrunners, managed to turn a profit of over fourteen thousand dollars on gross sales totaling almost sixty-four thousand dollars during the first half of 1922. The Bronfmans expanded their business by compounding denatured alcohol, declaring it a 'blend', and bottling and labeling it under various guises, both fictitious and legitimate. Eventually they purchased a distillery in the United States, dismantled it, and transported it to Canada, in order to open their own distillery. Establishing a partnership with the major Scotch producers in Britain, the Bronfmans purchased a separate Canadian distillery, Seagram. In 1929, the company showed net earnings in excess of $2.5 million for the previous year.[6]

In 1926 the Canadian government initiated an investigation of the department of Customs and Excise that determined fraud and corruption were extensive in the liquor export business. Fictitious names and destinations were used on export documentation, and false certifications of foreign landings led to a loss of dominion tax revenue. Corruption of Customs and Excise officers who operated in collusion with the liquor industry was also documented. Accusations of bribery eventually led Harry Bronfman to be arrested for attempted bribery and tampering with witnesses, only to be acquitted in 1930. Harry, along with brothers Allan, Abe, and Sam, faced trial again for conspiracy to avoid payment of customs duties, but the case was dismissed in 1935.[7]

The Bronfmans are an exceptional exemplar of Sutherland's five points comparing the criminality of corporations to the criminality of the underworld and professional thieves, and their example supports his argument that white-collar crime was also a form of organized crime. Their criminality was 'persistent', extending over the entire thirteen-year period of Prohibition.[8] 'Second, the illegal behavior [was] much more extensive than the prosecutions and complaints indicate'.[9] After years of conspiring to smuggle liquor into the United States, there were few legal actions against the corporation or its officers and associates. 'Third, the businessman who violates the laws which are designed to regulate business does not customarily lose status among his business associates'.[10] In the Bronfmans' case, the Scottish whiskey industry partnered with them instead of treating them as pariahs. 'Fourth, businessmen customarily feel and express contempt for law, for government, and for governmental personnel'.[11] The Bronfmans' ongoing conspiracy over the years of Prohibition speaks for itself. Finally, 'white collar crimes are not only deliberate; they are also organized'.[12] The family's informal organization, their partnership with the Scots in developing their business empire, and the family's reported collusion with Customs and Excise are but three examples. Besides showing the criminality of the Bronfmans in relation to professional criminals, these points, along with the Bronfmans' seeming failure to 'conceive of themselves as criminals',[13] justify the conclusion that the Bronfmans' violations qualify under Sutherland's definition as organized crime.[14]

A second Canadian liquor magnate also spent time on the Canadian prairie in his youth. Harry Hatch, born in the East, had worked in the family's hotel in Saskatchewan. He moved east again in 1908, also entering the retail liquor trade. With Canadian prohibition, like the Bronfmans, Hatch and his brother transferred their skills to the mail order liquor business. In 1921, Harry Hatch then joined Canadian Industrial Alcohol Company, owners of Corby and Wiser distilleries under Sir Mortimer Davis, as a sales manager with an agreement that the firm would pay brother Herb Hatch's company, Hatch and McGuiness, a dollar for every case of whiskey Hatch and McGuiness sold. The brothers recruited Larry McGuiness to enlist commercial fishermen to transport Sir Mortimer's liquor to buyers in the United States. Hatch's Navy was so successful at moving whiskey across the Ontario that by December 1923, Hatch had the funds to purchase the Gooderham and Worts distillery in Toronto. By 1925, the corporation had gone public. By Christmas 1926, Hatch had bought into the Hiram Walker distillery in Walkerville across from Detroit. A new company, Hiram Walker-Gooderham and Worts, was created and continued the Prohibition sales that the Hiram Walker and Corby and Wiser distilleries had developed, including the extension of operations to St. Pierre and other foreign ports. Harry and Herb Hatch were so successful that the corporation reported a profit of more than $3.4 million in the twelve months prior to November 1928. Harry and Herb Hatch, Larry McGuiness, and a number of associates in the liquor trade faced indictment in the United States in December 1928 for conspiracy to smuggle liquor into the United States. The charges against Hatch were ultimately dismissed by the government.[15] The Hatch family, like the Bronfmans, was Prohibition's exemplar of Sutherland's white-collar crime.

Heading south from Montreal, Quebec was another 'rum road' leading directly to New York City. Montreal, located fifty miles north of the U.S. border, provided unlimited alcohol. The numerous roads that crossed the border with few customs checkpoints in place at the start of Prohibition offered the opportunity to run the contraband across the line. With New York less than three hundred miles south of the border via Saratoga Springs and Albany, a ready market awaited the early entrepreneurs. Besides the highway, opportunities were also presented by railroads connecting the two great metropolitan areas and by Lake Champlain, a waterway transiting the border that allowed a vessel to travel for over one hundred miles from Montreal southward toward New York City.

As with the Western states, the border was lightly manned in 1920, with customs checkpoints located in small communities up to a mile from the actual border. With numerous roads crossing the line, with no controls in place, and with customs facilities not manned around the clock, the opportunities for local talent to become rumrunners was legend. As in the

West, it was not until the mid-1920s that the federal government finally established a border patrol. Thanks to New York passing a state prohibition statute though, state troopers and local law enforcement also enforced Prohibition.

As in Detroit, the railroad system was also used to move large quantities of beer and distilled spirits southbound. Besides the suitcase smugglers transporting small quantities as passengers bound for New York, the use of false walls and legitimate cargo in freight cars to conceal contraband allowed numerous bulk loads to be moved by rail with little chance of arrest for the organizers of these commercial shipments. A false wall in a freight car could easily conceal a couple hundred cases of beer. If a freight car was used with only a counterfeit manifest and was shipped fully loaded, nine hundred cases of beer could be moved south in one shipment. Inspectional techniques, along with intelligence and informants, helped in interdicting some of these loads. One shipment was found to have been manifested as baled hay bound for Newburg, New York. Under the hay, however, were 7,200 bottles of beer. Financial records reflected a transportation cost of less than thirty cents a quart for the contraband brew.[16]

Boats were also used during most of the year when Lake Champlain was not frozen. From using row boats to fifty-foot vessels capable of moving four hundred cases of beer a run, the lake was simply another road south. With minimal government vessels in use (it wasn't until 1922 that customs even had a boat on the lake) every dusk provided another daily opportunity for profit. One vessel, the *Massagna*, was apprehended while unloading forty-eight thousand bottles of beer south of the lake. Carrying numerous cases onboard, the crews of these craft risked arrest and seizure before all the evidence could be either offloaded or jettisoned overboard if likelihood of apprehension appeared eminent. Some rumrunners used a type of submersible barge that was towed behind the vessel and cut loose prior to apprehension for possible recovery at a later and potentially safer time. One submersible was seized with 5,000 quarts of beer onboard, another with 4,000 quarts, and a third with 4,800 quarts.[17]

It did not take long for smugglers to recognize that an empty auto northbound didn't contribute to the bottom line. Some rumrunners started to run stolen silks, cigarettes, narcotics, and industrial alcohol north into Canada, circumventing Canadian law and duties. With silk carrying a duty rate of 42.5 percent, the profit was more than worth the effort and a Montreal merchant could easily be found to purchase the contraband. Raw alcohol brought seventeen dollars a gallon in Canada yet could be purchased for four to seven dollars in the United States.[18]

Yet, during the early years of Prohibition, it was not the Rum Road from Montreal to New York that supplied the majority of smuggled whiskey to the city. Another highway, the sea lanes of the northern Atlantic, led to the infamous anchorage off the east coast of the United States known as Rum Row.

RUM ROW

For those along the southern Atlantic seaboard, the closest legal landfall for liquor was the British colony of the Bahamas. An archipelago almost six hundred miles long and slightly less than four hundred miles at its widest, its island of North Bimini lies less than fifty miles off eastern Florida. A base for privateers seizing American shipping during the Revolution in the eighteenth century and a depot for Confederate supplies running the Union blockade in the nineteenth, the port of Nassau was a critical cog in the machinery of rum running in the early twentieth century.[19]

With the start of Prohibition, liquor exports held at the level of the previous decade but quickly climbed tenfold. By 1922, over twenty liquor organizations were involved in the trade on New Providence. Agents representing English and Scotch distilleries marketed their wares to any potential buyers. Shipping traffic departing the Bahamas more than tripled from 1919 to 1922 to 1,681 vessels with total tonnage climbing more than eightfold to 718,110 tons. With duty on imported liquor up to six dollars a case, the income for the colony was enormous. Collected customs duties increased sixfold from 1919 to 1923. Prohibition profited the government of the Bahamas while its enforcement plundered the coffers of the U.S. government.[20]

One of the earliest to personally profit was the American adventurer and eventual legend William 'Bill' McCoy. Educated for the sea on the Pennsylvania Nautical School's *Saratoga*, McCoy served as a mate, boat builder, and motorboat service operator prior to being offered the opportunity to skipper the seventy-foot vessel *Dorothy W* with a load of rye whiskey from Nassau to Atlantic City, New Jersey. Though declining the original offer, he decided to take advantage of the opportunity offered by purchasing his own vessel, the *Henry L. Marshall*. The *Marshall* was the first of a series of vessels he owned over the next few years to run liquor to the United States. A ninety-foot fishing schooner built for the northeast fishing industry, the *Marshall* carried 1,500 cases of liquor in the original cases or twice that quantity if the lot was repackaged in burlap sacks (six bottles to a bag, known as 'hams'). Purchased for sixteen thousand dollars and refitted prior to sailing for another four thousand dollars, McCoy sailed to Nassau in early 1921 to obtain her first consignment of liquor for the United States.[21]

Immediately offered a charter upon arrival for 1,500 cases to Savannah, Georgia, at ten dollars a case, McCoy was in business. After clearing Nassau, a small under-the-table remuneration at the port of West End enabled McCoy to arrange for a second set of clearance papers, falsely indicating travel in ballast in lieu of carrying a cargo. Those papers offered an explanation to any future port official for an empty ship after the illicit cargo was discharged. Sailing to the coast but finding the seas too rough for lightering the load to shore, the *Marshall* sailed into St. Catherine's Sound south of Savannah, offloading in the night. The next morning, McCoy and the *Marshall* were bound for Nassau, McCoy fifteen thousand dollars richer for his few days' work.[22]

Back at Nassau, a second charter was offered to run a shipment of U.S. whiskey, being held in bond, from Bimini back into stateside commerce. The shipment had previously been legally exported from the United States, but the owners wanted to avoid the expense of paying the Bahamian duty on the imported goods. Bound for Norfolk, Virginia, after being advised that the market was not available there for the cargo of expensive, quality whiskey, the *Marshall* continued north to New York. Working with the organization that owned the liquor, they eventually arranged for two contact boats to offload the contraband for seven dollars a case. After offloading, the *Marshall* returned again to Nassau and McCoy had made another fifteen thousand dollars. That trip became the claim for the original vessel to start Rum Row off the New York shoreline. Another soon followed. Within three months McCoy's net profit was thirty-five thousand dollars from his rum running adventures.[23]

Shortly afterward, McCoy had another offer to move five thousand cases but was directed to obtain a ship that could haul the entire load in one trip. That led McCoy to purchase the most famous vessel in his growing fleet, the *Arethusa*. With a potential gross of fifty thousand dollars a trip to Rum Row, he was able to purchase this Gloucester schooner for twenty-one thousand dollars with another eleven thousand dollars used for refitting. After registering her under a British flag with the name of *Tomoka*, later to be renamed again as the *Marie Celeste*, McCoy avoided U.S. law being enforced against her while in international or foreign waters. To crew the *Marshall* and his future vessels, McCoy paid his captains one thousand dollars a month when he was not on board, five hundred dollars when he was. He also allowed the captain to ship up to five hundred dollars of his own contraband liquor on those journeys. The mate earned five hundred dollars unless McCoy was on board, in which case his salary was two hundred fifty dollars with two hundred fifty dollars of liquor allowed for shipment. The cook earned one hundred fifty dollars with the opportunity to ship another one hundred fifty dollars of liquor of his own per journey. Deckhands earned one hundred dollars a month with a bonus of a month's salary at the end of the trip.[24]

Rumors of unidentified vessels operating off the Atlantic seaboard either running liquor or possibly even hijacking legitimate shipping caused a Massachusetts reporter to track down the *Arethusa* as she operated off the Massachusetts coastline. The subsequent publicity and enforcement effort to apprehend the *Arethusa* and her contact boats led McCoy to depart immediately. Instead of being bound for the Bahamas, the *Arethusa* sailed north for Halifax. Approximately two weeks prior, on August 1, 1921, McCoy's schooner the *Henry L. Marshall* had been seized nine miles off Atlantic City, leading to McCoy's first indictment. His notoriety as a rumrunner precluded official entry into Halifax at the time (though in later years it too became a shipping port for Canadian liquor), so the port of St. Pierre on the barren and windswept French territorial islands of St. Pierre and Miquelon served as his alternate port in the current political storm.[25]

Located at the entrance to the Gulf of St. Lawrence about fifteen miles off the coast of Newfoundland, the fishing community of St. Pierre developed into a northern Nassau in its business dealings with the rum fleet. McCoy would go down in legend as opening the town to the opportunity for export trade and for being one of the first of many rumrunners to obtain an illicit cargo for the American coast here. He also opened the opportunity for Ontario distilleries to expand their white-collar criminality to the eastern seaboard. In 1923, over one thousand vessels entered St. Pierre with five hundred thousand cases of liquor being traded. By the mid-1920s, the distillers of Canada and Britain, including the Bronfman family and Harry Hatch of the Hiram Walker-Gooderham and Worts distillery empire, had established partnerships with local interests at St. Pierre to market their product south. Legal exports from Canada to St. Pierre increased by a factor of almost four. In the late 1920s, as American political pressure and a parliamentary investigation led to Canadian attempts to curtail the most egregious examples of shipments bound to the United States (by closing some of the export docks on the Detroit River, for example), St. Pierre became even more critical to the profits of the Canadian export houses and distilleries.[26]

One of the leading merchants on the St. Pierre prior to Prohibition was Paul Chartier, owner of the C. P. Chartier and Company. Chartier's business connections and expertise led him to serve as a broker for the liquor industry on both sides of the Atlantic and also as an agent for one of the major steamship corporations. At least one Scot served as agent for overseas distilleries, as did the French company of Société d'Importation et d'Exploration controlled by Morue Française, the powerful fishing concern that dictated St. Pierre's economic life. As the industry moved toward consolidation, Chartier eventually merged his interests with the Bronfman empire, as did at least one other local, Bill Miller and his St. Pierre Distributing Company. The Bronfmans' Northern Export Company came to dominate the export business along with the other Canadian distillery organizations. As consolidation continued, St. Pierre simply served as a convenient distribution and warehousing facility for the Canadian liquor concerns, while orders were placed via corporate offices in cities such as Montreal. Even the fish processing facility was turned into a warehouse allowing ships to offload liquor directly to storage from dockside. From agent and broker to stevedore and deckhand, all profited from the organized smuggling of contraband liquor into the United States, and none more so than the distillery owners of Canada and Britain. Besides the earnings from selling their liquor for an illegal market, evidence also substantiated numerous schemes used by these white-collar criminals to avoid paying Canadian taxes and duties.[27]

McCoy bought two more schooners, the *J. B. Young* and the *M. M. Gardner*, to expand his operations. Both were eventually seized only to be released at some further expense. McCoy also ventured more than once to Jamaica to buy duty-free loads of liquor for the *Arethusa*. When successfully entered into the United States, the loads held the potential for an enormous profit.

McCoy's own figures claimed a load for the *Arethusa* bought in Nassau ran $171,000, selling on Rum Row for double that at $342,000. Landed, the cargo doubled in value again with the consumers ultimately paying $2 million retail at a minimum. That largesse attracted numerous entrepreneurs to Rum Row in the next few years. As early as January 1922, the Coast Guard claimed to have identified about twenty ships in the trade. By 1924, that number had grown to 158 and doubled by 1925, the British ensign being the dominant flag by a ratio of ten to one.[28]

The fleet was a hodge-podge of sea craft in the early years. Though primarily fishing vessels like McCoy's, Gloucester schooners—originally built for Grand Banks fishing in the North Atlantic—were appropriated for the illicit trade. Coastal steamers, former yachts, ex sub-chasers, sea-going tugs, and even old windjammers also were used. Smaller contacts boats ran the loads to shore. From fishing dories to speedboats, whatever could carry some cases on the open sea and make it back to shore was used. Eventually custom-made speedboats with multiple aircraft engines to outrun the Coast Guard were built as the Coast Guard extended its boarding range from the three mile international maritime borderline to twelve miles off the coast and increased the number of boats in their fleet to interdict Rum Row.[29]

Vessels such as McCoy's had other types of individuals attracted to the trade, including the 'go-through guys' or hijackers. These characters led to McCoy being armed with a couple of machine guns when doing business on Rum Row. Willing to go-through whatever it took to get the money, these hijackers targeted the fleet on Rum Row as well as the off-load boats ship- or shore-bound. If the hijackers successfully overcame a Rum Row ship and crew, they pirated the cargo, transshipping it to their own vessel or even staying on board and marketing the cargo at cut-rate prices to clear the inventory quickly while the crew was held hostage. Other times the hijackers intercepted a load being carried to shore by a contact boat or going outbound to pick one up, in the latter case targeting the cash that was to be used to purchase the illicit liquor. A two-masted schooner carrying the name of *Patricia M. Behan* was boarded by the Coast Guard in April 1923 off New York, dragging her anchor. Upon boarding, no crew or skipper was found but evidence of a gunfight, including shell casings and bullet holes, was discovered as was evidence that she had carried a load of liquor; empty whiskey cartons and burlap sacks were found in her cargo hold.[30]

At times even the hired crew came under suspicion. One theory given for the abandonment of the *Behan* was that it had been robbed by the crew who then departed on one of the off-load boats to shore. The supercargo of the four-masted schooner *Cask* from Glasgow, carrying about twenty thousand cases of whiskey, suspected the mate and his brother of planning a hijacking after the mate offered to put four or five crewmen on board to work solely for passage. The crewmen supposedly wanted only the opportunity to be smuggled into the United States. Believing that the mate and his brother were arranging a hijacking, the mate was quickly discharged.[31]

It was the French steamer *Mulhouse*, however, that embodied the two views of organized crime: one as portrayed by Hollywood and the media of violent gun-toting toughs and the second as the respectable business-men pursuing a strong bottom-line via organized white-collar crime. The *Mulhouse* lost approximately thirty-six thousand cases of whiskey fourteen months after the discovery of the *Patricia M. Behan* when she was boarded at gun-point, and her crew was forced to offload the whiskey to a number of schooners by the mobsters. The vessel was not independently owned and operated, as McCoy's schooners were. The vessel instead reflected the inter-ests of a modern corporation, in this case one that warned its stock hold-ers that yearly dividends might be curtailed since the piracy of liquor had been so costly to the overall business, the cargo being valued at over half a million dollars. As prosecution was attempted against one of the suspected pirates, the corporation that owned the *Mulhouse*, Morue Françoise, the great French fishing concern with a fleet of vessels operating out of France and St. Pierre, pursued civil litigation against its underwriters for the loss of the cargo. The underwriters, in attempting to avoid payment, challenged the claim based on the illegality of the cargo as it was admitted that the liquor on board was bound of America. In 1928, a French court directed payment to Morue Françoise since no French laws were violated and the *Mulhouse* had lost her cargo in neutral waters. Yet within the year prior to her piracy, the skipper of the *Mulhouse* had been publicly accused by a captain of the Coast Guard of having offered the captain two dollars a case to permit rum-runners to run a load of liquor on the beach without interference.[32]

The ultimate antithesis to the image of gangster-trafficker well may have been Sir Broderick Cecil Denham Arkwright Hartwell, Baronet. Having reportedly decided to enter the smuggling business in partnership with an American in July of 1923, instead of creating a syndicate of private finan-ciers to stake his venture, Sir Broderick choose to issue a circular to as many as one hundred thousand individuals, offering them an opportunity to invest their personal funds in the business and guaranteeing a profit of 20 percent within sixty days. He received funds from ten thousand subscribers, more than covering the expenses of that first load. He kept his word at least on the first four loads, returning a full profit to his subscribers. Later subscribers were offered 25 percent profit. A total of seven shipments were dispatched but a portion of the sixth and most of the seventh was lost to seizure and other causes. By the spring of 1925, this led to bankruptcy and a loss of over one million dollars.[33]

In the fall of 1923, the *Arethusa* was boarded and seized by the Coast Guard cutter *Seneca*; McCoy and his crew were placed under arrest. After bailing out of custody, McCoy continued using the *M. M. Gardner* as his Rum Row vessel with two other chartered ships running loads of liquor to her. The following June, McCoy arranged to purchase the *Arethusa* at auc-tion, re-registering her under the French flag as the *Marie Celeste*. McCoy continued running liquor with her to his Rum Row ship. In March of 1925,

McCoy pled guilty to one of his indictments in federal court in New Jersey and was sentenced to nine months. Shortly afterward he sold the *Arethusa*.[34]

McCoy's run of systematic smuggling, involving numerous vessels and crews, characterizes the 'blue collar' organized crime found in the early years of Prohibition. Like the early rumrunners across the Detroit River and Great Lakes, he was an entrepreneur taking advantage of opportunity. As the government recognized that their early expectations of a self-enforcing prohibition had failed, they tailored the one available maritime organization at hand, the Coast Guard, to address the rum fleet. In 1924, Congress passed a funding bill to increase both the equipment and personnel of the Coast Guard, enabling it to acquire a fleet of twenty surplus navy destroyers for its enhanced enforcement mission, with five more destroyers added shortly afterward. Congress also paid for the construction of numerous seventy-five-foot patrol boats and thirty-six-foot picketboats for offshore and inshore operations. Between the three types of vessels, the Coast Guard was able to establish a series of defense lines against Rum Row and its contact boats. With destroyers at sea, the seventy-five-footers off shore, and the thirty-six-footers inshore, the gauntlet created by Washington drove the gentlemen-adventurers out of the trade, leaving gangsters such as William Dwyer, Frank Costello, and Charles (Vannie) Higgins in their wake. They and their associates came to dominate the liquor racket in the United States as much as the white-collar owners of the distilleries dominated the business in Canada.[35]

Yet the expanded Coast Guard, customs, and Prohibition Bureau were simply another challenge to be overcome for the later mobsters. Subterfuge came into play. The American freighter *Ansonia* simply sailed into the port of New York in 1927 with a half-million dollar cargo of liquor. A police bicycle patrolman noticed unusual activity at a landing pier in the middle of the night, bicycled to the nearest telephone, and called for back-up. A dozen officers responded by auto, arrested thirty-four men, and seized six trucks and two automobiles. The *Ansonia* had by then departed. Delayed in tying up to the pier by a low tide, she may have realized that law enforcement was en route. The Coast Guard, responding by patrol boat, pursued her. One guardsman boarded her and, with weapon drawn, took custody of the freighter and her crew of thirty-six. Though the off load crew at the dock was simply charged with trespassing and their vehicles returned, the crew was charged with transporting liquor, and the ship and cargo were forfeited. In court, the owner of the Ansonia Steamship Company—William Nelson, a banker in Ansonia, Connecticut—claimed that since he held a mortgage against the *Ansonia* valued at $39,250, that mortgage should have priority in any libel procedure. The pretense did not stand as the court determined that Nelson could not claim the rights of a mortgagee to a corporation of which he was also the owner and that owned the vessel in question. As a banker using the tools of his profession, the documents of stock certificates and mortgages, and facing little consequence for his actions, Nelson epitomized Sutherland's later characterization of a 'professional' as a white-collar criminal.[36]

Five years later, the 120-foot yacht *Prudence*, while transiting Boston bound for her homeport of New York, was boarded and searched. A secret panel inside a false bulkhead was discovered concealing 1,500 cases of liquor. During the search, an officer was playing with one of the light fixtures. When the fixture came loose, he found five feet of cord that, when pulled, released a lock allowing a panel to open, exposing the contraband.[37] The *Prudence* was but one of many vessels seized with hidden compartments.[38]

Blockade running also continued. Faster sixty-foot off-load boats running with multiple aircraft engines were built to outrun the shore-side patrol boats. Large, low-profile, and fast vessels up to one hundred feet long capable of carrying three thousand cases were constructed in Nova Scotia shipyards to replace the slow and easily overtaken Rum Row schooners and tramp steamers of earlier years. Other ports, including Halifax, Havana, and Belize in British Honduras came into play. Cuba's history of smuggling, with goods previously coming into Spanish Cuba from English Jamaica and later serving as a market in the Caribbean slave trade, gave a patina of legitimacy to the practice in the greater Cuban community. Less than one hundred miles from the Southern United States and being developed as a tourist destination, Cuba's logistical network was easily available for the trade's use. Besides serving as a transit port for British and French liquors, Cuba also had twenty-six rum distilleries that welcomed a northern market legally denied to them.[39]

The two-masted British schooner *I'm Alone* created an international incident in March 1928 when, after loading in Belize with a cargo of liquor, she sailed to the Louisiana coast and eventually off-loaded her cargo to a group of lightering small craft. Being pursued by a Coast Guard cutter, she had the temerity to run, only to be shelled and sunk by the gunfire. Rescuing her surviving captain and crew, one of which had been mortally wounded, the Coast Guard arrested them and placed them in irons. All were transported to New Orleans, only to have the U.S. district attorney drop all charges against the captain and seven surviving crew members. Six years later, the captain and crew were awarded compensation for the tragedy by a joint Canadian-American Arbitration Commission that had been formed to determine if the sinking of the *I'm Alone* was legally justified and what recompense might be appropriate.[40]

In arguing that the U.S. government owed no compensation to the owner of the *I'm Alone*, counsel proved to the satisfaction of the commission that ownership was fraudulent; American citizens actually owned and operated the vessel and its current claimed ownership, Eugene Creaser Shipping Company of Lunenburg, Nova Scotia (with George Hearn identified as its agent) was a sham meant to conceal the real owners. As such, if the commission determined compensation was due the owners, it would mean that the Dominion was arguing to compensate American citizens for damages

from the American government, a politically unsustainable position especially as the vessel in question was a flagrant rumrunner. Evidence pointed
to a Boston mobster, John Magnus, as a possible owner. When offered an
early release from a prison sentence he was serving, Magnus admitted to
owning the *I'm Alone* at one time and that he had been offered eight thousand dollars in 1928 by Dan Hogan. He also believed that Hogan was
part-owner of the vessel at the time of her last load. It took the assistance of
another associate of Hogan's to bring the sham ownership to light. Marvin
Clark had been indicted along with Dan Hogan as part of the conspiracy
to smuggle liquor into Louisiana, utilizing the *I'm Alone*. He disappeared
prior to sentencing but had been recognized and arrested in 1931. Clark
cut a deal and offered his testimony regarding the true ownership of the
vessel. Clark stated that, in November 1928, he had purchased the vessel in
partnership with Hogan and a third individual, Frank Reitman, after having been approached by the two. The *I'm Alone* had been put in the name
of the Eugene Creaser Shipping Company by the seller, after having been
paid twenty thousand dollars, a quarter put up by both Clark and Hogan
with Reitman fronting half the price. George Hearn, also indicted in the
Louisiana federal case, served as the company agent and was rewarded with
five hundred dollars by Clark. Over the next three months, Clark helped
offload the *I'm Alone* cargo in the Louisiana bayous. Though Clark was
gunned down on an unrelated issue prior to giving his testimony to the
commission, his affidavit, along with other evidence, successfully prevented
the claimed owners from receiving compensation from the U.S. government
for their loss. Nonetheless, the captain and crew were granted various sums
totaling $25,666: the captain was awarded $7,906 and the widow of the
slain crewman $10,185 with the rest of the crew receiving approximately
$1,000 apiece. The Canadian government was awarded $25,000 and a letter of apology.[41]

THE PACIFIC COAST

The Canadian white-collar smugglers operating out of British Columbia
created another maritime rum road from the Straits of Juan de Fuca all
the way to Southern California and Mexico, and continued to profit from
it throughout Prohibition. Again the distilleries created export houses to
move their product and were happy to market it to any purchasers. The
closest and easiest market to service was Seattle and the greater state of
Washington. With a simple one- to two-hour boat trip south from Victoria,
British Columbia, across the Strait of Juan de Fuca to the wooded north
shore of Washington state or east past the numerous San Juan Islands to the
U.S. shoreline stretching over one hundred miles south into the Puget Sound
onward to Seattle, a rumrunner in the early years of Prohibition had a minimal chance of being intercepted. Business was so good that in 1922, an open

convention took place in Seattle among almost one hundred smugglers and bootleggers to discuss future business practices.[42]

As times changed and enforcement agencies acquired the vessels and personnel to effectively interdict rumrunners, the smugglers improved their own craft. One smuggler who operated throughout the next decade started with an eighteen-foot, one-cylinder boat capable of doing five knots while carrying seventy-five cases of liquor at eleven dollars a case on contract, moved up to a thirty-two-footer with a seventy-five horsepower engine able to do fifteen knots, then built a thirty-five-foot vessel, eventually installing a three hundred horsepower Fiat aircraft engine—that cost five hundred dollars—which allowed it to run at thirty knots. That was followed by two more boats, the first running twin Fiat engines (the engines costing three thousand dollars a piece by then) the second one a thirty-six-foot craft carrying a twelve-cylinder four hundred horsepower Liberty engine (which cost four thousand dollars) allowing her to carry 125 cases at thirty knots. His penultimate rumrunner was built with twin Liberty engines and empty could do almost forty knots. At forty-five feet long and with a ten-foot beam she handled two hundred cases of liquor and could still do over thirty knots. When Canadian law eventually prevented dockside loading for U.S. bound liquor, a final boat, costing twenty-two thousand dollars, was built to be able to run out the strait to a mothership for a cargo. At fifty-six feet long and carrying a couple of 860 horsepower Packard aircraft engines—at seventy-five hundred dollars each—with the exhausts exiting underwater to minimize noise while underway, she burned 120 gallons of fuel an hour at full speed, 'only' using 40 gallons at cruise and, requiring two 600-gallon gas tanks for operation. Doing forty knots with 250 cases allowed her to outrun most of her competition. As the quality of the Coast Guard boats improved, so did many of the rumrunners.[43]

The Seattle market came to be dominated by a former cop, Roy Olmstead. Spotted at an off-load site a few months into national prohibition, Olmstead was fired from his position as a lieutenant of the Seattle Police Department. As the historian Norman Clark commented, that simply 'made it possible for him to give his full time to his business' and that business was the illegal liquor trade including smuggling.[44] Olmstead was the most obvious example of white-collar criminality and corruption being hand-in-glove. Olmstead built a rum running organization funded on the investments of eleven individuals, each of which put up a thousand dollars while Olmstead contributed ten thousand dollars himself for half-interest in the operation. Building an integrated structure from smuggling to sales over the next four years and undercutting the competition in price during that period, he successfully drove out many of his competitors. With sales reaching two hundred cases a day at times, even in a bad month sales totaled $176,000 with yearly revenues believed to exceed $2 million. Sometimes using contract boats, other times his own rum running vessels, it would take years for the government to penetrate his organization, eventually achieved through the use of wiretaps. Aware of the ongoing government activity, Olmstead continued moving alcohol across the straits, at times storing some of it at a ranch south of Seattle prior to distribution.[45] Different from the stereotypical gangster, Olmstead was a cross between the white-collar criminals of business and the stereotyped mobsters to come to the forefront of American crime in the 1930s. With a reputation for quality liquor, à la McCoy, and for forsaking violence, many did not place Olmstead in the same group of criminals as the Capones or the New York mobsters.[46]

Eventually, even with a network of sources in his old department yet without the protection of an international border from seizure and arrest, Olmstead was indicted, along with his wife and eighty-nine other individuals, for conspiracy to violate the National Prohibition Act and the Tariff Act of 1922. Though some of the indicted fled to Canada, Olmstead eventually faced trial and on March 8, 1926, was sentenced to four years at the federal penitentiary at McNeil Island, Washington, and fined eight thousand dollars, along with court costs. Though Elise Olmstead, his wife, was found not guilty, numerous others that faced trial were also convicted. Beginning his sentence in June 1928, after being out on bond pending his appeals, he was released in May of 1931. Unlike most of his professional associates in the rum running trade, Olmsted was given a full and unconditional pardon along with having his fine and court costs remitted in 1935 by President Franklin Delano Roosevelt.[47]

But the small boats of the Puget Sound arena were little match for the West Coast markets of Portland, San Francisco, Los Angeles, and San Diego. With the storms of the West Coast developing their power from traveling thousands of miles eastward across the Pacific Ocean, larger vessels, as well as a larger organization, were needed to deal with the accompanying surge and surf encountered while distributing Canadian alcohol to American bootleggers. To achieve that end, in 1922 nineteen dealers and exporters (who were also attempting to avoid paying a ten-thousand dollar federal tax on each individual selling agent) merged as the Consolidated Exporters Corporation Ltd., and for the next decade, the organization's name was synonymous with West Coast smuggling.[48] The corporation was a legitimate business in Canada, operating with but one objective: the circumvention of the prohibition laws of the United States. The firm was possibly the apex of white-collar criminality in the years of Prohibition.

Starting with a single vessel, Consolidated Exporters operated at least five ocean-going vessels while also supplying an unlimited number of smaller rumrunners in the Vancouver-Seattle area by 1927. Over the next five years, a variety of vessels cleared from Vancouver with liquor for Consolidated reputedly bound for Mexico, Central and South America, and Tahiti. The final, undocumented destination of the cargo was always the United States. Their fleet included the former sub-chaser *Ettamac*; the schooners *Haysport II*, *Jessie*, *Noble*, *Ouitachouan*, and *Coal Harbour*; the five-masted schooner *Malahat*; the steamships *Quadra* and *Federalship*; the motor ship *Principio*;

and the steam yacht *Chasina*, along with various other vessels. The *Coal Harbour*, *Malahat*, *Quadra*, *Federalship*, and *Principio* made headlines in the service of Consolidated Exporters and led many to be indicted in the United States.[49]

Though in international waters, the 175-foot *Quadra*, registered in Britain, was seized in October 1924 off the Farallon Islands, near San Francisco by the Coast Guard. The vessel and the cargo of twelve thousand cases of champagne and whiskey, valued at five hundred thousand dollars, were seized and the crew arrested. The crew was convicted some months later. Eventually appealed to the Supreme Court, the verdict was upheld, the court determining that the seizure was legal under the recent Anglo-American Liquor Treaty. The precedent-setting decision allowed for the future prosecution of rumrunners who conspired to smuggle but were beyond the geographical sovereignty of the United States.[50]

The seizure of the three-masted schooner *Coal Harbour* followed in February 1925, while she was operating twenty-three miles off the Farallons outside the Golden Gate. Towed into San Francisco, prosecution proceeded, but it came to light that the captain of the Coast Guard cutter had perjured himself as to their location at the time of seizure. The *Coal Harbour*, along with all personnel, was released after a jury declared them 'not guilty'.[51]

The admitted perjurer's testimony may have been caused by the frustration of dealing with the rumrunners as the *Coal Harbour*, *Malahat*, and other vessels had made numerous trips south from Vancouver with little success achieved by the Coast Guard in interdicting them or their contact boats operating from shore. By its own lenient actions against Chief Boatswain's Mate Sigvard Johnson, the Coast Guard itself may have also admitted to its organizational frustration in dealing with this criminal conspiracy of smugglers. Court-martialed, the twenty-nine-year veteran guardsman was only sentenced to six month's suspension on half-pay even though his false testimony and enforcement actions initiated an unsustainable indictment and trial. This created a major expense for the government, running into thousands of dollars for witness transport fees from numerous countries, court costs entailed in a major trial, and losses suffered by the corporate owner of the *Coal Harbour* and the numerous defendants. Within sixty days of the announcement of the sentence, the chief was under federal indictment for perjury. Possibly reflecting the U.S. district attorney's frustration with the Coast Guard, the district attorney stated that he believed that the punishment failed to address the severity of the crime. Found guilty, Johnson was eventually sentenced to two years for his perjury.[52]

Two years later the *Federalship*, a 222-foot Panamanian registered steamer, having been used for the previous two years as another mothership by the Consolidated Exporters, was tracked south from Vancouver and boarded almost three hundred miles off the California coastline. Within two months the ship was released and underway once again with its cargo of

12,500 cases of liquor. The courts had determined that its seizure failed to comply with the Anglo-American Liquor Treaty.[53]

These and other seizures of associated vessels along with the numerous indictments of personnel both in the United States and in Canada, as well as Canadian pressure from a Royal Commission investigating the export businesses, led to a change in operations for Consolidated. The company recognized that the procedure of simply loading in Vancouver, running south along the U.S. coastline and off-loading to various contact boats was compromised as the Coast Guard grew in the mid-1920s. Instead of simply claiming that shipments were destined for Mexico, motherships such as the *Malahat*, the steamship *Prince Albert*, and the motor vessels *Principio* and *Lillehorn* served as floating warehouses off the Mexican coast for liquor that was eventually bound northward. The *Malahat*, for example, carried up to one hundred thousand cases, eighty-five thousand below deck and fifteen thousand topside. The motherships off-loaded contraband to smaller vessels, including the *Ragna*, a ninety-five-foot former sub-chaser; the *Ruth B* and the *Ryou II*, a couple of sixty-foot fish packers; and the *Chief Skugaid*, a seventy-seven-foot packer. Coded radio traffic then directed these vessels north to a position where a shore boat could make contact and transfer a predetermined portion of the load over for the run to shore. The new procedures, as described by one former rumrunner, meant that the number of ships involved increased to two dozen, almost three times the number in use in the early years with an even greater increase in total time at sea for the fleet. This prevented the Coast Guard from seizing large, headline-making loads as they had done earlier. If one or two of the smaller 'blacks' were temporarily put out of commission when the Guard shadowed them for an extended time, one of the numerous other transport vessels could then make deliveries with minimal opposition. Until the end of Prohibition in 1933, these corporate tactics were effective in keeping the West Coast supplied with their chosen vice. Similar operations were also extended to Belize, British Honduras. Motherships operated off the Gulf Coast of the Southern United States and eventually distributed loads into the interior.[54]

Henry Reifel and his sons, Harry and George, operated in a similar vein. In front of the Lemieux-Brown Commission in 1926, Henry Reifel testified that he made payments in excess of one hundred thousand dollars in contributions to politicians in British Columbia over the previous eighteen months, apparently to influence local enforcement and regulation of his enterprises. Reifel controlled the Brewers and Distillers Ltd., a holding company for the British Columbia Distillery Company, Ltd., a second distillery, and some breweries. He also owned a liquor export company, Joseph Kennedy, Ltd., and served as a director of another holding company that concealed the ownership of various trafficking vessels. In 1927, his sons, along with twenty-two others, were named in an indictment for conspiring to violate the National Prohibition Act after a boat, the *Zev*, was seized with a load of contraband liquor. The boat became *CG-816* in the service of the Coast

Guard and the Reifels faced criminal charges years later. In 1934, Henry and his son George were arrested on conspiracy charges upon entering the United States. Charged with conspiring to smuggle liquor and to avoid payment of duty and taxes, they were accused of having smuggled more than two hundred thousand cases of liquor into the United States since July 1929. After being served in the civil suit for the 'recovery of $17,500,000, the forfeiture value of the liquors and other charges due the United States', they posted bail of $100,000 each. The two immediately re-entered Canada and in a settlement with the United States a year later, the family offered $500,000 to resolve the criminal case and civil suit against them for the back taxes, duties, and penalties. The posted bail was also forfeited with their failure to appear in court as they originally agreed to do upon release from detention.[55] As Sutherland remarked regarding white-collar criminals, they 'can employ skilled attorneys and in other ways can influence the administration of justice in their own favor' and 'their illegal behavior receives the attention of administrative commissions and of courts operating under civil or equity jurisdiction'.[56] In the Reifels' case, both applied.

MEXICAN-AMERICAN BORDER

For the American communities along the Southwest U.S. border, alcohol was available with a simple trip across the line to the Mexican border towns ready and willing to offer liquid refreshment. Whether Tia Juana (Tijuana) and Mexicali for San Diegans and Los Angelinos, or Juarez for El Pasoans, entertainment and refreshment were available for those motivated enough to pursue it. Railroad corporations also took advantage of the opportunities offered. The San Diego and Arizona Railway attached a buffet car onto its train, allowing alcohol service to its customers when the train transited Mexico on its run between San Diego and Yuma. The Golden State Limited would stop in Mexico for thirty minutes to complete an engine swap, which also permitted thirty minutes of perfectly legal imbibing.[57]

For the previous decade, Mexico had been dealing with a revolution and the violence born of it, with much of the activity happening in the border country. A culture and an infrastructure had developed for smuggling guns south into Mexico to supply the various armies, offering a borderland norm for easily accepting the violation of a new American law and the attendant smuggling of liquor northward. Though the population along the Southwest border was minimal in comparison to Detroit, New York, and the other northern cities, the violence on the southern line more than equaled those other areas. Besides bordering a country that was in a state of revolution, with fighting in Juarez taking place as late as 1929, the homicide rate in the Southwest historically was higher than in the Northeast.[58] That violence was also reflected in federal officer homicides. Out of twenty-four line-of-duty deaths in the U.S. Border Patrol from 1920 to 1933, eighteen were killed while serving in the Southwest, fourteen by gunfire—primarily in Texas. Of the six killed on the northern border, only one died from gunfire. Customs lost twenty-five officers in the same period, thirteen in the Southwest, eleven of them by gunfire—all but one in Texas. In the rest of the United States, customs lost twelve officers but only two of them by gunfire and one by a bomb.[59] The Coast Guard lost at least three guardsmen by gunfire during Prohibition.[60]

The violence of the revolution did not cease at the formal termination of Mexican hostilities. The bloodshed continued to carry over into the conflict inherent in enforcing the United States' prohibition laws. Unlike the Canadian-American border country where violence tended to be initiated by government forces when smugglers attempted to flee, violence was instigated along the southern border by both smugglers and government agents. In a three month period less than a year into Prohibition in just one border town, El Paso, Texas, a civilian was wounded and three prohibition officers were killed, as were two smugglers, along with one customs officer, one immigration officer, three army soldiers, and four smugglers in confrontations with smugglers running loads across the border. Six months later no one had been convicted for the homicides. As late as 1930, El Paso averaged one smuggler fatality a month in the first quarter. Moving liquor across the Rio Grande on the back of a man carrying two cases a crossing or in a train of burros carrying three to four times as much per pack animal, many smugglers operating in groups of twenty to thirty men did not hesitate to become involved in a running shoot-out with government agents. Gun battles lasting hours might be fought over fewer than a hundred cases of whiskey or tequila.[61]

As Prohibition progressed, the government added few men to the Southwest border in order to enforce the smuggling laws. With fewer than seventy customs mounted inspectors across the Southwest in 1922, many cases were made in cooperation with other federal, state, and local agencies. In Texas, a group of Rangers operated with one or two customs officers working the border area smuggling trails. Over the years, a given individual might serve as a deputy marshal, a Ranger, a customs mounted inspector, and then possibly as an elected sheriff or appointed FBI agent. With so many positions held due to political connections, many an officer's career was wide-ranging. In all of them, the potential for violence was ever present in the Southwest. In late 1921, for example, the Rangers were in three gunfights in five days, casualties totaling at least twenty smugglers with four thousand quarts of whiskey and sixty-three horses seized.[62]

Even when only one or two smugglers were encountered, thanks to the remoteness and isolation of much of the border and the few enforcement officers working the line, a contrabandista might just as easily take his chances with a fight instead of facing arrest, imprisonment, and loss of the contraband. One agent, in attempting to apprehend a 'woman' crossing the border with a sack of liquor on her back, was immediately knocked to the ground with a swing of the sack. While fighting, the agent came to realize that this six-foot-tall smuggler was, in actuality, a locally stationed soldier in disguise. Only after looking down the barrel of the agent's revolver and realizing that bringing a knife to a gun fight might cost him his life did the soldier surrender. In the scuffle, he had still managed to stab the customs agent.[63] As one former officer explained, ' "We shot a lot of men then, and we had to—for we ourselves had the highest casualty rate of any police force in the country." [He] made it clear that the Mexicans whom patrolmen faced were expert gunmen. "Most of them had seen service in one or more revolutions before they became smugglers. They were tough, game and knew how to shoot.' "[64]

Warehouses along the Mexican side of the line aided and abetted the smuggling. Many were loaded with American whiskey in anticipation of Prohibition. In the case of one general store on the U.S. side and a wholesale liquor facility on the other that were both owned by the same individual, liquor was moved by raft to the northern side with little difficulty. When one load was intercepted, one smuggler was killed and three others were arrested, and enough evidence was obtained to file conspiracy charges against the warehouse owner and his two primary associates.[65]

When breweries and distilleries closed in the United States, some individuals took advantage of the proximity of the northern Mexican states to establish facilities south of the border. A new distillery owned by American and Mexican citizens was built in 1920 at Piedras Negras, one hundred miles upriver from Laredo, Texas. A second distillery was built six years later in Juarez, sister city across the line from El Paso, Texas, by some Americans from Colorado. That same year Americans were also given permission to build a brewery in Matamoros in the lower Rio Grande valley. All of these entrepreneurs recognized a U.S. market for their products.[66]

Yet Mexico would never match Canada's notoriety for brewing, distilling, and distributing liquor into the United States. Sixteen of the largest twenty cities in the United States were located in the northeast, Kansas City being the city furthest west. Three of the other four were the Pacific ports of Seattle, San Francisco, and Los Angeles with New Orleans being the only city in the South on the top twenty list.[67] The distillery and brewery owners in Canada had the facilities for producing the contraband and the distribution chain to move the liquor—in some cases, such as Detroit, they needed only to move the contraband a mile across the Detroit River to their customers. Unlike in the Southwest, the roads and rails were ubiquitous in the border and port areas with many of the major markets being port cities themselves. Even when Mexico was utilized, it served as a transit area for the movement of Canadian alcohol to the west or Gulf coasts of the United States. Ensenada served as a key facility in the endeavors of the Consolidated Exporters of Vancouver, British Columbia, and Perez Island eighty miles off the northern coast of the Yucatan served as a storage facility for Gulf coast entrepreneurs.[68]

As in the Northeast, aircraft became an accepted mode of transportation for contraband in the early years of Prohibition. Originally developed as observation platforms by the military and used as such when the Coast Guard adopted their first seaplane in October 1926, by 1928 the Coast Guard operated aircraft along the entire Atlantic seaboard. In the Southwest, at the instigation of General Billy Mitchell, the Army Air Service had pioneered the use of aircraft along the Mexican border from 1919 to 1921, providing surveillance, photography, and observation support to army units deployed along the border in an attempt to suppress border lawlessness. Originally operating with eighteen WWI vintage DH4 bombers, propelled by 440 horsepower V-12 Liberty engines (of later fame in various rum running vessels), the Army Air Service Border Patrol eventually operated from fields in McAllen, Laredo, Eagle Pass, Sanderson, Marfa, and El Paso (Fort Bliss), Texas; Douglas and Nogales, Arizona; and San Diego, California, with approximately 175 flying officers and eighty-five aircraft to cover the border. At one point even an airship was sent south to Fort Bliss. Though it made numerous flights, none were known to be patrol missions along the Rio Grande. Flying patrols the length of the border in an effort to stop raids from south of the line, when suspected bandits and smugglers were located, the information was passed to the cavalry and federal agents from customs or immigration. By 1921, all of the aero squadrons were off the border with the exception of the Fort Bliss unit, which delayed its departure for another five years.[69]

Also by 1921, reports of aircraft being used to transport alcohol from Mexico into the interior of Texas were being received. Not until 1931 did a couple of customs agents and a Prohibition agent seize a plane (running ten five-gallon cans of alcohol), which gave them the opportunity to actually pursue the smugglers they had watched disappear over the northern horizon in earlier years. Attempting to use information they developed that identified potential aircraft flying northbound, the agents staged their own plane at locations that allowed them to observe and intercept the airborne smuggler. When sighted, they launched their newly seized aircraft from a makeshift strip in pursuit, and used hand signals to direct the smuggler-pilot to land or to be fired upon, the presence of a rifle—and later a submachine gun—offering convincing proof of that capability. After seizing a second plane by this very technique, the agents had created an air patrol. Eventually climbing to a fleet of eight airframes, service-wide customs seized thirty-five airplanes in the twelve months ending on June 30, 1932, with another thirty seized the following year and fourteen more in the next. On the West Coast a Ryan monoplane was put into service after its seizure. Shortly after the end of Prohibition, the Treasury consolidated aviation assets under the Coast Guard, transferring fifteen customs aircraft, the majority of which were burned at San Antonio, Texas. With the loss of the customs air fleet, some of the flight officers joined the Coast Guard to continue flying as enlisted pilots.[70]

By 1932, the newly elected president, Franklin Delano Roosevelt, and the American populace had a more important issue to address: the Great Depression. Recognizing the expense of continued enforcement, the lost revenue from the lack of taxes collected on contraband alcohol, and the potential for an expanded market for the economically hard-hit farmers whose crops were grain and hops, Congress approved legislation to void the Eighteenth Amendment within months of the election. A year later, ratification by two-thirds of the states was complete and national Prohibition was finally brought to an end, along with the profitability of smuggling contraband liquor into the United States for most. Some continued in the trade at least for a few years, however, in an attempt eke out a profit by avoiding import duties and local taxes.[71]

It was during Prohibition that the media created the stereotypical image of the organized criminal gangster, all but pushing aside the knowledge of those in legitimate business involved in the same crimes. Al Capone, Frank Costello, and the like were identified as organized crime figures, but the distiller families of Bronfman, Reifel, and Hatch; the directors of the French fishing organization Morue Française; Sir Broderick Hartwell, baronet; the vice president of a Connecticut bank claiming ownership of a rumrunner to avoid the forfeiture of the vessel; or another bank vice president serving as a trustee for the transfer of funds for the purchase of smuggled liquor were also, though rarely overtly identified as such, 'organized crime'. These individuals embodied a white-collar version of organized crime, with an objective of achieving the American Dream of the good life, defined by wealth and material comfort at the expense of the law.[72] All exemplified Sutherland's white-collar criminal as much as did the executives of the corporations that Sutherland later documented, including those at American Sugar, General Motors, National Dairy, Warner Brothers, Westinghouse, and sixty-five other corporations.[73]

NOTES

1. Janice Cheryl Beaver, *U.S. International Borders: Brief Facts*, RS21729, Congressional Research Service, Library of Congress, 2006.
2. Edmund Fahey, *Rum Road to Spokane* (Missoula: University of Montana Press, 1972), pp. 108–113; Michael R. Marrus, *Mr. Sam: The Life and Times of Samuel Bronfman* (Toronto: Viking, 1991), p. 76; Gary A. Wilson, *Honky-Tonk Town: Havre, Montana's Lawless Era* (Guilford, CT: Globe Pequot, 2006), pp. 52, 90.
3. Fahey, *Rum Road to Spokane*, pp. 7–9; Wilson, *Honky-Tonk Town*, pp. 51–52.
4. Fahey, *Rum Road to Spokane*, pp. 72–77, 114–115.
5. Marrus, *Mr. Sam*, pp. 55–71.
6. Marrus, *Mr. Sam*, pp. 75–81, 129–131; Royal Commission on Customs and Excise, *Interim Reports (Nos. 1 to 10)* (Ottawa, Ontario, Canada: F. A. Acland, 1928), p. 53.

7. Dave McIntosh, *The Collectors: A History of Canadian Customs and Excise* (Toronto: New Canada Publications, 1984), pp. 273–285; Royal Commission on Customs and Excise, *Interim Reports (Nos. 1 to 10)*, pp.18–21, 51–52.

8. Edwin H. Sutherland, *White Collar Crime: The Uncut Version* (New Haven, CT: Yale University Press, 1983), p. 227.

9. *ibid.*, p. 228.

10. *ibid.*, p. 228.

11. *ibid.*, p. 229.

12. *ibid.*, p. 229.

13. *ibid.*, pp. 229–230.

14. *ibid.*, p. 239.

15. 'Hiram Walker-Gooderham & Worts', *The Wall Street Journal*, October 12, 1928, p. 10; C. W. Hunt, *Booze, Boats and Billions: Smuggling Liquid Gold!* (Toronto: McClelland and Stewart, 1988), pp. 73–94, 202–215; Stephen Schneider, *Iced: The Story of Organized Crime in Canada* (Mississauga, Ontario, Canada: John Wiley and Sons, 2009), p. 199; 'Thirty Indicted in Border Rum Plot', *New York Times*, December 5, 1928, p. 24.

16. Allan S. Everest, *Rum across the Border: The Prohibition Era in Northern New York* (Syracuse, NY: Syracuse University Press, 1978), pp. 33–34.

17. *ibid.*, pp. 34–35, 98–99.

18. *ibid.*, pp. 14–15, 41–43; Royal Commission on Customs and Excise, *Interim Reports (Nos. 1 to 10)*, pp. 30, 32, 52.

19. Michael Craton, *History of the Bahamas* (London: Collins, 1962), pp. 11, 149–161, 217–237.

20. *ibid.*, pp. 264–269; 'Bahamas Sent US 2,000,000 Gallons', *New York Times*, January 29, 1923, p. 17; Gertrude Lythgoe, *The Bahama Queen: The Autobiography of Gertrude 'Cleo' Lythgoe* (Mystic, CT: Flat Hammock Press, 2006), pp. 44–49.

21. Frederic F. Van de Water, *The Real McCoy* (Garden City, NY: Doubleday, Doran & Company, 1931), pp. 6–13.

22. *ibid.*, pp. 14–22; 'Rum Running Vessels Listed by Government', *New York Times*, January 12, 1922, p. 10.

23. Van de Water, *The Real McCoy*, pp. 23–36.

24. *ibid.*, pp. 37–41.

25. Everett S. Allen, *The Black Ships: Rumrunners of Prohibition* (Boston, MA: Little, Brown and Company, 1965), pp. 28–36; 'Forfeit Wet Ship Taken 9 Miles Out', *New York Times*, June 21, 1923, p. 2; 'Arethusa Quits the Coast', *New York Times*, August 15, 1923, p. 24; Royal Commission on Customs and Excise, *Interim Reports (Nos. 1 to 10)*, pp. 55–56; 'Says Arethusa Sells Rum by Drink or Barrel', *New York Times*, August 12, 1923; Van de Water, *The Real McCoy*, pp. 49–61; Malcolm F. Willoughby, *Rum War at Sea* (Washington, D.C.: Government Printing Office, 1964), p. 23.

26. J.P. Andrieux, *Prohibition and St. Pierre* (Lincoln, Ontario, Canada: W.F. Rannie, 1983), pp. 14–25; Marrus, *Mr. Sam*, pp. 139–141; Van de Water, *The Real McCoy*, pp. 61–72; National Commission on Law Observance and Enforcement, *Report on the Enforcement of the Prohibition Laws of the United States* (Washington, D.C.: Government Printing Office, 1931), pp. 24–25.

27. Andrieux, *Prohibition and St. Pierre*, pp. 23, 27–54; William A. Christian, Jr., *Divided Island: Faction and Unity on Saint Pierre* (Cambridge, MA: Harvard University Press, 1969), p. 18; Marrus, *Mr. Sam*, p. 141; Royal Commission on Customs and Excise, *Interim Reports (Nos. 1 to 10)*, pp. 51–52, 55, 67–68, 114–116.

Fifty years later another town, Everglades City, this time located in southwestern Florida, became synonymous with smuggling. Located eighty miles from Miami and surrounded by the waterways and isolated islands of the National Everglades Park, the community of about three hundred, whose old-time residents were crabbers and net fisherman, had, by the late 1970s, numerous residents involved in marijuana trafficking. At fifty thousand dollars a night for boat captains and ten thousand dollars for a loader, the temptation to make up to five times a yearly salary in one night was too great for many. In July 1983 the Drug Enforcement Administration (DEA) sealed off the town and arrested a couple dozen residents and seized 350,000 pounds of marijuana, almost two-dozen boats, twenty-one cars, and three planes. One indicted individual posted bail, in cash, of $1.25 million pending trial. Within four years 144 Everglades City residents and associates eventually faced indictment. See Roy Thomas Dye, 'A Social History of Drug Smuggling in Florida' (unpublished doctoral dissertation, Florida State University, 1998), pp. 73–107.

28. Van de Water, *The Real McCoy*, pp. 114–120, 161–162; ' "Rum Running" Vessels Listed by Government', *New York Times*, January 12, 1922, p. 10; 'Reports Increase in Liquor Running', *New York Times*, February 22, 1924, p. 17; '332 Foreign Ships Found in Rum Trade', *New York Times*, February 3, 1925, p. 6.

29. Van de Water, *The Real McCoy*, pp. 136–137; Willoughby, *Rum War at Sea*, p. 17.

30. 'Real Sea Wolves Prey on Rum Ships', *New York Times*, August 1, 1923, p. 21; 'Think Pirates Slew Crew of Liquor Ship Abandoned at Sea', *New York Times*, April 16, 1923, p. 1; Van de Water, *The Real McCoy*, pp. 172–177; Willoughby, *Rum War at Sea*, pp. 34–37.

31. Alastair Moray, *The Diary of a Rum-runner* (London: Phillip Allan and Company, 1929), p. 119; 'Treasury Men Visit Liquor Smugglers', *New York Times*, April 26, 1923, p. 21.

32. 'Coast Guard Spurns $70,000 Liquor Bribe', *New York Times*, July 11, 1924, p. 19; 'French Court Awards Mulhouse Insurance; Owners of Liquor Pirated Off New Jersey Win', *New York Times*, March 20, 1928, p. 4; 'French Magistrate Names Bootleg King', *New York Times*, October 3, 1924, p. 6; 'Must Pay for Stolen Rum' *New York Times*, February 4, 1926, p. 5; 'Pirates Seize Liquor Valued at $500,000', *New York Times*, July 11, 1924, p. 4; Willoughby, *Rum War at Sea*, pp. 40, 54.

33. 'Hartwell Testifies to Loss of £232,759', *New York Times*, May 6, 1926, p. 12; Donald Lawder, 'Rum Row's Baronet Speaks Out', *New York Times*, November 9, 1924, p. SM1; Eric Mills, *Chesapeake Rumrunners of the Roaring Twenties* (Centreville, MD: Tidewater, 2000), p. 96; 'Rum-running Baronet Loses a Liquor Cargo', *New York Times*, April 20, 1925, p. 12.

34. 'Cutter's Guns Halt British Liquor Ship Beyond 3-mile Line', *New York Times*, November 26, 1923, p. 1; 'Dry Agents Arrest Chicago Delegate', *New York Times*, June 27, 1924, p. 40; Van de Water, *The Real McCoy*, pp. 266–267, 279–282.

35. Andrieux, *Prohibition and St. Pierre*, pp. 89–90; 'Biggest Liquor Ring Smashed by Arrest of 20 Accused Here', *New York Times*, December 4, 1925, p. 1; 'Higgins Acquitted of Liquor-running', *New York Times*, January 21, 1932, p. 44; 'Seize Higgins at Sea near Liquor Ship', *New York Times*, May 5, 1932, p. 14; Harold Waters, *Smugglers of Spirits: Prohibition and the Coast Guard Patrol* (New York: Hastings House, 1971), pp. 59–64; Willoughby, *Rum War at Sea*, pp. 46–59. For life on a Coast Guard seventy-five-footer, see Harold Waters and Aubrey Wisberg, *Patrol*

Boat 999 (Philadelphia: Chilton, 1959); from a rumrunner's perspective, see James Barbican (pseudonym of Eric Sherbrooke Walker), *The Confessions of a Rum-runner* (New York: Ives Washburn, 1928) and Scott Corbett with Captain Manuel Zora, *The Sea Fox: The Adventures of Cape Cod's Most Colorful Rumrunner* (New York: Thomas Y. Crowell, 1956), as well as Fraser Mile's *Slow Boat on Rum Row* (Madeira Park, B.C., Canada: Harbour Publishing, 1992), Moray's *The Diary of a Rum-runner*, Marion Parker and Robert Tyrrell's *Rumrunner: The Life and Times of Johnny Schnarr* (Victoria, B.C., Canada: Orca Book Publishers, 1988), and Van de Water's *The Real McCoy*.

36. 'Lone Guard Seizes 36 on Liquor Ship', *New York Times*, August 13, 1927, p.1; 'Ship Held Forfeit as Liquor Carrier', *New York Times*, December 30, 1927, p. 3.

37. '$250,000 in Liquor Found Behind Secret Panel on Costly New York Yacht, Seized in Boston', *New York Times*, September 12, 1932, p. 1.

38. Robert Carse, *Rum Row* (New York: Reinhart, 1959), p. 14.

39. Geoff Robinson and Dorothy Robinson, *It Came by the Boat Load* (Self-published, 1983), pp. 54–81; Eduardo Saenz Rovner, *The Cuban Connection: Drug Trafficking, Smuggling, and Gambling in Cuba from the 1920s to the Revolution* (Chapel Hill: University of North Carolina Press, 2008), pp.17–29; Willoughby, *Rum War at Sea*, pp. 101–102; Van de Water, *The Real McCoy*, pp. 296–299.

40. 'Rum Boat Shipper Tells of Sinking Under Fire in Gale', *New York Times*, March 25, 1929, p. 1; 'I'm Alone Crew Freed as U.S. Drops Charges', *New York Times*, April 10, 1929, p. 10; 'I'm Alone Skipper Describes Cruises', *New York Times*, December 30, 1934, p. 17; 'I'm Alone Sinking to Cost U.S. $50,666', *New York Times*, January 10, 1935, p. 10; Robinson and Robinson, *It Came by the Boat Load*, pp. 54–81; Willoughby, *Rum War at Sea*, pp. 128–130.

41. 'I'm Alone Sinking to Cost U.S. $50,666', *New York Times*, January 10, 1935, p. 10; Nancy Galey Skoglund, 'The *I'm Alone* Case: A Tale from the Days of Prohibition', *University of Rochester Library Bulletin*, 23 (1968), www.lib.rochester.edu/index.cfm?PAGE=1004 [Date accessed: August 8, 2011]; Lawrence Spinelli, *Dry Diplomacy: The United States, Great Britain, and Prohibition* (Wilmington, DE: Scholarly Resources, 1989), pp. 130–132, 141–142.

42. Norman H. Clark, *The Dry Years: Prohibition and Social Change in Washington* (Seattle: University of Washington Press, 1988), p. 153.

43. Parker and Tyrrell, *Rumrunner: The Life and Times of Johnny Schnarr*, pp. 66, 67–68, 75, 86, 105, 120, 126, 129, 178–181.

44. Clark, *The Dry Years*, pp. 163.

45. *ibid.*, pp. 161–169; *Olmstead v. United States*, 277 U.S. 457 (1928).

46. Clark, *The Dry Years*, p. 166.

47. *ibid.*, pp. 172–175; *United States of America v. Roy Olmstead, et al*, Indictment (November 1924), Term, Record Group 56, Bureau of Prohibition, National Archives and Records Administration, Pacific Alaska Region, Seattle, WA; Presidential Pardon of Roy Olmstead, Record Group 56, Bureau of Prohibition, National Archives and Records Administration, Pacific Alaska Region, Seattle, WA.

48. 'Bootleg Trade Revealed', *Los Angeles Times*, December 9, 1926, p. 3; Ruth Greene, *Personality Ships of British Columbia* (West Vancouver, B.C., Canada: Marine Tapestry Publications, 1969), p. 240; Douglas L. Hamilton, *Sobering Dilemma: A History of Prohibition in British Columbia* (Vancouver, B.C., Canada: Ronsdale Press, 2004), p. 187.

49. Ernest L. Harris, American Consul General to Charles S. Emery, Special Agent, U.S. Prohibition Service, July 12, 1928, Record Group 56, Bureau of Prohibition, National Archives and Records Administration, Pacific Alaska Region, Seattle, WA.

50. 'Rum Treaty Fight Lost', *Los Angeles Times*, April 12, 1927, p. 1; Spinelli, *Dry Diplomacy*, p. 116; Willoughby, *Rum War at Sea*, pp. 81–82; 273 U.S. 593 (1927).

51. 'Liquor Ship Case Compromised', *New York Times*, May 26, 1928, p. 28; Willoughby, *Rum War at Sea*, p. 82.

52. 'Cutter Skipper Perjures Self', *Los Angeles Times*, March 7, 1928, p. 8; 'Guard Must Serve Term', *Los Angeles Times*, May 20, 1930, p. 6; 'Long Service Saves Sailor', *Los Angeles Times*, May 2, 1928, p. 7; 'Mate Again in Trouble in Case of Liquor Ship', *Los Angeles Times*, June 25, 1928, p. 5; 'Perjury Suspect in Special Plea', *Los Angeles Times*, July 6, 1928, p. 5; 'Rum Ship Captor Admits Perjury', *Los Angeles Times*, April 4, 1928, p. 1; 'Rum-ship Case Man Indicted', *Los Angeles Times*, June 28, 1928, p. 1; Willoughby, *Rum War at Sea*, pp. 82.

53. 'Rich Fugitive Taken at Sea', *Los Angeles Times*, May 3, 1927, p. 3; 'Suit Impending in Rum Seizure', *Los Angeles Times*, May 5, 1927, p. 5; Willoughby, *Rum War at Sea*, pp. 83–85.

54. 'Indictment of 104 Bares Big Rum Ring'. *New York Times*, February 13, 1932, p. 22; Fraser, *Slow Boat on Rum Row*, pp. 235–239, 255–270.

55. *Annual Report of the Secretary of the Treasury on the State of the Finances for the Fiscal Year Ended June 30, 1934* (Washington, D.C.: Government Printing Office, 1935), p. 91; 8 F. Supp. 647; Case 48-S, Roy Olmstead, et al, Bureau of Prohibition correspondence, Record Group 56, Bureau of Prohibition, National Archives and Records Administration, Pacific Alaska Region, Seattle, WA; Hamilton, *Sobering Dilemma*, p. 186; 'Seven Canadians Are Indicted By Jury in Seattle', *Washington Post*, August 27, 1927, p. 4; Schneider, *Iced*, p. 192.

56. Sutherland, *White Collar Crime*, p. 6.

57. Lucy Bender, 'New Year's Eve at Juarez', *Los Angeles Times*, January 27, 1924, p. B21; 'Border Fence Is No Bar to Booze', *Los Angeles Times*, February 15, 1920, p. II1; Jim Brown with additional material by Rand Careaga, *Riding the Line: The United States Customs Service in San Diego, 1885–1930: A Documentary History* (Washington, D.C.: U.S. Customs Service, 1991), pp. 79–80.

58. Roger Lane, 'Murder in America: A Historian's Perspective', *Crime and Justice*, 25 (1999), 191–224; Leon C. Metz, *Border: The U.S.-Mexico Line* (El Paso, TX: Mangan, 1989), pp. 236–238; U.S. Bureau of Investigation, *Uniform Crime Report for the Fourth Quarterly Bulletin, 1932* (Washington, D.C.: Government Printing Office, 1933).

59. National Law Enforcement Officers Memorial Fund, URL: www.nleomf. com/ [Date accessed: August 14, 2011]; Officer Down Memorial Page, www. odmp.org/ [Date accessed: August 14, 2011]; U.S. Customs and Border Protection, *Valor Memorial Brochure* (Washington, D.C.: Customs and Border Protection, 2011).

60. Robert Erwin Johnson, *Guardians of the Sea: History of the United States Coast Guard, 1915 to the Present* (Annapolis, MD: Naval Institute Press, 1987), p. 98. Four customs officer ODMP death records failed to identify the cause of death, one officer identified in Customs Service records was not in the NLEOMF database, and one customs officer identified in the NLEOMF database was not identified in Customs Service records. At least one coast

guardsmen was also not identified in NLEOMF and ODMP records when accessed—Boatswain's Mate Carl Gustafson, killed by machine-gun fire while on patrol off of Long Island, New York, in April 1925. See Johnson, *History of the United States Coast Guard*, p. 98, and Allen, *The Black Ships*, p. 119.

61. 'Border War against Liquor Smugglers', *Fort Worth Star-Telegram*, May 1, 1921, p. 1; 'Rangers Kill 2 Smugglers; Find Whisky', *Fort Worth Star-Telegram*, January 7, 1921, p. 13; 'Rum Runners Battle Border Patrol, Two Are Believed Killed', *Dallas Morning News*, July 24, 1929, p. 1; 'Rum Smuggler Shot to Death', *Dallas Morning News*, April 4, 1930, p. 1.; 'Stage of Rio Grande Regulates Texas Liquor Supply', *Fort Worth Star-Telegram*, November 20, 1921, p. 8.

62. Chas. Schreiner III, Audrey Schreiner, Robert Berryman, and Hal F. Matheny, *A Pictorial History of the Texas Rangers* (Mountain Home, TX: Y-O Press, 1969), pp. 53–111; Laurence F. Schmeckebier, *The Customs Service: Its History, Activities and Organization* (Baltimore, MD: Johns Hopkins Press, 1924), p. 123; Robert M. Utley, *Lone Star Lawmen: The Second Century of the Texas Lawmen* (New York: Oxford University Press, 2007), p. 97.

63. 'Border Yankee Sahara Oasis', *Los Angeles Times*, March 8, 1920, p. 13; Garland Roark, *The Coin of Contraband: The True Story of United States Customs Investigator Al Scharff* (Garden City, NY: Doubleday, 1964), pp. 154–155.

64. John Myers Myers, *The Border Wardens* (Englewood Cliff, NJ: Prentice-Hall, 1971), p. 42.

65. 'Barrels of Joy Now in Mexico', *Los Angeles Times*, January 17, 1920, p. II6; 'Border Fence Is No Bar to Booze', *Los Angeles Times*, February 15, 1920; Roark, *The Coin of Contraband*, pp. 174–177.

66. 'Mexico Looks for a Boom', *Los Angeles Times*, February 6, 1922, p. 16; Gabriela Recio, 'Drugs and Alcohol: US Prohibition and the Origins of the Drug Trade in Mexico, 1910–1930', *Journal of Latin American Studies*, 34 (2002), 21–42 (pp. 31–32).

67. U.S. Bureau of the Census, *Fourteenth Census of the United States Population: Number and Distribution of Inhabitants, Summary of Results* (Washington, D.C.: Government Printing Office, 1921).

68. Miles, *Slow Boat on Rum Row*, pp. 129–135, 235–239; Recio, 'Drugs and Alcohol', p. 33; Willoughby, *Rum War at Sea*, p. 79.

69. Stacy C. Hinkle, *Wings Over the Border: The Army Air Service Armed Patrol of the United States-Mexico Border, 1919–1921* (El Paso: Texas Western Press, 1970), pp. 6–12.

70. *Annual Report of the Secretary of the Treasury on the State of the Finances for the Fiscal Year Ended June 30, 1932* (Washington, D.C.: Government Printing Office, 1932), p. 140; *Annual Report of the Secretary of the Treasury on the State of the Finances for the Fiscal Year Ended June 30, 1933* (Washington, D.C.: Government Printing Office, 1933), p. 85; *Annual Report of the Secretary of the Treasury on the State of the Finances for the Fiscal Year Ended June 30, 1934*, p. 89; Brown, *Riding the Line*, p. 81; Eric S. Ensign, *Intelligence in the Rum War at Sea, 1920–1933* (Washington, D.C.: Joint Military Intelligence College, 2001), pp. 34–35, 61; Sheridan J. Finney, personal correspondence, September 12 and October 3, 1993; Roark, *The Coin of Contraband*, pp. 292–295; Clifford James Walker, *One Eye Closed the Other Red: The California Bootlegging Years* (Barstow, CA: Back Door, 1999), pp. 222–224.

71. Thirty-five years later the Customs Service would again create an air wing to pursue marijuana and narcotics smugglers that were using general aviation

aircraft to transport the contraband over the border from Mexico, Jamaica, and South America. Eventually the force grew to almost one thousand personnel, three hundred of which were pilots. By the early 1990s the original seized aircraft, from single engine planes to executive jets and a WWII attack plane, were replaced with specially designed interceptors. Congress funded the purchase of twenty-six Cessna Citation II business jets modified with F-16 fighter radar systems and night vision cameras to hunt down the traffickers. Sikorsky Blackhawk helicopters were also acquired and tasked with landing behind the smugglers and apprehending the aircraft, pilots, off-load crews, and contraband. Establishing bases across the southern tier of the United States from Miami to San Diego and using a second fleet of surplus navy four-engine Orion sub-hunters heavily modified for air interdiction missions, the program became extremely effective in deterring aviation smuggling. The success of the mission allowed the aircraft to operate further south in support of Mexico, Peru, and Colombia in an attempt to intercept smuggling aircraft en route to transit countries such as the Bahamas or Mexico prior to a marine or land smuggling attempt. Once again, the Coast Guard attempted to absorb the mission but, in this later case, only managed to share it with the Customs Service, primarily in supporting its own marine assets and in sharing the management of operations/radar facilities. See Henry M Holden, *Aerial Drug Wars: The Story of U.S. Customs Aviation* (Niceville, FL: Wind Canyon Books, 2000) for further background.

Edward Behr, *Prohibition: Thirteen Years That Changed America* (New York: Arcade, 1996), pp. 234–236; Sean Dennis Cashman, *Prohibition: The Lie of the Land* (New York: Free Press, 1981), pp. 230–240; David Heron, *Night Landing: A Short History of West Coast Smuggling* (Central Point, OR: Hellgate, 1998), pp. 48–49; Daniel Okrent, *Last Call: The Rise and Fall of Prohibition* (New York: Scribner, 2010), pp. 351–353.

72. 'Dry Agents Arrest a Miami Banker', New *York Times*, March 22, 1922, p. 13.

73. Sutherland, *White Collar Crime*, pp. 13–25.

8   The Drug Trade

Alcohol was but one item that federal law prohibited in the early twentieth century. In 1914, opium and cocaine were, as alcohol would be a few years later, prohibited for non-medicinal use. Like alcohol, the use of narcotics in America dated to the colonial era. Yet throughout the first 150 years of the United States' existence, American business interests have had an intimate relationship with narcotics and narcotics have been a major feature of white-collar criminality—all in the name of achieving the American Dream, achieved, as Merton remarked, 'by fair means if possible and by foul means if necessary'.[1] On more than one occasion, foul means were more than necessary, but some of Sutherland's 'respected business or professional men' did not hesitate to achieve success by those necessary means.[2]

American business interests continually returned to narcotic trafficking as a source of profit, commencing first in the China trade and emulating the British opium trade, only to have later generations follow the precedent set by their shipping forefathers by smuggling opium directly into the United States with no less enthusiasm. Eventually, though the nation came to demonize the use of narcotics, American and foreign business interests continued to contribute excess quantities of narcotics to the world's markets, knowing they were also contributing to the contraband trade. In all of these cases, businesses, in the quest for profit, performed an act—smuggling—that was socially harmful and that was subject to punishment by one or more nations. As such, under Sutherland's definition, their actions qualified as white-collar criminality.[3]

When Thomas Hobbes remarked that the condition of mankind was 'solitary, poor, nasty, brutish and short'[4], his observation applied as much to the late eighteenth century as it did to the mid-seventeenth century period of civil strife. Little had changed for many, especially in dealing with the pain of injury or illness. One natural product known for centuries as a medicinal aid for numbing pain was the opaque, milky sap of the opium poppy. Found in an Egyptian tomb and mentioned in Homer's *Odyssey* and Virgil's *Aeneid*, the Venetians, and later the Portuguese, traded in the poppy's by-product after the Crusades, which found a home in the pharmacopeia of European physicians.[5]

A painkiller in colonial times, opium's use climbed in the early part of the nineteenth century with a variety of nostrums being sold directly to the public that included a quantity of the narcotic. Mixed with alcohol or water, opium was distributed as laudanum; opium's derivative, morphine, was later marketed in liquid, powder, or tablet form. Prescribed widely for a variety of ailments, opium was especially effective in dealing with medical emergencies, offering solace and comfort otherwise unavailable with a major injury. That capability led to its widespread use in the Civil War, so much so that opium addiction became known as the 'soldier's disease' to many.[6]

With opium coming primarily from Turkey or other areas in Asia, many believed that opium poppy growing should be developed in the United States in order to limit foreign dependence. Efforts in the Southwest and California along with various attempts in the Northeast were initiated; by the Civil War even the Confederate Atlantic coastal states and Tennessee were growing poppies. In the end the venture was not considered economically feasible.[7]

Imports continued to rise and patent medicine use climbed also, almost seven times faster than the population growth of the country. In a country instilled with an image of self-sufficiency, having few if any doctors available, self-medication and care was a major characteristic of American cultural individualism. Yet with limited understanding of the properties of opium, even doctors at times failed to acknowledge its dangers. Many, including those self-same doctors, faced the risk of daily dependence on opium. The addictive properties led to estimates of between 100,000 and 200,000 addicts in the nation by the turn of the century. By 1924, the most accurate number settled at something under 110,000, with an estimate of 246,000 as a previous maximum in 1900, prior to federal prohibition. Possible cocaine addiction added another 18,000 to the total.[8]

Opium usage also became associated with city life and personal stress born of the competitiveness of industrialization. As city life, with its anonymity and personal isolation, personified evil for many in the coming century, individualism was suspected of having the potential to lead to anomie with which the rootless 'tends to self-indulgence and excess' as a means to cope.[9] As more immigrants continued to obtain passage to the United States, they too were seen as a corrupting influence and a threat to the community previously established. Whether the whiskey of the Irish, the beer of the Germans, or the opium of the Chinese, all were seen as dangers to the mores of conventional American society. Alcohol would be addressed with local and national prohibition, but the opium problem, a vice not as widely used and with few allies, was attacked generations earlier.

Opium smoking was associated with Chinese immigrants, a group who had like many before them traveled to the United States for economic opportunity. California's gold rush in 1849 offered a destination with financial potential, as did the Central Pacific and later, both the Northern Pacific and the Canadian Pacific railroads, all needing vast numbers of laborers to construct these transnational railways. Willing to provide labor at below market rates, Chinese communities spread throughout the West and even to major northeastern industrial centers. Yet their acceptance was, at best, minimal with a widespread Western belief that the Chinese would not acclimate to American society and its existing culture. With distinctively different language, customs, and dress, and tending to congregate within their own, in many cases, bachelor communities, the functional and physical distancing of the Chinese contributed to a prejudice that easily developed against them. With an economic depression in the 1870s impacting opportunity for many in the West, the Chinese became an easy scapegoat for labor interests. By 1882, the Chinese Exclusion Act passed the federal legislature, preventing Chinese laborers from entering the United States, as well as preventing Chinese immigrants from becoming naturalized citizens.[10]

The association of opium smoking with the Chinese dates back to the British opium trade of the eighteenth century and the later Opium Wars in which the British forced the opening of China to British-controlled, Indian-grown opium. As the British developed a taste for tea, particularly Chinese tea, the trade required payment in silver bullion or specie, since the British could offer no cargo in comparable demand by their Chinese trading partners. A second commodity was needed to balance the increased demand of tea, and that product proved to be opium for the Chinese market. Though the emperor attempted to curtail its use by edict as early as 1729, the British simply smuggled it into China with the connivance of corrupt local officials and the endorsement of the Crown. Merchant houses that served as the middlemen between the Chinese buyers and the East India Trading Company developed, holding a monopoly on Indian opium. When China attempted to force compliance with their prohibitions, two separate wars broke out. Both ended to China's detriment and allowed a further expansion of the opium trade in Britain's favor, the second conflict allowing the dutiable import of opium into China.[11]

Yet it was not only the British who were involved in the opium trade to China. An estimated 10 percent of the trade was handled by the merchant houses of the United States. Precluded from the Indian opium market, the earliest trade by Americans in Turkish opium from the port of Smyrna dates from the 1790s, but by 1804 the trade to China had become significant. The Turkish opium, though inferior to the British product, had a market available for it, and American merchants entered the trade in earnest. The Wilcocks family of Philadelphia and the Perkins family of Boston became early representatives in the trade with others joining in. Benjamin Wilcocks also served as the American consul in Canton, allowing him to influence if not to control U.S. relations with the Chinese government and its local representatives to the benefit of American opium traders—an early example of Sutherland's premise that a 'less critical attitude of government toward businessmen' is formed by the numerous interpersonal relationships between government and business.[12] Robert Bennet Forbes entered the trade as early as 1823 with the support of his uncles, the owners of J. and T.H. Perkins. John Perkins Cushing, at the age of sixteen, had established Perkins and Company, as the Canton entity of the family partnership. Forbes himself was so successful in his ventures in the China trade that he became a managing partner of Russell and Company, the successor to the Perkins opium enterprise. Joseph Peabody, a merchant out of Salem, and another in the China trade at the same time as Forbes, eventually parlayed his own opium profits into a fleet of over eighty ships operating throughout the world.[13]

The 'Boston Concern' also included the Sturgis, Cushing, and Cabot families with competition in some cases from John Jacob Astor and Stephen Girard. Eventually the Americans extended their trade into Indian opium, merging their interests with those of the British merchant houses in their dealings with the Chinese government. Even after the trade was acknowledged via treaty provisions in 1844 between the nations and after Washington condoned the prosecution of Americans by the Chinese government for smuggling opium, more than one continued to smuggle the contraband in exchange for the all but guaranteed profit available in handling the prohibited product.[14] As late as 1872, American ships were still moving opium into the Chinese island of Formosa.[15]

As discussed earlier, these traders were from among the upper socioeconomic class of America. In violating the laws of China in the course of their occupation, they fulfilled Sutherland's concept of white-collar crime.[16] By resorting to the corruption of Chinese officials to realize their objectives these traders further reinforced their identification as white-collar criminals.[17] Finally, these businessmen failed to accept that they were in any way involved in criminal activity. Robert Bennet Forbes wrote:

> Dealing in opium was not looked upon by the British government, by the East India Company, or by the merchants as a smuggling transaction; it was viewed as a legitimate business as long as the drug was sold on the coast, outside the professed jurisdiction of China. [. . .] I shall not go into any argument to prove that I considered it right to follow the example of England, the East India Company, the countries that cleared it for China, and the merchants to whom I have always been accustomed to look up as exponents of all that was honorable in trade, the Perkins's, the Peabodys, the Russells and the Lows.[18]

Forbes' excuse clearly shows that he, and one can assume his fellow traders, did not see his actions as criminal, confirming a Sutherland specification of white-collar criminals: '[e]ven when they violate the law, they do not conceive of themselves as criminals'.[19] Sutherland continued, '[t]heir consciences do not ordinarily bother them, for they have the support of their associates in the violation of the law'.[20] Forbes, in identifying such a wide range of entities and respectable families in the trade, obviously believed he was in good company.

With the continued prejudice against the Chinese in the Western United States and the identification of opium smoking as an addiction believed to be endangering the general community, a political effort similar to alcohol prohibition developed. With only a minority group viewed disparagingly considered to be primarily involved, first local and then national legislation was introduced to control the import and use of smoking opium. In the mid-1870s, some western cities passed municipal regulations outlawing opium dens, and by 1881 a second treaty prohibited the importation of opium by Chinese nationals into the United States. Americans, however, were allowed to continue importing opium themselves, though at a high duty rate for smoking opium, eventually reaching a rate of twelve dollars a pound in 1890, all but doubling the cost of the otherwise illicit goods, and offering a profit large enough to entice many a trafficker.[21]

Quantities of opium found their way to San Francisco on the same boats that transported typical merchandise and Chinese immigrants to North America. From 1849 to 1854, over forty thousand Chinese had been attracted to San Francisco and the gold rush of Northern California. By 1880, over one hundred thousand Chinese immigrants lived in the United States with over eight thousand arriving during the twelve months preceding July 1883, the last year prior to the enactment of the Chinese Exclusion Act. With the immigrants came the habit of opium use. Importation of opium reached 298,000 pounds in 1883, but by 1885, legal imports had dropped to under 40,000 pounds with the increase in the duty rate from six to ten dollars a pound. Importation of opium through San Francisco alone climbed back to 138,000 pounds by 1895. A year later, the duty for imported smoking opium was reduced to six dollars a pound, also reducing the potential profit from avoiding the payment of duty. The previous year's total of only 49,000 pounds of declared opium easily supports an assumption that at least 90,000 pounds of contraband opium passed through the port during the same period.[22]

In January 1882, San Francisco police officers, while patrolling the harbor, spotted a boat near the steamship *City of Tokio*, recently arrived from Hong Kong, China. Giving chase, the boat was stopped and two individuals were detained, along with a cargo of ninety-seven packages of tinned opium, three packages having been thrown overboard prior to seizure. The prepared opium, including the three thrown packages, weighed two thousand pounds and was valued at twenty thousand to twenty-five thousand dollars. Approached shortly afterward by Henry Kennedy, the brother of one of the detainees, and claiming to be in the smuggling business when questioned, the officers were offered two thousand dollars to release the suspects. The offer eventually was raised to ten thousand dollars along with the suggestion that the officers could retain the seized opium, with the brother offering assistance locating a buyer for the contraband. Though failing to sway the officers, the smuggler eventually challenged the seizure and forfeiture in federal court, claiming that the opium was not manufactured in

Hong Kong but had been purchased domestically and was being shipped out of the United States to be smuggled into the Kingdom of Hawaii on a second ship at anchor at the time of the seizure, the *City of Sydney*.[23] After a thirteen day trial to determine liability, with testimony from associates of Kennedy and letters introduced in evidence that were en route to Hong Kong further identifying other associates overseas, a total of 3,880 boxes of opium were forfeited to the government.[24]

As early as 1864 the courts were dealing with opium seizures from the port of Victoria, British Columbia, bound for the United States. Having its own Chinese settlement and being the major seaport for western Canada, Victoria developed into a hub for the opium trade in the Northwest. Though sellers were locally licensed, it was not until 1871 that the importation of opium required the payment of a duty to the Canadian government; Vancouver Island, the location of the city of Victoria, had merged with British Columbia earlier and British Columbia then joined the Confederation. Even that duty was exempt if the opium was in transit through Victoria's harbor to a foreign destination. In later years when it had become illegal for Chinese residents to import opium into the United States, duty paid or not, the smuggling of Victoria opium became widespread. The duty in Canada was only one dollar a pound on the raw opium imported for preparation in comparison to U.S. rates reaching as high as twelve dollars a pound for a period of time. With numerous opium factories in Victoria refining raw opium for smoking, totaling more than a dozen by 1888, more than ninety thousand pounds of the potential contraband was available for the U.S. market.[25] Being a legitimate business providing revenue for the Victoria, British Columbia, and Canadian governments, those primarily involved in the opium trade in Victoria were the influential and privileged of the Chinese community, the successful merchants and businessmen of the population. Like the liquor distillers of later years, they too had few qualms regarding the smuggling of their product into the United States. And as in Prohibition, the same waterways and islands used by liquor smugglers to conceal their entry into Washington were utilized by drug runners of the Northwest two generations prior to the Volstead Act.[26]

In many cases, opium was shipped on commercial vessels operating between Canada and the United States. One shipping firm conspired to smuggle in thirty thousand pounds of opium in one year while also moving 1,500 Chinese laborers into the United States illegally. Approximately sixty people were indicted with numerous principals pleading guilty or being convicted and one of the company's steamships being forfeited to the government.[27] The owners of the Merchant Steamship Company—Nathan Blum, William Dunbar, and E. P. Thompson—had arranged a business agreement with the Canadian Pacific Railroad to transport illegal Chinese immigrants across the Canadian-U.S. border as needed by the railroad. By 1892, they had also arranged to add opium to their inventory of cargo, working with the Chinese merchants and labor contractors in both Victoria and Portland,

Oregon. Operating two steamships, the *Haytian Republic* and the *Wilmington*, and utilizing a Canadian agent to represent their interests with the opium factories of Victoria, the owners of the Merchant Steamship Company also worked at compromising the customs collector of the port of Portland—the senior federal position within customs locally—and a Treasury agent responsible for overseeing customs activity in the Northwest. Continuing to move immigrants south with fraudulent papers, they also arranged to move opium as far south as San Francisco. Though loads generally ran between one hundred and five hundred pounds, one thousand to two thousand pound loads were also shipped directly to San Francisco and to San Francisco by way of Portland where they were divided for distribution between the two communities. Using a network of local Chinese merchants, the opium would be picked up dock-side in Portland, for example, and distributed as previously determined. At other times the opium was secured in barrels to be dumped overboard and recovered by trailing boats prior to the ship's docking. When encountering difficulties with at least one government agent, they arranged for his transfer to a port out of which the smuggling ring did not operate. Eventually the multiple indictments led to various criminal trials and appeals extending over the next three years. Of the three co-owners and the associated principals, Blum turned state's evidence and received no jail time, while Dunbar was sentenced to two years in county jail and fined. E. P. Thompson succeeded in obtaining a hung jury while the treasury special agent received a year in jail and a thousand-dollar fine. The collector of customs was simply fined eight thousand dollars. Wilson, the Canadian agent, was never extradited to face the federal court. Blum and another conspirator later had the temerity to attempt to claim half of the government proceeds from the sale of the forfeited *Haytian Republic*, alleging their testimony was instrumental in convicting their co-conspirators. The U.S. attorney's position was simply that they had already more than benefited by avoiding incarceration.[28]

This conspiracy involved a wide spectrum of respected individuals fulfilling a broad range of occupations: attorneys (and a law student); appointed governmental positions, including the collector of customs along with at least two underlings—a deputy collector and the captain of the inspectors; a treasury department investigator; ship's officers and owners; and Chinese merchants. Utilizing the skills and networks of their professions, they typified the border between legitimate business and crime that characterizes organized white-collar crime. Even after the trial and various convictions, most continued to have successful careers in the Portland area, obviously burdened with little, if any, disrepute for their smuggling of both opium and Chinese laborers into the United States.[29] As Sutherland writes, '[t]he businessman who violates the laws which are designed to regulate business does not customarily lose status among his business associates. [. . .] The public, likewise, does not think of the businessman as a criminal; that is, the businessman does not fit the stereotype of criminal'.[30] Both attitudes toward white-collar criminals aided the conspirators in their criminal cases and in their reintegration into the community afterward.

With the completion of the Canadian Pacific Railway in 1885 and the Northern Pacific Railway in 1883, two parallel rail lines existed, one on each side of the international border. Various connections existed between the two lines in Washington state east of Vancouver, via water through Idaho, multiple routes through Winnipeg, Manitoba, and on to North Dakota or Minnesota, and numerous opportunities were viable for transporting opium east via the Canadian Pacific Railway and eventually southbound by the Northern Pacific. Further east, the Canadian Pacific eventually continued onward to Windsor, located across the river from Detroit, and to Toronto and Montreal, offering further opportunities to move Victoria opium into the U.S. market.[31] One former chief inspector of customs was arrested in Ogdensburgh (Ogdensburg), New York, attempting to smuggle 780 pounds of opium after its transport via the Canadian Pacific Railway having previously moved over 3,500 pounds in the commerce.[32]

Yet it was not just opium that was smuggled from Canada. Druggists north and south moved opium and analgesics across the line in an attempt to avoid paying customs duty. About a dozen men, including two train car porters, were arrested for trafficking in phenacetine and sulfonal, some implicating numerous Canadian druggists from Montreal in the ongoing conspiracy.[33] Two years later in 1897, customs received information from an associate of the owner of the Bayer patent for phenacetine that a Detroit resident identified as 'J. Lewis' was selling phenacetine in New York at a price low enough to suspect that import duty had not been paid on the drug. An investigation determined that the address identified as that of 'J. Lewis' was Lewis J. Fulmer's, a druggist with a store in Detroit and that Fulmer was reported to be in New York marketing some patent medicines. The two individuals present at his store were his partner, George Schumacker, and a clerk named Herbert Jenkins. When one of the customs agents eventually entered the drug store, he recognized Schumacker as an individual he had known for many years. He later suspected that Schumacker had also recognized him as a customs agent because the store and all its contents were destroyed in a fire later that very night. Shortly afterward, Fulmer returned from New York. He and Jenkins were arrested, and a quantity of sulfonal, phenacetine, various other drugs, and business papers were seized at a newly established office. After determining that the missing Schumacker was across the river in Canada with his family, surveillance was established at the ferry landing where he was arrested upon his return journey. Fulmer's brother-in-law was also identified as a conspirator but had been on a western marketing trip only to return and flee to Canada after becoming aware of the investigation. Two other clerks of a Windsor, Ontario, drug store were also implicated. The papers seized from the business identified numerous individuals who received goods shipped by the two conspirators located in various cities in Ohio, Missouri, New York, North Carolina,

Pennsylvania, and Kentucky. The conspirators' affidavits stated that the smuggling of phenacetine had occurred for at least a year and a half with various individuals, including Fulmer, Schumacker, Jenkins, and the clerks of the Canadian drug store bringing bulk quantities across to be broken down and shipped to consignees that had ordered them from the alias 'J. Lewis'. Women associated with Fulmer were involved in smuggling quantities across the river, hiding the contraband under their clothing while traveling via carriage over the ferry.[34] One of the two Canadian drug store clerks was later linked to a second business in Detroit used as a distribution hub for smuggled phenacetine with papers again tying the owner of the Canadian drug store to the contraband business.[35] These druggists were simply the latest iteration of Sutherland's respected businessmen committing crimes in the course of their occupations.

Six months later three individuals, one a porter on a parlor car operating between Toronto, Canada, and Detroit, were apprehended while exiting the train with 374 ounces of phenacetine, 52 ounces of sulfonal, and various other drugs (the aggregate total equaling 530 ounces) packaged for shipping to eleven consignees across the Central and Eastern United States. Investigation confirmed that at least sixty-four shipments had been forwarded in the previous sixty days. It was suspected that the goods were furnished by a Toronto individual 'who had been doing this kind of business under the name of Radcliffe & Co., for some time.'[36] The porter was eventually sentenced to nine months in the Detroit House of Correction and fined two hundred fifty dollars with one of his associates having his sentence suspended 'being young and inexperienced.'[37] A treasury report summarized the drug smuggling problem best:

> It is well understood in Customs circles that certain New York importing firms have copyright patents of certain drugs manufactured in Germany and the same are sold in this country at high values as compared with the original cost, hence the large drug firms in Canada and New Brunswick ship large quantities of the drugs to the United States, and while no doubt some of the firms would not knowingly defraud our Customs revenue laws, yet it is true there are a number of firms in the cities of Halifax, N.S., St. John, N.B., Montreal and Toronto who are actively engaged in undervaluing as well as aiding in the illegal importation of the merchandise.[38]

That description of many drug firms on both sides of the border was applied as easily to other businesses in the import-export trade over the years as it was to various drug firms.

With an international movement to suppress opium production and use at the start of the twentieth century, the Canadian government outlawed the importation, manufacturing, and sale of opium for non-medical use in 1908 with the passage of the Opium Act.[39] Yet the drug trade of

Mexico would more than fulfill future supply needs of the United States for illicit opium. As Canada and the United States had built railroads, creating a demand for labor, Mexico was little different. As American investors entered the Mexican economic arena, labor was needed for railroad construction, mining, and agriculture and the Diaz government concluded a treaty with China in 1899, allowing for increased immigration. After the United States initiated the Chinese Exclusion Act in 1882, Mexico became the country of choice for many Chinese who planned to enter the United States surreptitiously. With the Chinese immigrants came the addiction of smoking opium.[40]

The port of Ensenada in Baja California was one port of entry for opium with the governor of Baja California profiting from the trade. Governor Esteban Cantu was somewhat autonomous in his working relationship with Mexico City thanks both to distance and to limited transportation services between his state and the capital city. That power and political independence allowed Cantu's family to control the opium traffic within the state, his corruption allowing the contraband to be moved north to the United States.[41] Eventually as drug laws were passed and enforced on both sides of the American-Mexican border, the market for opium and its derivatives, morphine and heroin, stimulated the development of opium fields in the northwestern states of Mexico with the same area becoming the distribution hub for American-bound drugs. During the Prohibition era, border communities such as Mexicali became infamous as much for drugs as for alcohol.[42] Yet in 1926, Mexico was still importing narcotics, with fifty kilograms of opium and morphine being discovered on a French vessel in Veracruz, for example.[43]

Even in the late 1930s U.S. Customs was still addressing Mexico as both a destination and a transit base. In 1936, Maria 'Molly' Wendt, reportedly a Eurasian and the daughter of a Chinese official, was apprehended in San Pedro, California, after arriving on the *Heiyo Maru* from the Orient with fifty-four pounds of heroin valued at one hundred thousand dollars concealed in her baggage. The heroin was determined to be from China and bound for Mexico. Wendt's Shanghai associate, Nastali Lefenholtz Brandstatter, was implicated and then indicted; after traveling from Shanghai to Spain, and later on to Cuba—only to be deported within a month of his arrival—he boarded the liner *Oriente*. While the liner was approaching New York, a customs agent attempted to arrest him under the indictment. Knocking on his cabin door and not receiving a response, the agent requested a steward enter only to find Brandstatter had committed suicide by hanging himself. Wendt was sentenced to ten years.[44] Though she claimed that she had simply been a 'tool' in the smuggling venture, that persona may have been merely a guise to avoid prosecution. 'With her multi-cultural background and a powerful father, Wendt was highly educated, urbane, Western, and well-traveled', undercutting any reputed innocence in such a major smuggling venture.[45]

Though prior to the twentieth century various communities and states passed laws, generally focused on Chinese immigrants, limiting the use of drugs, federal legislation was slow in coming. With the possession of the Philippines in 1898, the opportunity for America to offer a moral example to the rest of the colonial powers came into play while also allowing the United States to cater to the opium suppression interests of China. Governmental action led to the prohibition of opium for non-medical use in the islands in 1908.[46] As the United States attempted to influence other nations in addressing America's own concern with narcotics, recognition that federal legislation was critical prior to demanding other nations divest themselves of a lucrative source of revenue led to the submission of further narcotics legislation to Congress. In 1909, the Smoking Opium Exclusion Act was passed, followed by the Harrison Narcotics Tax Act five years later.[47] Signed into law in 1914, the Harrison Act treated opium and cocaine as prohibited substances for non-medical use. This latter legislation became 'the cornerstone of US domestic drug law'[48] and led to a bureaucratic infrastructure designed to address narcotics prohibition within the United States. Though further legislative restrictions were passed by Congress, including the 1922 Narcotic Drugs and Import and Export Act, it would be Treasury regulations and state initiatives that addressed the domestic front.[49]

Yet with all the legislation and regulations addressing the control of narcotics smuggling enforcement was limited, at best. With a belief that there was a national consensus against narcotics and an acceptance that treatment and regulation could address the domestic scourge of drugs, enforcement efforts focused on the newly enacted prohibition with few assets directed toward smuggling of narcotics. Those involved in organized crime associated with the new breed of gangsters developed during Prohibition would fill the supply void, and a professional gambler by the name of Arnold Rothstein would be their banker.

Rothstein, the son of a respected New York businessman and factory owner, was credited by many with fixing the outcome of the 1919 World Series and was suspected of masterminding the theft of four million dollars worth of Liberty bonds.[50] A bookmaker, high stakes gambler, and former rumrunner, who invested in legitimate financial securities and real estate, he became a banker to the New York underworld.[51] Moving into the drug trade, Rothstein's name was connected over and over again to those actually handling the product. His personal secretary and a second associate were arrested in 1926 by French police on narcotics charges, and a year earlier, Rothstein had posted bail for two others arrested after taking delivery of 1,220 pounds of heroin, morphine, and cocaine from the liner *Arabic*. A year later another associate, Jack 'Legs' Diamond, also had his bail posted by Rothstein after a narcotics arrest.[52] In November of 1928, Rothstein was gunned down in a hotel in New York. After the seizure of business papers from his office in the course of the homicide investigation, information developed from them substantiated his involvement in narcotics trafficking and led to the seizure of two million dollars of narcotics a month later followed by four arrests and an additional two million dollars of narcotics being seized. On December 19, another two thousand pounds of narcotics were seized from the French liner *Rochambeau*.[53] Within the next eighteen months dozens more were indicted and the stench of corruption lingered on the Treasury's narcotic unit as it was revealed that, besides the New York office padding statistics, being guilty of numerous instances of dereliction of duty, and having at least one agent using narcotics, Rothstein had hired the son of the deputy commissioner over the narcotics unit to handle a federal tax appeal and that the deputy commissioner's son-in-law had borrowed sums in the thousands.[54] Demoted to the field, he was replaced by Harry Anslinger. Washington removed narcotics enforcement from the corrupt Bureau of Prohibition by creating a separate Bureau of Narcotics. With Rothstein's death, others replicated his importation methods but none duplicated his panache. His murder was never solved.[55]

Rothstein and his associates easily fitted into the newly minted image of the organized crime gangster with the major newspapers making the most of their notoriety to improve sales figures. The attraction for the readers was the 'success story [. . .] in which strife, grand achievement, and spectacular failures were the stuff of daily life [. . .] [T]he central theme of the narrative was an individual's escape from obscurity to wealth, power, and fame.'[56] Whether Capone or Rothstein's gangster associates, the story also easily transferred to cinema with the likes of newspaper reporters and crime writers turned screenwriters—Ben Hecht being the most famous example—pulling the narrative from the newsrooms to the Hollywood cinema cutting rooms to create the film image of the modern gangster.[57] Generally cut from the scripts were the 'legitimate' businessmen guilty of white-collar criminality with whom they were conspiring, allowing them to achieve their version of the American Dream—'wealth, power, and fame'—be it the owners of the pharmaceutical laboratories in Europe from whence the narcotics came or the distilleries in Canada where the rumrunners obtained their brand of contraband.

The Bureau of Narcotics, an organization solely focused on narcotics suppression and control, was established under the secretary of the Treasury. The bureau originally was developed from a unit in the Internal Revenue Service, eventually under the Prohibition office's organizational chart, and finally came into its own in 1930. Its original commissioner, Harry Anslinger, previously served as the chief of the Foreign Control Section of Treasury's Prohibition unit and recognized a need to address the supply sources of contraband in an attempt to minimize smuggling. He built on the diplomatic foundations against opium smuggling developed through the Shanghai Conference in 1909 and the Hague Convention of 1912, leading to national narcotics control policies. Eventually developing an intelligence network of international proportions among law enforcement, Anslinger assigned numerous narcotic agents overseas in order to interdict traffickers transporting narcotics into the United States.[58]

In 1930, intelligence developed through paid informants led to the seizure of 1,090 pounds of morphine valued at one million dollars from the French liner *Alesia* and concealed in a Russian fur shipment, followed four months later by more than three tons of various narcotics valued at over four million dollars from the German liner *Milwaukee*. This level of seizures gave the Bureau and the State Department leverage to pressure European nations to address the manufacturing source of supply.[59] The seizures also forced traffickers to ship in smaller quantities, recognizing that the seizure of large loads had the potential to bankrupt a smuggling organization.[60]

Legitimate pharmaceutical corporations, thanks to the unregulated nature of the business in the early twentieth century, were part of the problem as seen by the Bureau because they profited from both the legal and the illegal sides of the narcotics market. Drugs were shipped from the United States to phony firms in Canada and Mexico only to be smuggled back into the United States for the illegitimate market, much to the profit of American business.[61] With little control over opium-producing countries such as China, Turkey, Yugoslavia, and Persia, various governments attempted to regulate the production and movement of manufactured narcotics via an export-import certification process. This allowed government regulators to discover discrepancies that might identify a specific corporation's drugs that were being diverted into the contraband market. Major factories involved in the production of narcotics included C.H. Boehringer Sohn, E. Merck, and I.G. Farbenindustrie in Germany; Hoffman-La Rouche, Ciba and Sandoz (both predecessors of the current corporation, Novartis) in Switzerland; and Comptoir Français des Alcaloides and Société Industrielle de Chimie Organique (SICO) in France. Yet the identification of any discrepancies then required action by the host country. Not all were initially willing to do so, possibly 'influenced by financial gain and economic benefits that could be achieved from the manufacture and trade in drugs'.[62] When French export records showed a 440 kilo discrepancy of morphine to Germany in 1927 and a 346 kilo discrepancy to the United States in 1928, little follow-up was forthcoming by French authorities. With Turkish records identifying France as importing nearly three times the quantity of opium as the rest of the world combined in 1928—over 228,000 kilograms—France was recognized as the source of much of the manufactured contraband narcotic trade in the world. France eventually responded and in 1929, imports dropped to 80,000 kilos of opium, a third of the previous year's imports. France also shut down factories associated with diverted narcotics, including SICO and Comptoir Alcaloides, whose operations moved to Turkey.[63]

Yet the contraband of the European labs continued to impact American smuggling years later. In 1935, thirteen members of a smuggling organization were apprehended and convicted, including the corporate president of the Poydras Fruit Company, which operated the steamship *Gaston* between Honduras and New Orleans. After making a series of undercover purchases of heroin, the investigation revealed that an individual had recently arrived from

Honduras to sell a quantity of narcotics while also purchasing munitions for the return journey. Two individuals were arrested and eight pounds of narcotics were seized; eventually one of the arrestees indicated that the munitions obtained in any exchange for the narcotics were to be used to overthrow the Honduran government. After a further series of heroin purchases from numerous individuals who stated that the drugs originated in Honduras, law enforcement was able to connect four rings together to the one source. Lab tests and intelligence indicated that the heroin most likely originated from a European shipment several years earlier, one large enough to reportedly fulfill the medical requirements of Honduras for the next forty years.[64]

Though smaller seizures continued, law enforcement efforts, combined with diplomatic successes to bring manufacturing and producing nations into compliance with various treaties designed to control the production and transport of narcotics internationally, drastically reduced the number of major American seizures. From 1,400 kilos seized at the border or at seaports along with another 1,100 kilos seized domestically in 1931, only 300 kilos were seized by customs with another 200 kilos seized domestically by 1935. Loads became smaller to avoid a financial nightmare with the loss of a large quantity in a single seizure. Smugglers became high visibility targets for the police of numerous nations, now cooperating in addressing the international drug trade. The onset of World War II eventually curtailed the movement of contraband from overseas.[65]

'After the Harrison Act became law, the growth in trafficking in the USA became increasingly controlled by gangsters', effectively driving out the white-collar organized criminals of the past.[66] With major prison terms given to traffickers, a history of jailing doctors and pharmacists since the passage of the Harrison Narcotics Act, and a society that viewed drugs as a scourge and danger to American youth, gangsters and a small cadre of professional narcotic traffickers came to dominate the market. Seizures plummeted, drug adulteration increased, and the price of narcotics climbed, together generally accepted, at least by American politicians, as reliable measures of determining success in narcotic enforcement.[67] Anslinger's policy of addressing the supply of narcotics was aided, as mentioned earlier, by the start of World War II, effectively eliminating the movement of narcotics in the international arena for the war's duration.

Almost since the founding of the United States, American business interests have profited from the illegal trafficking of narcotics in their quest for what Merton described as the success-theme in American culture and the achievement of the American Dream. In so doing they also personified, at least prior to the late 1920s, Sutherland's white-collar criminal. American merchants from as early as the 1790s were trafficking Turkish opium to China, in violation of Chinese law, having joined in a trade dominated by Great Britain. Involving the elite merchant interests of the northeastern seaports, the trade continued as late as the American Civil War with Boston vessels continuing to run opium to the island of Formosa.

Chinese immigration to North America also brought the use of smoking opium to the West Coast where American companies were implicated in smuggling large quantities of the narcotic into the United States to avoid customs duties. In some cases shipping directly from China, the city of Victoria, British Columbia, also became a major source of smuggled opium both by vessel south along the Pacific coast and by Canadian rail eastward to the cities of Windsor, Montreal, and Toronto for later movement across the border. Professional druggists from both sides of the border moved opium, along with other drugs, across the line in an attempt to avoid paying U.S. customs duties. Mexico also became a transit point in the movement of opium, having established a large Chinese community within its borders after the United States instituted exclusionary laws; Mexico subsequently opened its own borders to increased immigration.

With the possession of the Philippines in 1898, the United States proffered itself as an exemplar of moral probity and passed a series of anti-narcotic statutes, the most drastic being the Harrison Act, making opium and cocaine prohibited substances for non-medical use. Though organized crime associates then filled the supply void—men such as Arnold Rothstein and Al Capone in the United States—the legitimate pharmaceutical companies in America and Europe continued to produce narcotics for their corporate financial gain. Sometimes being shipped to 'front' firms in Canada or Mexico from the United States only to be smuggled back into the States or from Europe to countries such as Honduras for eventual transport to the United States, the businessmen of these corporations were well aware of the ultimate source of their products. The onset of World War II was more effective than any police force in curtailing the white-collar criminals involved in the international drug trade.

For almost 150 years, American and foreign business interests satisfied Sutherland's definition of both white-collar crime and organized crime in their handling of the international narcotics trade, at first with the eighteenth-century merchants continuing their normal business practices in order to achieve wealth and thereby their version of the American Dream, one of power and success achieved via money. To succeed they used their businesses in order to corrupt Chinese government officials, to be allowed to transport their contraband into China, learning and continuing the techniques and practices from their fellow British business associates. They were followed by later generations of businessmen who used their own occupational pursuits to smuggle smoking opium into the United States, again corrupting government officials to acquiesce to their smuggling enterprises. With the prohibition of non-medicinal narcotics in the United States, laboratories both domestic and foreign continued to manufacture and distribute quantities of narcotics at a level obviously beyond the medicinal needs of the world, allowing traffickers to develop an import trade for the newest contraband in the later years of Prohibition.

By the end of World War II, narcotics smuggling and the white-collar criminality tied to it all but disappeared, but with the trade routes opened again the opportunity to move contraband globally reestablished itself. As had developed prewar, the traffic was one dominated not by otherwise legitimate businessmen but instead organized crime and other 'traditional' criminals. In the 1950s and 1960s heroin was moved from Turkey to Marseilles by the Corsican underworld. Now processed from opium to heroin in illegal laboratories, the drugs were moved into the United States via various couriers. The failure of the Bureau of Narcotics and Dangerous Drugs (born from a recent merger of the reputedly corrupt Bureau of Narcotics and the recently created Bureau of Drug Abuse Control) and the growth of military personnel addicted to Asian heroin during America's war in Vietnam contributed to an effort to create yet a third anti-drug organization in 1973, the Drug Enforcement Administration. Merging a variety of drug-related federal agencies and personnel, including BNDD, approximately seven hundred customs personnel and at least a dozen former CIA agents, DEA became the lead agency responsible for addressing the flood of drugs entering the United States thanks to America's counterculture of the 1960s.[68]

MONEY LAUNDERING

Mexico, a continuing source of low quality heroin since the war, was also the United States' major source of marijuana. And with Turkey prohibiting opium growth, Mexico filled the void and became the primary source of heroin in the early 1970s.[69] Yet with the Mexican government's attempt to control the marijuana harvest through a program of eradication, Colombian traffickers stepped in to address the already developed market for marijuana by shipping tons of Colombian weed north via the Gulf of Mexico and the Eastern Pacific.[70] The early routes used to move cocaine were originally developed by, of all people, Corsicans operating out of South America. From moving French heroin northward in the 1960s and 1970s, the adjustment to marijuana and eventually cocaine was minor.[71] With the recognition that cocaine was as easily transported in quantity as marijuana, smugglers filled the demand for weed and white powder to the tune of seven billion dollars by 1980.[72] This traffic opened the door for white-collar crime once again as the currency had to be accounted for and eventually moved south. 'Bankers, lawyers, accountants, all kinds of ostensibly respectable citizens actively were aiding and abetting the Colombians'.[73] For many, that aiding and abetting was in assisting the drug traffickers in legitimizing their 'dirty money' by laundering the profits of the illegal trade and concealing its true source. By 1989 that profit was estimated at over eighty billion dollars.[74]

Money laundering, defined as 'the means used to convert funds that proceed from illegal activities, such as narcotics trafficking [. . .] into financial uses that involve legal instruments (such as bank deposits, investments in stock and bonds or real estate, etc.)',[75] was addressed via a variety of federal laws developed over two decades of penal and regulatory efforts pursuing smuggling and other high-dollar crimes. In an attempt to attack organized crime Congress had passed the Bank Secrecy Act in 1970. The act required documentation of major cash transactions but money laundering in itself was not yet a crime; as long as the reporting requirements were met, the law was being complied with. Even with this limited requirement more than one bank was prosecuted for violations. The Bank of Boston was the first of many, paying a half a million-dollar fine for illegal transactions totaling more than one billion dollars. Crocker National Bank was fined over two million dollars for handling almost four billion dollars without filing the appropriate paperwork. After Operation Greenback, a joint federal investigative operation in south Florida targeting money laundering, identified major weaknesses in reporting requirements under federal law, in 1986 and again in 1988 Congress strengthened the criminal code by making it a crime to conceal the ownership of any money obtained by criminal means as well as assisting a criminal activity through money laundering. Willful blindness to the underlying criminal activity was no longer an excuse to avoid prosecution.[76]

The act of money laundering was now a crime with a potential for civil fines and prison sentences.[77] In the following years the law and related regulations were continually strengthened to address techniques designed to circumvent the earlier statutes.[78] The 1988 UN convention against drug trafficking slowly extended the criminalization of money laundering worldwide.[79] 'Between 1986 and 1992 a total of 290 accountants, 151 certified public accountants, and 225 attorneys were charged with laundering drug money. Most were convicted'.[80]

With IRS and Customs having primary criminal enforcement responsibilities related to domestic and border related enforcement respectively, DEA addressed money laundering cases related to its primary drug enforcement mission as FBI did for traditional high-dollar criminal activities such as racketeering, gambling, and fraud, as well as those crimes it had dual jurisdiction over. The extent of money laundering led to the creation in 1990 of FINCEN, the Financial Crimes Enforcement Network under Treasury, responsible for coordinating intelligence activities across agencies.[81]

In 1982 an officer and two employees of the Great American Bank of Dade County, based in Miami, Florida, were indicted and later convicted of money laundering charges after they had willfully concealed monetary transactions from the government. The bank itself was fined five hundred thousand dollars after having suffered one million dollars in legal fees.[82]

Officers of the Republic National Bank in Miami, Florida, were indicted in 1988 and the president and two others eventually convicted of bank fraud and conspiracy. The same year the Bank of Credit and Commerce, known as BCCI, and five of its officers were also indicted in Tampa, Florida, for money laundering. BCCI, an international banking organization operating in seventy-two countries, had been successfully penetrated by a Customs undercover operation labeled Operation C-Chase that led to the conviction of various bank officers, the bank being fined fifteen million dollars, and its eventual demise.[83]

In 1994 the American Express Bank International, a subsidiary of American Express, paid thirty-two million dollars in fines for laundering Mexican and Colombian drug proceeds.[84] Yet even with the increased enforcement of the various federal statutes and regulations and a history of high profile actions against a variety of financial organizations, in 2007 an encore performance by the two corporations led to another civil fine totaling sixty-five million dollars.[85] Wachovia Bank, owned by Wells Fargo, would also be fined one hundred and sixty million dollars for laundering Mexican drug money.[86]

In the opening years of the twenty-first century one of the most egregious examples of the banking industry and money laundering was HSBC, Britain's largest bank. Accused of both laundering narcotics funds for Mexican traffickers and assisting individuals from various nations under U.S. sanctions in moving funds through the United States, HSBC forfeited $1.92 billion. Yet in choosing to enforce a civil penalty instead of pursuing criminal charges against the bank and its officers, the government affirmed Sutherland's argument that the elites of our culture had the power and influence to define crime to not necessarily encompass their own activities under the penal code. In HSBC's case they were in a position to argue that they were too big to fail; for being a global banking empire, extensive criminal penalties could lead to their probable collapse, potentially threatening the world's economy.[87]

With increased penalties for narcotics trafficking leading to definitions less favorable to direct violations of the narcotics laws, businesses in America instead became involved in ancillary services. From selling real estate, automobiles, vessels, and aircraft to providing legal and financial services to traffickers, American business profited from the marijuana and narcotic trade. The opium traffickers were simply an earlier iteration—similar to the 'robber barons'—of Sutherland's concept of white-collar criminality that were replaced by the modern institutional money launderers of America's global financial industry.

NOTES

1. Robert K. Merton, *Social Theory and Social Structure* (New York: The Free Press, 1968), p. 223.
2. Edwin H. Sutherland, 'White-collar Criminality', *American Sociological Review*, 5 (February, 1940), 1–12, (p. 1).
3. Edwin H. Sutherland, *White Collar Crime: The Uncut Version* (New Haven, CT: Yale University Press, 1983), p. 46.
4. Thomas Hobbes, *Leviathan* (New York: Oxford University Press, 1996), p. 84.

5. Martin Booth, *Opium: A History* (New York: St. Martin's Griffin, 1996), pp. 15–26.
6. *ibid.*, p. 73; H. Wayne Morgan, *Drugs in America: A Social History, 1800–1980* (Syracuse, NY: Syracuse University Press, 1981), pp. 2–4; Oscar Reiss, *Medicine in Colonial America* (Lanham, MA: University Press of America, 2000), p. 207.
7. Booth, *Opium*, p. 73; Morgan, *Drugs in America*, p. 2.
8. Lawrence Kolb and A. G. Du Mez, 'The Prevalence and Trend of Drug Addiction in the United States and the Factors Influencing It', *Public Health Reports*, 39 (1924), 1179–1204; Morgan, *Drugs in America*, pp. 32–33.
9. Charles H. Bass, 'Why Are We Not a Healthy People', *Atlanta Medical and Surgical Journal*, 5 (December 1859), cited in Morgan, *Drugs in America*, p. 47.
10. Act of May 6, 1882, 22 *Stat.* 58; Lucy E. Salyer, *Laws Harsh as Tigers: Chinese Immigrants and the Shaping of Modern Immigration Law* (Chapel Hill: University of North Carolina Press, 1995), pp. 2–18.
11. Booth, *Opium*, pp. 109–137, 144–145.
12. Jacques M. Downs, 'American Merchants and the China Opium Trade, 1800–1840', *Business History Review*, 42 (1968), 418–442; Sutherland, *White Collar Crime*, pp. 251–252.
13. J. P. Cushing, ' "Memo for Mr. Forbes Respecting Canton Affairs . . ." ', *Business History Review*, 40 (1966), 98–107; Geoffrey M. Footner, *Tidewater Triumph: The Development and Worldwide Success of the Chesapeake Bay Pilot Schooner* (Mystic, CT: Mystic Seaport Museum, 1998), p. 163; Steve Fraser and Gary Gerstle, *Ruling America: A History of Wealth and Power in America* (Cambridge, MA: Harvard University Press, 2005), p. 96.
14. Booth, *Opium*, p. 121; 'China', *Treaties, Conventions, etc., between China and Foreign States*, 2nd edn, 2 vols, (Shanghai: Statistical Department of the Inspectorate General of Customs, 1917), I, 677–712; Downs, 'American Merchants and the China Opium Trade'.
15. Samuel E. Morison, *The Maritime History of Massachusetts, 1783–1860* (Boston, MA: Houghton Mifflin, 1921), p. 279.
16. Sutherland, *White Collar Crime*, p. 7.
17. Jonathan Goldstein, *Philadelphia and the China Trade, 1682–1846: Commercial, Cultural and Attitudinal Effects* (University Park: Pennsylvania State University, 1978), pp. 57–61.
18. Robert Bennet Forbes, *Personal Reminiscences* (Boston, MA: Little, Brown, 1878), pp. 144–145.
19. Sutherland, *White Collar Crime*, p. 230.
20. *ibid.*, p. 232.
21. Booth, *Opium*, p. 110; Senate Report No. 698, *Customs Laws of 1894 Compared with the Customs Law of 1890 with Rates of the Mills Bill of 1880 and the Wilson Bill of 1894*, 2nd edn, 53rd Cong., 2nd sess. (Washington, D.C.: Government Printing Office, 1894), p. 9; David Chuenyan Lai, 'Chinese Opium Trade and Manufacture in British Columbia, 1858–1908', *Journal of the West*, 38 (1999), 21–26; Carl E. Prince and Mollie Keller, *The U.S. Customs Service: A Bicentennial History* (Washington, D.C.: U.S. Customs Service, 1989), pp. 220–223.
22. *Annual Report of the Secretary of the Treasury of the State on the Finances for the Year 1884* (Washington, D.C.: Government Printing Office, 1884), p. L; *Annual Report of the Secretary of the Treasury of the State on the Finances for the Year 1890* (Washington, D.C.: Government Printing Office, 1891), p. 782; *Annual Report of the Secretary of the Treasury of the State*

on the Finances for the Year 1895 (Washington, D.C.: Government Printing Office, 1896), p. 717; Lawrence Douglas Taylor Hansen, 'The Chinese Six Companies of San Francisco and the Smuggling of Chinese Immigrants across the U.S.-Mexico Border, 1882–1930', *Journal of the Southwest*, 48 (2006), 37–61 (p. 38); Salyer, *Laws Harsh as Tigers*, p. 8.

23. The Kingdom of Hawaii had outlawed the importation of opium in 1874 after the earlier introduction of Chinese laborers for the sugar plantations had created a market for the contraband. With few customs officers addressing increasing quantities of inbound commercial traffic from Asia, North America, and Europe, and even fewer preventive officers (limited to attempts to suppress the contraband trade in the late 1890s) by the turn of the century no fines or forfeitures were collected, a reflection of the lack of success against the smuggling trade. See Roland L. Delorme, 'Revenuers in Paradise: The Advent of United States Customs Regulations of the Hawaiian Trade', *Hawaii Journal of History*, 15 (1981), 69–79.

24. *Three Thousand Eight Hundred and Eighty Boxes of Opium v. United States*, 9 Sawy. 259, 23 F. 367 (1883).

25. Lai, 'Chinese Opium Trade and Manufacture', pp. 22–26.

26. *Annual Report of the Secretary of the Treasury on the State of the Finances for the Year 1887* (Washington, D.C.: Government Printing Office, 1887), p. 882; *Annual Report of the Secretary of the Treasury on the State of the Finances for the Year 1891* (Washington, D.C.: Government Printing Office, 1891), p. 852; Lai, 'Chinese Opium Trade and Manufacture', pp. 22–26; *Ten Cases of Opium*, Deady 62, 23 F.Cas. 840 (1864).

27. *Annual Report of the Secretary of the Treasury on the State of the Finances for the Year 1894* (Washington, D.C.: Government Printing Office, 1894), p. 958.

28. Sarah M. Griffith, 'Border Crossings: Race, Class, and Smuggling in Pacific Coast Chinese Immigrant Society', *Western Historical Quarterly*, 35 (2004), 473–492; 'An Enlarged Gall', *Los Angeles Times*, July 18, 1895, p. 3; 'Chinese Smuggling Conspirators', *Los Angeles Times*, September 7, 1895, p. 3; 'The Pacific Slope', *San Francisco Chronicle*, July 3, 1894, p. 5; 'The Pacific Slope', *San Francisco Chronicle*, May 28, 1895, p. 3; *Dunbar v. United States*, 156 U.S. 185, 15 S.Ct. 325 (1895); *United States v. Dunbar*, 60 F. 75 (1894); United States v. the Haytian Republic, 154 U.S. 118, 14 S.Ct. 992 (1894); *United States v. Wilson et al.*, 60 F. 890 (1894); *United States v. Wilson et al.*, 69 F. 584 (1895).

29. Griffith, 'Border Crossings', p. 491; 'More Frauds Found', *San Francisco Chronicle*, December 7, 1893, p. 4.

30. Sutherland, *White Collar Crime*, pp. 228, 232.

31. *Annual Report of the Secretary of the Treasury of the State on the Finances for the Year 1888* (Washington, D.C.: Government Printing Office, 1888), p. 855; Lai, 'Chinese Opium Trade and Manufacture', p. 24; Prince and Keller, *The U.S. Customs Service*, p. 225.

32. 'After Opium Smuggler', *New York Times*, February 15, 1888, p. 8; *Annual Report of the Secretary of the Treasury on the State of the Finances for the Year 1888*, p. 855; 'On Trial for Opium Smuggling', *New York Times*, November 28, 1888, p. 3.

33. 'Phenacetine Smuggling Is Checked', *New York Times*, May 30, 1895, p. 9.

34. Office of the Special Agent, Treasury Department, Report, Subject: Report of the arrest of Lewin J. Fulmer, Herbert T. Jenkins, and George L. Schumacker, for smuggling phenacetine, and the seizure of contraband goods in their possession, also of books, papers, counterfeit labels, etc., April 16, 1897,

Record Group 36 (RG 36.2.2), U.S. Customs Service, Case Files and Related Correspondence, 1833–1915, Records of the Special Agents Division, Office of the Commissioner of Customs; Bureau of Customs and its Predecessors, 1820–1974, National Archives Building, Washington, D.C.

35. Office of the Special Agent, Treasury Department, Report, Subject: Reporting the arrest of Frederick Rohns on the charge of receiving, concealing and facilitating the transportation of phenacetine imported contrary to law, May 1, 1897, *Record Group 36.2.2, U.S. Customs Service*, National Archives Building, Washington, D.C.

36. Office of the Special Agent, Treasury Department, Report, Subject: Seizure of 540 ounces of coal tar preparations, and 1000 phenacetine tablets. Arrest of three smugglers, November 15, 1897, *Record Group 36.2.2, U.S. Customs Service*, National Archives Building, Washington, D.C.

37. Office of the Special Agent, Treasury Department, Report, Subject: Benjamin Hunton and James Nevels convicted of smuggling coal tar preparations; Hunton sentenced to imprisonment in Detroit House of Corrections for nine months and to pay a fine of $250. Sentence suspended on Nevels. January 8, 1898, *Record Group 36.2.2, U.S. Customs Service*, National Archives Building, Washington, D.C.

38. Office of the Special Agent Treasury Department, Report, Subject: Report, enclosing a summary statement concerning the Transactions of the First Special Agency District for the Fiscal Year ended June, 30/96, pp. 5–6, *Record Group 36.2.2, U.S. Customs Service*, National Archives Building, Washington, D.C.

39. Canada, Statutes, 7–8 Edward VII, chapter 50, An Act to Prohibit the Importation, Manufacture and Sale of Opium for other than Medical Purposes.

40. Evelyn Hu-DeHart, 'Indispensable Enemy or Convenient Scapegoat? A Critical Examination Sinophobia in Latin America and the Caribbean, 1870s to 1930s', in *The Chinese in Latin American and the Caribbean*, ed. by Walton Look Lai and Tan Chee-Beng (Boston, MA: Brill Academic, 2010), 65–102 (pp. 69–71).

41. Cantu's entrepreneurial spirit wasn't limited to opium. In 1919 a Cantu representative offered, in talks with California prohibitionists, to establish a twenty mile 'dry zone' bordering the United States for a personal payment of four hundred thousand dollars for a period of two years, subject to renegotiation at the end of the stipulated time. See Gabriela Recio, 'Drugs and Alcohol: US Prohibition and the Origins of the Drug Trade in Mexico, 1910–1930', *Journal of Latin American Studies*, 34 (2002), 21–42 (pp. 30–31).

42. 'Smuggling of Dope Alarms', *New York Times*, August 21, 1922, Section 2, p. 1.

43. Recio, 'Drugs and Alcohol', pp. 33–41.

44. 'Accused in Narcotic Plot', *New York Times*, August 30, 1936, p. 17; Elaine Carey, 'Women with Golden Arms: Narco-Trafficking in North America, 1910–1970', *History Compass*, 6 (2008), 774–795 (pp. 780–781); Garland Roark, *The Coin of Contraband: The True Story of United States Customs Investigator Al Scharff* (Garden City, NY: Doubleday, 1964), pp. 324–332; 'Smuggler Pursuit Ended by Suicide', *New York Times*, September 5, 1936, p. 30.

45. Carey, 'Women with Golden Arms', p. 781.

46. Arnold H. Taylor, 'American Confrontation with Opium Traffic in the Philippines', *Pacific Historical Review*, 36, (1967), 307–324; P.L. 58–141, 33 *Stat*. 928, 944 (1905).

47. P.L. 60–100, 35 *Stat*. 614 (1909); P.L. 63–223, 38 *Stat*. 785 (1914).

48. David R. Bewley-Taylor, *The United States and International Drug Control, 1909–1997* (New York: Pinter, 1999), p. 16.
49. P.L. 227, 42 *Stat*. 596 (1922); Morgan, *Drugs in America*, p. 119.
50. 'Charges Rothstein Had $4,000,000 Loot of Bond Theft Ring, *New York Times*, November 11, 1928, p. 1; 'Rothstein a Power in Gambling World', *New York Times*, November 7, 1928, p. 28.
51. Leo Katcher, *The Big Bankroll: The Life and Times of Arnold Rothstein* (New York: Harper and Brothers, 1958), pp. 116–118, 233–237, 300–309.
52. Jill Jonnes, *Hep-cats, Narcs, and Pipe Dreams: A History of America's Romance with Illegal Drugs* (New York: Scribner, 1996), pp. 75, 78–79.
53. 'Four Caught in Raids on Rothstein Ring; More Drugs Seized', *New York Times*, December 9, 1928, p. 1; '$4,000,000 Narcotics Seized Here, Traced to Rothstein Ring', *New York Times*, December 19, 1928. p. 1; '$2,000,000 Narcotics of "Rothstein Ring" Seized in Hotel Here', *New York Times*, December 8, 1928, p. 1; 'Unger Is Indicted in Drug Conspiracy', *New York Times*, December 11, 1928, p. 26.
54. 'Federal Men Face Narcotic Inquiry', *New York Times*, January 14, 1930, p. 27; '14 Taken in Roundup of 3 Narcotic Rings Linked to Rothstein', *New York Times*, December 29, 1929, p. 1; 'Grand Jury Accuses Highest Officials in Narcotics Bureau', *New York Times*, February 20, 1930, p. 1; 'Never Saw Rothstein, Nutt's Son Declares', *New York Times*, February 22, 1930, p. 2; '23 Men Indicted in Drug Ring Case', *New York Times*, January 4, 1930, p. 16.
55. Jonnes, *Hep-Cats*, pp. 72–86; Katcher, *The Big Bankroll*, pp. 1–7, 290–299.
56. David E. Ruth, *Inventing the Public Enemy: The Gangster in American Culture, 1918–1934* (Chicago: University of Chicago Press, 1996), pp. 122–123.
57. *ibid*., p. 119.
58. Harry J. Anslinger and William F. Tompkins, *The Traffic in Narcotics* (New York: Funk and Wagnalls, 1953), pp. 29–34; Ethan A. Nadelmann, *Cops across Borders: The Internationalization of U.S. Criminal Law Enforcement* (University Park: Pennsylvania State University Press, 1993), pp. 93–95.
59. Jonnes, *Hep-Cats*, p. 98; '$1,000,000 of Morphine Seized at Pier Here', *New York Times*, December 17, 1930, p. 4; '3 Tons of Narcotics Seized on Pier Here', *New York Times*, April 25, 1931, p. 1.
60. The same year as the *Alesia* and the *Milwaukee* seizures a third one took place off of the *Ile de France* totaling 612 kilos of morphine and heroin. See Kathryn Meyer and Terry Parssinen, *Web of Smoke: Smugglers, Warlords, Spies, and the History of the International Drug Trade* (Lanham, MD: Rowman and Littlefield, 1998), pp. 251–252.
61. House of Representatives, *Exportations of Opium: Hearings before a Subcommittee of the Committee on Ways and Means*, 66th Cong., 3rd sess., 1920–1921, pp. 53, 132, as mentioned in Jones, *Hep-cats*, p. 77.
62. Bewley-Taylor, *The United States and International Drug Control*, p. 33.
63. Alan A. Block, 'European Drug Traffic and Traffickers between the Wars: The Policy of Suppression and Its Consequences', *Journal of Social History*, 23 (1989), 315–337.
64. Bureau of Narcotics, *Traffic in Opium and Other Dangerous Drugs for the Year Ended December 31, 1935* (Washington, D.C.: U.S. Treasury Department, Bureau of Narcotics, 1936), pp. 24–26.
65. Jonnes, *Hep-Cats*, pp. 107–115; Meyer and Parssinen, *Webs of Smoke*, pp. 251–264; Bureau of Narcotics, *Traffic in Opium and Other Dangerous Drugs for the Year Ended December 31, 1935*, p. 55.
66. Booth, *Opium*, p. 243.

67. *Annual Report of the Secretary of the Treasury on the State of the Finances for the Fiscal Year Ended June 30, 1940* (Washington, D.C.: Government Printing Office, 1941), p. 372.
68. Jonnes, *Hep-cats*, pp. 265, 297; Prince and Keller, *The U.S. Customs Service*, pp. 235–237.
69. William O. Walker, *Drug Control in the Americas*, revised edn (Albuquerque: University of New Mexico Press, 1989), p. 192.
70. Jonnes, *Hep-cats*, p. 339.
71. *ibid.*, pp. 338–339.
72. *ibid.*, p. 345.
73. *ibid.*, p. 345.
74. U.S. General Accounting Office, *Money Laundering: The U.S. Government Is Responding to the Problem, GAO/NSIAD-91-130* (Washington, D.C.: General Accounting Office, 1991), p. 12.
75. Robert E. Grosse, *Drugs and Money: Laundering Latin America's Cocaine Dollars* (Westport, CT: Praeger, 2001), p. 3.
76. Anti-Drug Abuse Act of 1986 (P.L. 99–570); Anti-Drug Abuse Act of 1988 (P.L. 100–690); Grosse, *Drugs and Money*, p. 57.
77. 18 USC 1956 and 1957.
78. Grosse, *Drugs and Money*, pp. 56–63.
79. Jonnes, *Hep-cats*, p. 438.
80. Ron Chepesiuk, *The War on Drugs: An International Encyclopedia* (Santa Barbara, CA: ABC-CLIO, 1999), p. 144.
81. U.S. General Accounting Office, *Money Laundering*, pp. 17–18.
82. John G. Edwards, 'Drug Money Laundering Gaining Sophistication', *Sun Sentinel*, May 26, 1985, p. 3E; 'Miami Bank Indicted on Charges of Laundering Illicit Drug Money', *New York Times*, December 14, 1982, p. A28.
83. Grosse, *Drugs and Money*, pp. 74–75, 93–103; Jeffrey Schmalz, 'Bank Is Charged by U.S. with Money-laundering', *New York Times*, October 12, 1988.
84. Allen R. Myerson, 'American Express Unit Settles Laudering (sic) Case', *New York Times*, November 22, 1994, p. D2.
85. 'American Express Is Fined $65 Million', *Wall Street Journal*, eastern edn, August 7, 2007, p. A2.
86. 'Wachovia and U.S. Settle a Money Laundering Case', *New York Times*, March 17, 2010, p. B8.
87. Jessica Silver-Greenberg, 'HSBC Agrees to Pay $2 Billion to Settle Charges of Illegal Transfers', *New York Times*, December 12, 2012, p. B3; 'Too Big to Indict', *New York Times*, December 12, 2012, p. A38.

Conclusion

When Edwin Sutherland introduced the concept of white-collar crime, he referred to the respectable businessmen of his day who had, in the course of their occupations, violated the law whenever 'definitions' favored them doing so. He presented numerous examples of twentieth-century corporations violating various statutes while also effectively avoiding both criminal sanctions as well as the placement of personal responsibility on their corporate officers. He further remarked that the 'robber barons' of the nineteenth century also qualified as white-collar criminals.

Yet since at least the founding of the American Republic, various individuals other than the notorious 'robber barons' have been involved in white-collar criminality. Using organized smuggling as an exemplar, this study establishes that white-collar crime always has been an integral part of America when conditions offered 'definitions' in favor of violating the law. Each period of smuggling in American history is a link in the continuous chain of white-collar criminality in the 150 years prior to Sutherland's assertion. The objective of that criminality was to achieve monetary success, an economic version of the American Dream, one that mandated success by legal methods if possible but, in any case, by whatever means necessary, including smuggling.

This dark side of the American Dream originally exposed itself in colonial times, with the elite merchants of communities such as Boston trafficking contraband into the colonies; these included John Hancock, one of the signatories of the Declaration of Independence. Violating British law and regulations in the course of their occupations, they manipulated the legal system and the population to their own interests, having little recognition of their criminality. They instead justified their actions as a positive good and helped to thrust the colonies into war.

By 1809, with a change of political control in Washington, the administration of Thomas Jefferson created conditions for business to resort, yet again, to smuggling by enacting a series of embargo and nonimportation statutes meant to keep the nation out of war. These same laws became a new justification for smuggling, using techniques developed years earlier to circumvent governmental restrictions. For the merchant elite of the Northeast, as it was for many who followed, money was the path to power and social success, and neither law nor a distant administration was allowed to interfere in that objective. Within thirty years, these same merchant houses began smuggling opium into China, following in the wake of the British and finding little reason to question their own morality in violating the law, substantiating Sutherland's recognition that white-collar criminals do not see themselves as criminals. Years later other businessmen trafficked opium into the United States to serve the local Chinese communities, only to be replaced by pharmacists and pharmaceutical corporations who also conspired to introduce narcotics illegally into domestic commerce. All were businessmen fulfilling their occupational roles, the merchants in trade and the pharmacists and pharmaceutical businesses in their own chosen profession, focused on profit instead of the morality or legality of their transgressions. All provide evidence of Robert Merton's depiction of an American Dream that constitutes a moral mandate to achieve success by whatever means, including ignoring the criminality and the morality of trafficking in narcotics.

When Sutherland contended that various war crimes qualified as white-collar crimes, his focus had been on the recent world wars. Yet as the evidence in the previous chapters substantiate, the numerous conflicts in which America has been involved over its history offered some in business numerous 'definitions' in favor of violating the law. For example wars, by their very nature create instability. For white-collar criminals, instability was seen as opportunity. Some Northern merchants, sympathetic to the Southern cause and to their own personal profit during the Civil War, moved contraband goods south via neutral ports, moving coin or cotton north in exchange. Blockade running into Southern ports became the norm until effectively interdicted by Union forces. Yet others traveled to Mexico in an attempt to buy Southern cotton shipped south across the Texas-Mexico border. One U.S. senator, William Sprague, was investigated for conspiring to do so but, just as Sutherland had characterized how white-collar criminals avoid the consequences of their actions, Sprague was able to use his political power and influence to avoid serious repercussions for his treasonous actions. Cotton was also moved across the extended and porous dividing lines of the fighting forces in a quest for profit, with Union General Benjamin Butler condoning a criminal conspiracy, coordinating the movement of Southern cotton northward by fraud and by manipulation of the law. His position, both militarily and politically, also offered him the opportunity to protect those in business with him from critical 'definitions' by government, much to his financial benefit. The involvement of both of these otherwise elite Union officials, as well as the earlier merchant house elites of the nineteenth century, demonstrates the thesis that white-collar crime does not date from the twentieth-century corporations as Sutherland expressed but extends back much earlier in American history, involving respectable individuals willing to forgo or circumvent the law in their quest for financial success in the course of their occupations, be they merchant house traders, military officers, or textile manufacturers.

Conflict was again an issue with over a hundred years' worth of filibustering efforts documenting a similar, if longer lasting, criminality. In an effort to achieve financial and personal success, numerous individuals participated or supported various filibustering attempts, justifying their actions, in many cases, under the politically expedient concept of Manifest Destiny. Whether attempting to extend slavery, to enlarge business markets, or to spread democracy, filibusters and associated businesses saw their self-interest, specifically their financial self-interest, in alignment with the national self-interest and offering 'definitions' in favor of their war crimes. At the start of the twentieth century, another conflict, the Mexican Revolution, offered businesses located along the southern border of the United States similar opportunity for profit, marketing arms and ammunition to the various military forces in spite of national policy. As shown in this work, these business ventures, including national corporations such as Phelps-Dodge, were able to manipulate the interests of law to their financial advantage, avoiding the legal consequences of their actions through their political relationships with both the judiciary and with the administration in power.

The most famous era of smuggling awaited the nation, however, when the political efforts of the temperance movement bore fruit and established national prohibition. This intersection of political, legal, and business interests allowed some entrepreneurs in business to use the political conflict to their own profitable advantage, knowing there was an extensive market for the contraband of alcohol. With the political interests of Canada all but acquiescing to the smuggling traffic in exchange for the revenue contributed to the treasury, enterprise and innovation coupled with corruption and guile allowed business interests such as the Bronfmans and the Reifels to dominate the market through their white-collar criminality. Manipulating the laws, as well as their own financial books, to maximize profit and to minimize governmental interference, these businessmen were no less white-collar criminals involved in organized crime than the corporate businessmen whom Sutherland described when originally introducing his concept of white-collar criminality a few years later. They were persistent, were extensive in their criminality, lost little, if any, public status for their smuggling endeavors (the Scottish whiskey industry partnered with them), obviously had contempt for Prohibition, and seemed to have little recognition that they were criminals by any definition of the law. These same traits identified by Sutherland apply, as is recognized in this work, as easily to the merchant house elites of America's Northeast in the nineteenth century and to the filibusters attempting to extend the nation's supposed Manifest Destiny as they do to the distillery owners who shipped their product south to the United States.

When Sutherland presented his conception of white-collar crime and criminality, he referred to the corporations of his day, with the muckrakers of the previous generation offering examples of turn-of-the century corporate malfeasance. Later criminologists documented contemporary examples of white-collar crime in various fields, from the price-fixing of the electrical equipment industry to the Enron corporation collapse. Yet, in reality, and as is argued in this work, since the founding of the American nation, there have been white-collar criminals. The concept may have been formulated and publicly presented in the 1930s but, also like the notion of the American Dream, white-collar crime predated its own definition. The evidence presented demonstrates that white-collar crime is not simply a twentieth-century form of deviant behavior, let alone a twenty-first-century one. It has been part of American culture since the birth of the nation as is demonstrated by America's history of organized smuggling over the 150 years prior to Sutherland's original introduction of his concept. Each period of smuggling in the Republic's history was a link in the continuing chain of white-collar criminality now extending forward into the twenty-first century, involving various businessmen who believed that the 'definitions' in favor of violating the law were present for a window of time. In their efforts to achieve the American Dream, they put profit and financial success above the law and, in some cases, above patriotism. Otherwise respected in their communities, they did not see themselves as criminals even when violating the law. Committing their crimes in the course of their occupations, they were as much white-collar criminals as Sutherland's corporate businessmen of later years. Sutherland's concept of white-collar crime is not only a filament of criminality wired throughout modern American business but a thread of lawlessness woven through the American past.

Bibliography

PRIMARY SOURCES

Annual Report[s] of the Secretary of the Treasury on the State of the Finances, for the years 1884, 1887, 1888, 1890, 1891, 1894, 1895, 1919, 1920, 1932, 1933, 1934, and 1940 (Washington, D.C.: Government Printing Office, publication dates vary)

Barbican, James (pseudonym of Eric Sherbrooke Walker), *The Confessions of a Rum-runner* (New York: Ives Washburn, 1928)

Bureau of Prohibition, Record Group 56, National Archives and Records Administration, Pacific Alaska Region, Seattle, WA

Bush, Ira Jefferson, *Gringo Doctor* (Caldwell, ID: Caxton Printers, 1939)

'Comision Pesquisadora de la Frontera del Norte: Report to the President,' *U.S.-Mexico Borderlands: Historical and Contemporary Perspectives*, ed. by Oscar J. Martinez (Wilmington, DE: Scholarly Resources, 1996), pp. 58–61

'China', *Treaties, Conventions, etc., between China and Foreign States*, 2nd edn, 2 vols (Shanghai: Statistical Department of the Inspectorate General of Customs, 1917)

Coolidge, Thomas Jefferson, *Thomas Jefferson Coolidge: An Autobiography* (Boston, MA: Houghton Mifflin, 1900)

Davies, K. G. (editor), "America and West Indies: March 1737, 1–15," Calendar of State Papers Colonial, America and West Indies, Volume 43: 1737, British History Online, www.british-history.ac.uk/report.aspx?compid=72900&strquery=

Eastland Company, *The Acts and Ordinances of the Eastland Company*, ed. by Maud Sellers (London: Royal Historical Society, 1906)

Finney, Sheridan J., personal correspondence and interview, September 12 and October 3, 1993

Firth, C.H. and R.S. Rait, (eds), *Acts and Ordinances of the Interregnum, 1642–1660*, British History Online, www.british-history.ac.uk/source.aspx?pubid = 606

Forbes, Robert Bennet, *Personal Reminiscences* (Boston, MA: Little, Brown, 1878)

Fortescue, J.W. (editor), "America and West Indies: February 1686," Calendar of State Papers Colonial, America and West Indies, Volume 12: 1685–1688 and Addenda 1653–1687, British History Online, www.british-history.ac.uk/report.aspx?compid=70499

—— "America and West Indies: August 1696, 17–31," Calendar of State Papers Colonial, America and West Indies, Volume 15: 1696–1697, British History Online, www.british-history.ac.uk/report.aspx?compid=70866

Gallatin, Albert, *Selected Writing of Albert Gallatin*, ed. by E. James Ferguson (Indianapolis, ID: Bobbs-Merrill, 1967)

Grant, W.L. and J. Mason (eds), *Acts of the Privy Council of England, Colonial Series*, 6 vols (London: Anthony Brothers, 1908–1912)

Hamilton, Alexander, (as Publius), *Federalist No. 35* (1788)

——*The Papers of Alexander Hamilton*, ed. by Harold C. Syrett, 27 vols (New York: Columbia University Press, 1969)

Headlam, Cecil (editor), "America and West Indies: February 1714," Calendar of State Papers Colonial, America and West Indies, Volume 27: 1712–1714, British History Online, www.british-history.ac.uk/report.aspx?compid=73930&strquery=

Headlam, Cecil (editor) and Arthur Percival Newton (introduction), "America and West Indies: October 1724, 16-31," Calendar of State Papers Colonial, America and West Indies, Volume 34: 1724–1725, British History Online, www.british-history.ac.uk/report.aspx?compid=72399&strquery=

Ingersoll, Henry, "Diary and Letters of Henry Ingersoll, Prisoner of Carthagena, 1806–1809", *American Historical Review*, 3 (1898), 674–702

Lythgoe, Gertrude, *The Bahama Queen: The Autobiography of Gertrude 'Cleo' Lythgoe* (Mystic, CT: Flat Hammock Press, 2006)

Madison, James, *The James Madison Papers*, http://memory.loc.gov/ammem/collections/madison_papers/ [Date accessed: September 17, 2011]

Mercator, Gerhard, *Orbis Terrae Compendiosa Descripitio* [Amsterdam, 1637?], Map Division, John H. Levine Bequest 97–7397, New York Public Library, New York, NY, http://digitalgallery.nypl.org/nypldigital/dgkeysearchdetail.cfm?strucID= 773787&imageID=1524650#_seemore [Date accessed: December 25, 2013]

Miles, Fraser, *Slow Boat on Rum Row* (Madeira Park, B.C., Canada: Harbour Publishing, 1992)

Moray, Alastair, *The Diary of a Rum-runner* (London: Phillip Allan and Company, 1929)

National Commission on Law Observance and Enforcement, *Report on the Enforcement of the Prohibition Laws of the United States* (Washington, D.C.: Government Printing Office, 1931)

Records of the Special Agents Division, Office of the Commissioner of Customs, Bureau of Customs and its Predecessors, 1820–1974, U.S. Customs Service, Record Group 36 (RG 36.2.2),National Archives and Records Administration, National Archives Building, Washington, D.C.

A Report of the Record Commissioners of the City of Boston Containing the Records of Boston Selectmen, 1736–1742 (Boston, MA: Rockwell and Churchill, 1886)

Royal Commission on Customs and Excise, *Interim Reports (Nos.1 to 10)* (Ottawa, Ontario, Canada: F. A. Acland, 1928)

Sherman, William Tecumseh, *Home Letters of General Sherman,* ed. by M. A. DeWolfe Howe (New York: Charles Scribner's Sons, 1909)

U.S. Bureau of Narcotics, *Traffic in Opium and Other Dangerous Drugs for the Year Ended December 31, 1935* (Washington, D.C.: U.S. Treasury Department, Bureau of Narcotics, 1936)

U.S. Bureau of the Census, *Fourteenth Census of the United States Population: Number and Distribution of Inhabitants, Summary of Results* (Washington, D.C.: Government Printing Office, 1921)

U.S. Bureau of Investigation, *Uniform Crime Report for the Fourth Quarterly Bulletin, 1932* (Washington, D.C.: Government Printing Office, 1933)

U.S. Census Office, *The Seventh Census of the United States: 1850* (Washington, D.C.: Robert Armstrong, 1853)

U.S. Congress, American State Papers: Finance 1.

——, American State Papers: Foreign Relations 1.

——, American State Papers, Military Affairs 6.

——, *Annals of Congress,* Senate, 10th Cong., 1st sess.

——, *Congressional Globe*, 28th Cong., 1st sess.

——, *Congressional Globe*, 37th Cong., 3rd sess.

——, *Congressional Globe*, 38th Cong., 2nd sess.

——, *House Journal*, 5th Cong., 3rd sess., January 14, 1799.

——, House, Report from the Committee on Public Expenditures, New York Custom-House, 38th Cong., 1st sess., Report No. 111.

——, House, Report from the Committee on Public Expenditures, New York Custom-House, 38th Cong., 2nd sess., Report 25.

——, Senate Bill 1, 37th Cong., 1st sess., July 6, 1861.

——, Senate Executive Document No. 1, *Report of the Secretary of the Treasury on the State of the Finances for the Year Ending June 30, 1857,* 35th Cong., 1st sess.

——, Senate Executive Document No. 10, Part 3, 41st Cong., 3rd sess.

——, *Senate Executive Journal*, 30th Cong., 1st sess., March 9, 1848.

——, *Senate Executive Journal*, 33th Cong., 1st sess., April 25, 1854.

——, *Senate Journal*, 5th Cong., 1st sess., July 7, 1797.

——*Senate Journal*, 5th Cong., 1st sess., July 8, 1797.

——, *Senate Journal*, Cong., 3rd sess., January 14, 1799.

——, *Senate Journal*, 27th Cong., 3rd sess., August 11, 1842.

——, Senate Report No. 108, Part 3, 37th Cong., 3rd sess.

——, Senate Report No. 377, 41st Cong., 3rd sess.

——, Senate Report No. 698, 53rd Cong., 2nd sess.

——, Subcommittee of the Committee of the Judiciary, *National Prohibition Hearings*, 69th Cong., 1st sess., April 5-24, 1926.

U.S. Customs Service, Record Group 36, National Archives and Records Administration, Southwest Region, Fort Worth, TX

U.S. General Accounting Office, *Money Laundering: The U.S. Government Is Responding to the Problem, GAO/NSIAD-91–130* (Washington, D.C.: General Accounting Office, 1991)

U.S. Naval War Records Office, *War of the Rebellion: A Compilation of the Official Records of the Union and Confederate Navies,* 30 vols (Washington, D.C.: Government Printing Office, 1874–1922)

U.S. War Department, *War of the Rebellion: A Compilation of the Official Records of the Union and Confederate Armies*, 128 vols (Washington, D.C.: Government Printing Office, 1880–1900)

Waters, Harold and Aubrey Wisberg, *Patrol Boat 999* (Philadelphia, PA: Chilton, 1959)

NEWSPAPERS AND PERIODICALS

American Citizen [New York], December 16, 1806

Atlanta Constitution, March 9, 1916

Boston Chronicle, April 4–April 11, 1768

Boston Evening Post, June 1, 1761–May 31, 1762

Boston Post-Boy, June 21, 1742

Boston Weekly News-Letter, May 29, 1760

Boston Weekly News-Letter and New-England Chronicle, May 31, 1764–June 23, 1768

Chicago Daily Tribune, December 23, 1853–November 3, 1915

Columbian Centinel [Boston], April 30, 1791

Commercial Advertiser [New York], April 23, 1802; July 26, 1806

Daily Ohio Statesmen [Columbus] January 1–January 25, 1838

Dallas Morning News, January 16, 1892–March 23, 1895; July 24, 1929–April 4, 1930

Evening Post [New York], April 26, 1802
Fort Worth Star-Telegram, January 7–November 20, 1921
Gazetteer [Boston], June 25, 1803
Hartford Daily Courant [CT], June 1, 1850–November 12, 1857
Impartial Herald [Newburyport, MA], January 26, 1796
Literary Digest [New York], October 9, 1920–October 8, 1927
Los Angeles Times, July 18, 1895–May 20, 1930
Macon Daily Telegraph [GA], August 14, 1921
Massachusetts Mercury [Boston], May 20, 1796–December 5, 1800
Morning Chronicle [New York], May 16, 1803
New England Palladium [Boston], July 26, 1803–August 8, 1803
New York Daily News, October 24, 1851–January 1, 1856
New York Daily Times, October 30, 1851–November 14, 1855
New York Herald, June 11, 1803–October 4, 1860
New York Times, November 13, 1857–December 12, 2012
Newburyport Herald [MA], June 12, 1801–May 4, 1802
Newport Mercury [RI] July 24, 1789
Oregonian [Portland], February 21, 1921
Providence Gazette and Country Journal [RI], September 23–September 30, 1769
San Francisco Chronicle, December 7, 1893–April 11, 1917
Sun (Dover, NH],May 3, 1802–October 8, 1851
Sun Sentinel [Ft. Lauderdale, FL], May 21, 1985
Times-Picayune [New Orleans], published as *Daily Picayune*, October 22, 1850–
    May 28, 1857
Wall Street Journal, October 12, 1928–Aug. 7, 2007
Washington Post, August 27, 1927
Western Star [Stockbridge, MA], June, 23, 1795

SECONDARY SOURCES

Articles and Chapters

Agnew, Robert, 'A Revised Strain Theory of Delinquency', *Social Forces*, 64 (1985),
    151–167
——'Building on the Foundation of General Strain Theory: Specifying the Types of
    Strain Most Likely to Lead to Crime and Delinquency', *Journal of Research in
    Crime and Delinquency*, 38 (2001), 319–361
Albertson, Dean, 'Puritan Liquor in the Planting of New England', *New England
    Quarterly*, 23 (1950), 477–490
Anes, Rafael Donoso, 'Accounting and Slavery: The Accounts of the English South
    Sea Company, 1713–22', *European Accounting Review*, 11:2 (2002), 441–452
Barrile, Leo G., 'A Soul to Damn and a Body to Kick: Imprisoning Corporate Crimi-
    nals', *Humanity & Society*, 17 (1993), 176–199
Beaver, Janice Cheryl, *U.S. International Borders: Brief Facts*, RS21729, Congres-
    sional Research Service, Library of Congress, 2006
Beckert, Sven, 'Merchants and Manufacturers in the Antebellum North', in *Rul-
    ing America: A History of Wealth and Power in a Democracy*, ed. by Steve
    Fraser and Gary Gerstle (Cambridge, MA: Harvard University Press, 2005),
    pp. 92–122
Blaisdell, Lowell L., 'Was It Revolution or Filibustering? The Mystery of the Flores
    Magon Revolt in Baja California', *Pacific Historical Review*, 23 (1954), 147–164
——'Harry Chandler and Mexican Border Intrigue, 1914–1917', *Pacific Historical
    Review*, 35 (1966), 385–393

Block, Alan A., 'European Drug Traffic and Traffickers between the Wars: The Policy of Suppression and Its Consequences', *Journal of Social History*, 23 (1989), 315–337

Bolster, W. Jeffery, 'The Impact of Jefferson's Embargo on Coastal Commerce', *Log of Mystic Seaport*, 37 (1986) 111–123

Brynn, Edward, 'Patterns of Dissent: Vermont's Opposition to the War of 1812', *Vermont History*, 40 (1972), 10–27

Carey, Elaine, 'Women with Golden Arms: Narco-Trafficking in North America, 1910–1970', *History Compass*, 6 (2008), 774–795

Chenault, William W. and Robert C. Reinders, 'The Northern-born Community of New Orleans in the 1850s', *Journal of American History*, 51 (1964), 232–247

Coatsworth, James H., 'American Trade with European Colonies in the Caribbean and South America, 1790–1812', *William and Mary Quarterly*, 3rd ser., 24 (1967), 243–266

Cohen, Andrew W., 'Smuggling, Globalization, and America's Outward State, 1870–1909', *Journal of American History*, 97 (2010), 371–398

Conley, John A., 'Historical Perspective and Criminal Justice', *Journal of Criminal Justice Education*, 4 (1993), 349–360

Coulter, E. Merton, 'Commercial Intercourse with the Confederacy in the Mississippi Valley, 1861–1865', *Mississippi Valley Historical Review*, 5 (1919), 377–395

Cumberland, Charles C., 'Precursors of the Mexican Revolution of 1910', *Hispanic American Historical Review*, 22 (1942), 344–356

Cushing, J. P., '"Memo for Mr. Forbes Respecting Canton Affairs . . ."', *Business History Review*, 40 (1966), 98–107

De Fleur, Melvin L. and Richard Quinney, 'A Reformulation of Sutherland's Differential Association Theory and a Strategy for Empirical Verification', *Journal of Research in Crime and Delinquency*, 3 (1966), 1–22

Delorme, Roland L., 'Revenuers in Paradise: The Advent of United States Customs Regulations of the Hawaiian Trade', *Hawaii Journal of History*, 15 (1981), 69–79

Dickerson, O. M., 'John Hancock: Notorious Smuggler or Near Victim of British Customs Racketeers?', *Mississippi Valley Historical Review*, 32 (1945–1946), 517–540

Downs, Jacques M., 'American Merchants and the China Opium Trade, 1800–1840', *Business History Review*, 42 (1968), 418–442

Eckberg, Douglas, 'Stalking the Elusive Homicide', *Social Science History*, 25 (2001), 67–91

Ellis, L. Tuffley, 'Maritime Commerce on the Far Western Gulf, 1861–1865', *Southwestern Historical Quarterly*, 77 (1973), 167–226

Eves, James H., '"The Poor People Had Suddenly Become Rich": A Boom in Maine Wheat, 1793–1815', *Maine Historical Society Quarterly*, 27 (1987), 114–141

Forbes, John D., 'Boston Smuggling, 1807–1815', *American Neptune*, 10 (1950), 144–154

Geis, Gilbert, 'The Heavy Electrical Equipment Antitrust Cases of 1961', in *Criminal Behavior Systems*, ed. by Marshall Clinard and Richard Quinney (New York: Holt, Rinehart & Winston, 1967), pp. 139–150

——'White-collar Crime: What Is It?', *Current Issues in Criminal Justice*, 3 (1991), 9–24

Gerhard, Peter, 'The Socialist Invasion of Baja California, 1911', *Pacific Historical Review*, 15 (1946), 295–304

Goff, John S., 'The Organization of the Federal District Court in Arizona, 1912–1913', *American Journal of Legal History*, 8 (1964), 172–179

Griffith, Sarah M., 'Border Crossings: Race, Class, and Smuggling in Pacific Coast Chinese Immigrant Society', *Western Historical Quarterly*, 35 (2004), 473–492

Hansen, Lawrence Douglas Taylor, 'The Chinese Six Companies of San Francisco and the Smuggling of Chinese Immigrants across the U.S.–Mexico Border, 1882–1930', *Journal of the Southwest*, 48 (2006), 37–61

Harris, Charles H., III, and Louis R. Sadler, 'The Underside of the Mexican Revolution: El Paso, 1912', *Americas*, 39 (1982), 69–83

Hartung, Frank E., 'White-collar Offenses in the Wholesale Meat Industry in Detroit', *American Journal of Sociology*, 56 (1950), 25–34

Higham, Robin D. S., 'Port of Boston and the Embargo of 1807', *American Neptune*, 16 (1956), 189–210

Holli, Melvin G., 'The Founding of Detroit by Cadillac', *Michigan Historical Review*, 27 (2001), 129–136

Hu-DeHart, Evelyn, 'Indispensable Enemy or Convenient Scapegoat? A Critical Examination of Sinophobia in Latin America and the Caribbean, 1870s to 1930s', in *The Chinese in Latin American and the Caribbean*, ed. by Walton Look Lai and Tan Chee-Beng (Boston, MA: Brill Academic, 2010), pp. 65–102.

Johansen, Robert W., 'The Meaning of Manifest Destiny', in *Manifest Destiny and Empire: American Antebellum Expansionism*, ed. by Sam W. Haynes and Christopher Morris (College Station: Texas A&M University, 1997), pp. 7–20

Johnson, Ludwell H., 'Contraband Trade during the Last Year of the Civil War', *Mississippi Valley Historical Review*, 49 (1963), 635–652

——'Northern Profit and Profiteers: The Cotton Rings of 1864–1865', *Civil War History*, 12 (1966), 101–115

——'Commerce between Northeastern Ports and the Confederacy, 1861–1865', *Journal of American History*, 54 (1967), 30–42

Johnstone, Peter, 'Serious White Collar Fraud: Historical and Contemporary Perspectives', *Crime, Law and Social Change*, 30 (1999), 107–130

Jones, Douglas Lamar, ' "The Caprice of Juries": The Enforcement of the Jeffersonian Embargo in Massachusetts', *American Journal of Legal History*, 24 (1980), 307–330

Knapp, Frank A., 'A Note on General Escobedo in Texas', *Southwestern Historical Quarterly*, 55 (1952), 394–401

Kolb, Lawrence and A. G. Du Mez, 'The Prevalence and Trend of Drug Addiction in the United States and the Factors Influencing It', *Public Health Reports*, 39 (1924), 1179–1204

Lai, David Chuenyan, 'Chinese Opium Trade and Manufacture in British Columbia, 1858–1908', *Journal of the West*, 38 (1999), 21–26

Lane, Robert E., 'Why Business Men Violate the Law', *Journal of Criminal Law, Criminology, and Police Science*, 44 (1953), 151–165

Lane, Roger, 'Murder in America: A Historian's Perspective', *Crime and Justice*, 25 (1999), 191–224

Langlois, Janet, 'Smuggling Across the Windsor-Detroit Border: Folk Art, Sexual Difference and Cultural Identity', *Canadian Folklore*, 13 (1991), 23–34

Lawson, W. R., 'United States Banking in 1893', *Bankers', Insurance Managers' and Agents' Magazine*, 56 (1893), 371–388

Lindsay, Diana, ed., 'Henry A. Crabb, Filibuster, and the *San Diego Herald*', *Journal of San Diego History*, 19 (1973), 34–42

Locker, John P. and Barry Godfrey, 'Ontological Boundaries and Temporal Watersheds in the Development of White-collar Crime', *British Journal of Criminology*, 46 (2006), 976–992

May, Robert, 'Manifest Destiny's Filibusters', in *Manifest Destiny and Empire: American Antebellum Expansionism*, ed. by Sam Haynes and Christopher Morris (College Station: Texas A&M University, 1997), pp. 146–179

Merton, Robert K., 'Social Structure and Anomie', *American Sociological Review*, 3 (October, 1938), 672–682

——'On the Evolving Synthesis of Differential Association and Anomie Theory: A Perspective from the Sociology of Science', *Criminology*, 35 (1997), 517–525

Monkkonen, Eric H., 'Estimating the Accuracy of Historic Homicide Rates', *Social Science History*, 25 (2001), 53–66

Muller, H. N., 'Smuggling into Canada: How the Champlain Valley Defied Jefferson's Embargo', *Vermont History*, 38 (1970), 5–21

——'A "Traitorous and Diabolical Traffic": The Commerce of the Champlain-Richelieu Corridor during the War of 1812', *Vermont History*, 44 (1976), 78–96

O'Sullivan, John Louis, 'Annexation', *United States Magazine and Democratic Review*, 17 (July and August, 1845), 5–10

Parkes, Henry Bamford, 'Morals and Law Enforcement in Colonial New England', *New England Quarterly*, 5 (1932), 431–452

Perry, Charles, 'Clandestine Commerce: Yankee Blockade Running', *Journal of Confederate History*, 4 (1989), 89–111

Potter, Gary and Larry Gaines, 'Underworlds and Upperworlds: The Convergence of Organized and White-collar Crime', in *Definitional Dilemma: Can and Should There Be a Universal Definition of White-collar Crime*, ed. by James Helmkamp, Richard Ball, and Kitty Townsend (Morgantown, WV: National White Collar Crime Center and West Virginia University, 1996), pp. 30–52

Quinney, Earl R., 'Occupational Structure and Criminal Behavior: Prescription Violation by Retail Pharmacists', *Social Problems*, 11 (1963), 179–185

Recio, Gabriela, 'Drugs and Alcohol: US Prohibition and the Origins of the Drug Trade in Mexico, 1910–1930', *Journal of Latin American Studies*, 34 (2002), 21–42

Sibley, Marilyn McAdams, 'Charles Stillman: A Case Study of Entrepreneurship on the Rio Grande, 1861–1865', *Southwestern Historical Quarterly*, 77 (1973), 227–240

Skoglund, Nancy Galey, 'The *I'm Alone* Case: A Tale from the Days of Prohibition', *University of Rochester Library Bulletin*, 23 (1968), URL: www.lib.rochester.edu/index.cfm?PAGE = 1004 [Date accessed: August 8, 2011]

Strum, Harvey, 'Smuggling in the War of 1812', *History Today*, 29 (1979), 532–537

——'Smuggling in Maine during the Embargo and the War of 1812', *Colby Library Quarterly*, 19 (1983), 90–97

Surdam, David G., 'Traders or Traitors: Northern Cotton Trading during the Civil War', *Business and Economic History*, 28 (1999), 302–312

Sutherland, Edwin H., 'White-collar Criminality', *American Sociological Review*, 5 (February 1940), 1–12

——'Is "White-collar Crime" Crime?', *American Sociological Review*, 10 (1945), 132–139

Tappan, Paul W., 'Who Is the Criminal?', *American Sociological Review*, 12 (1947), 96–102

Taylor, Arnold H., 'American Confrontation with Opium Traffic in the Philippines', *Pacific Historical Review*, 36 (1967), 307–324

Terry, Clinton W., ' "Let Commerce Follow the Flag": Trade and Loyalty to the Union', *Ohio Valley History*, 1 (2001), 2–14

U.S. Customs and Border Protection, *Valor Memorial Brochure* (Washington, D.C.: Customs and Border Protection, 2011)

Valeri, Mark, 'Calvin and the Social Order in Early America: Moral Ideals and Transatlantic Empire', in *John Calvin's American Legacy*, ed. by Thomas J. Davis (New York: Oxford University Press, 2010), pp. 19–41

Ward, Christopher, 'The Commerce of East Florida during the Embargo, 1806–1812: The Role of Amelia Island', *Florida Historical Quarterly*, 68 (1989), 160–179

Watson, D. H., 'Joseph Harrison and the Liberty Incident', *William and Mary Quarterly*, 3rd ser., 20 (1963), 585–595

Books

Abadinsky, Howard, *Organized Crime*, 9th edn (Belmont, CA: Wadsworth, 2010)

Adams, Henry, *History of the United States during the Administrations of Thomas Jefferson* (New York: Library of America, 1986)

Adams, James Truslow, *The Epic of America* (Boston, MA: Little, Brown and Company, 1931)

Albion, Robert Greenhalgh with the collaboration of Jennie Barnes Pope, *The Rise of New York Port, 1815–1860* (New York: Charles Scribner's Sons, 1939; Boston, MA: Northeastern University Press, repr. 1984)

——and Jennie Barnes Pope, *Sea Lanes in Wartime: The American Experience, 1775–1942* (New York: Norton, 1942)

Allen, Everett S., *The Black Ships: Rumrunners of Prohibition* (Boston, MA: Little, Brown and Company, 1965)

Allison, Graham and Philip Zelikow, *Essence of Decision: Explaining the Cuban Missile Crisis*, 2nd edn (New York: Longman, 1999)

Andreas, Peter, *Smuggler Nation: How Illicit Trade Made America* (New York: Oxford University Press, 2013)

Andrieux, J. P., *Prohibition and St. Pierre* (Lincoln, Ontario, Canada: W. F. Rannie, 1983)

Anslinger, Harry J. and William F. Tompkins, *The Traffic in Narcotics* (New York: Funk and Wagnalls, 1953)

Atton, Henry and Henry Hurst Holland, *The King's Customs, An Account of Maritime Revenue & Contraband, Traffic in England, Scotland, and Ireland, from the Earliest Times to the Year 1800*, 2 vols (London: John Murray, 1908; repr. New York: Augustus M. Kelley, 1967)

Barr, Andrew, *Drink: A Social History of America* (New York: Carroll and Graf, 1999)

Barrow, Thomas C., *Trade and Empire: The British Customs Service in Colonial America, 1660–1775* (Cambridge, MA: Harvard University Press, 1967)

Baxter, William T., *The House of Hancock: Business in Boston, 1724–1775* (Cambridge, MA: Harvard University Press, 1945)

Becker, Carl Lotus, *Beginnings of the American People* (Boston, MA: Houghton Mifflin, 1915)

Behr, Edward, *Prohibition: Thirteen Years That Changed America* (New York: Arcade, 1996)

Belden, Thomas Graham and Marva Robins Belden, *So Fell the Angels* (Boston, MA: Little and Brown, 1956)

Bergman, Andrew, *We're in the Money: Depression America and Its Films* (New York: New York University Press, 1971)

Bernath, Stuart L., *Squall across the Atlantic: American Civil War Prize Cases and Diplomacy* (Berkeley: University of California, 1970)

Bewley-Taylor, David R., *The United States and International Drug Control, 1909–1997* (New York: Pinter, 1999)

Booth, Martin, *Opium: A History* (New York: St. Martin's Griffin, 1996)

Braudel, Fernand, *The Mediterranean and the Mediterranean World in the Age of Philip II*, 2 vols (New York: Harper Colophon, 1976)

Brown, Charles H., *Agents of Manifest Destiny: The Lives and Times of the Filibusters* (Chapel Hill: University of North Carolina, 1980)

Brown, Jim with additional material by Rand Careaga, *Riding the Line: The United States Customs Service in San Diego, 1885–1930: A Documentary History* (Washington, D.C.: U.S. Customs Service, 1991)

Brown, N. Lowell, *High Crimes and Misdemeanors in Presidential Impeachment* (New York: Palgrave Macmillan, 2010)

Bryant, Keith and Henry Dethloff, *A History of American Business* (Englewood Cliffs, NJ: Prentice-Hall, 1983)

Butts, Edward, *Outlaws of the Lakes* (Toronto: Lynx Images, 2004)

Calhoun, Frederick S., *The Lawmen: United States Marshals and their Deputies, 1789–1989* (Washington, D.C.: Smithsonian Institution Press, 1989)

Canney, Donald L., *U.S. Coast Guard and Revenue Cutters, 1790–1935* (Annapolis, MD: Naval Institute Press, 1995)

Carman, Michael Dennis, *United States Customs and the Madero Revolution* (El Paso, TX: University Of El Paso Press, 1976)

Carse, Robert, *Blockade: The Civil War at Sea* (New York: Rinehart, 1958)

——*Rum Row* (New York: Rinehart, 1959)

Cashman, Sean Dennis, *Prohibition: The Lie of the Land* (New York: Free Press, 1981)

Catton, Bruce, *America Goes to War* (Middletown, CT: Wesleyan University Press, 1958; repr. 1986)

Chaffin, Tom, *Fatal Glory: Narciso Lopez and the First Clandestine U.S. War against Cuba* (Charlottesville: University Press of Virginia, 1996)

Chepesiuk, Ron, *The War on Drugs: An International Encyclopedia* (Santa Barbara, CA: ABC-CLIO, 1999)

Christian, William A., Jr., *Divided Island: Faction and Unity on Saint Pierre* (Cambridge, MA: Harvard University Press, 1969)

Clark, Norman H., *The Dry Years: Prohibition and Social Change in Washington* (Seattle: University of Washington Press, 1988)

Clinard, Marshall, *The Black Market: A Study of White Collar Crime* (New York: Rinehart, 1952)

Cloward, Richard and Lloyd Ohlin, *Delinquency and Opportunity: A Theory of Delinquent Gangs* (New York: The Free Press, 1960)

Cohen, Albert, *Delinquent Boys: Culture of the Gang* (Glencoe, IL: The Free Press, 1955)

Corbett, Scott with Captain Manuel Zora, *The Sea Fox: The Adventures of Cape Cod's Most Colorful Rumrunner* (New York: Thomas Y. Crowell, 1956)

Corey, Albert B., *Canadian-American Relations along the Detroit River* (Detroit, MI: Wayne State University Press, 1957)

Craton, Michael, *History of the Bahamas* (London: Collins, 1962)

Cullen, Jim, *The American Dream: A Short History of an Idea that Shaped a Nation* (New York: Oxford University Press, 2003)

Daddysman, James. W., *The Matamoros Trade: Confederate Commerce, Diplomacy and Intrigue* (Cranbury, NJ: University of Delaware Press, 1984)

Davis, Richard Harding, *Soldiers of Fortune*, ed. by Brady Harrison (Peterborough, Ontario, Canada: Broadview Press, 1897; repr. 2006)

Dickerson, Oliver M., *The Navigation Acts and the American Revolution* (Philadelphia: University of Pennsylvania Press, 1951)

Doherty, Thomas, *Pre-code Hollywood: Sex, Immorality, and Insurrection in American Cinema, 1930–1934* (New York: Columbia University Press, 1999)

Duffy, John, Samuel Hand, and Ralph Orth, *The Vermont Encyclopedia* (Burlington: University of Vermont Press, 2003)

Dyment, David, *Doing the Continental: A New Canadian-American Relationship* (Toronto: Dundurn, 2010)

Eltis, David, *Economic Growth and the Ending of the Transatlantic Slave Trade* (New York: Oxford University Press, 1987)

Engelmann, Larry, *Intemperance: The Lost War against Liquor* (New York: The Free Press, 1979)

Ensign, Eric S., *Intelligence in the Rum War at Sea, 1920–1933* (Washington, D.C.: Joint Military Intelligence College, 2001)

Evans, Stephen H., *The United States Coast Guard, 1790–1915: A Definitive History* (Annapolis, MD: U.S. Naval Institute, 1949)

Everest, Allan S., *Rum across the Border: The Prohibition Era in Northern New York* (Syracuse, NY: Syracuse University Press, 1978)

Fahey, Edmund, *Rum Road to Spokane* (Missoula: University of Montana Press, 1972)

Fedorowicz, J.K., *England's Baltic Trade in the Early Seventeenth Century: A Study in Anglo-Polish Commercial Diplomacy* (Cambridge: Cambridge University Press, 1980)

Fenwick, Charles G., *The Neutrality Laws of the United States* (Washington, D.C.: Carnegie Endowment for International Peace, 1913)

Fischer, David Hackett, *Liberty and Freedom: A Visual History of America's Founding Ideas* (New York: Oxford University Press, 2004)

Fitzgerald, F. Scott, *The Great Gatsby* (New York: Scribner, 1925; repr. 1995)

Footner, Geoffrey M., *Tidewater Triumph: The Development and Worldwide Success of the Chesapeake Bay Pilot Schooner* (Mystic, CT: Mystic Seaport Museum, 1998)

Francaviglia, Richard V., *From Sail to Steam: Four Centuries of Texas Maritime History, 1500–1900* (Austin: University of Texas, 1998)

Fraser, Steve and Gary Gerstle, *Ruling America: A History of Wealth and Power in America* (Cambridge, MA: Harvard University Press, 2005)

Friedrichs, David O., *Trusted Criminals: White Collar Crime in Contemporary Society*, 3rd edn (Belmont, CA: Thomson Wadsworth, 2007)

Fritz, Christian G., *Federal Justice in California: The Court of Ogden Hoffman, 1851–1891* (Lincoln: University of Nebraska Press, 1991)

Geis, Gilbert, *White-collar and Corporate Crime* (Upper Saddle River, NJ: Person Prentice Hall, 2007)

Gervais, H., *The Rumrunners: A Prohibition Scrapbook* (Scarborough, Ontario, Canada: Firefly, 1980)

Gillman, Peter with Paul Hamann, *The Duty Men: The Inside Story of the Customs* (London: BBC Books, 1987)

Goff, Richard D., *Confederate Supply* (Durham, NC: Duke University Press, 1969)

Goldstein, Jonathan, *Philadelphia and the China Trade, 1682–1846: Commercial, Cultural and Attitudinal Effects* (University Park: Pennsylvania State University, 1978)

Graham, Eric J., *Clydebuilt: The Blockade Runners, Cruisers and Armoured Rams of the American Civil War* (Edinburgh: Birlinn, 2006)

Grahn, Lance, *The Political Economy of Smuggling: Regional Informal Economics in Early Bourbon New Granada* (Boulder, CO: Westview Press, 1997)

Greene, Ruth, *Personality Ships of British Columbia* (West Vancouver, B.C., Canada: Marine Tapestry Publications, 1969)

Gregg, Robert D., *The Influence of Border Troubles on Relations between the United States and Mexico, 1876–1910* (Baltimore, MD: Johns Hopkins Press, 1937)

Gregory, Frances W., *Nathan Appleton: Merchant and Entrepreneur, 1779–1861* (Charlottesville: University Press of Virginia, 1975)

Grosse, Robert E., *Drugs and Money: Laundering Latin America's Cocaine Dollars* (Westport, CT: Praeger, 2001)

Haley, J. Evetts, *Jeff Milton: A Good Man with a Gun* (Norman: University of Oklahoma Press, 1948)

Hall, Linda B. and Don M. Coerver, *Revolution on the Border: The United States and Mexico, 1910–1920* (Albuquerque: University of New Mexico, 1988)

Hamilton, Douglas L., *Sobering Dilemma: A History of Prohibition in British Columbia* (Vancouver, B.C., Canada: Ronsdale Press, 2004)

Hannigan, Robert E., *The New World Power: American Foreign Policy, 1898–1917* (Philadelphia: University of Pennsylvania Press, 2002)

Haring, C.H., *The Spanish Empire in America* (New York: Harcourt, Brace and World, 1963)

Harrington, Virginia D., *The New York Merchant on the Eve of the Revolution* (Gloucester, MA: Peter Smith, 1964)

Haufman, Richard F., *The War Profiteers* (Indianapolis, IN: Bobbs-Merrill, 1970)

Heron, David, *Night Landing: A Short History of West Coast Smuggling* (Central Point, OR: Hellgate, 1998)

Hickey, Donald R., *The War of 1812: A Forgotten Conflict* (Urbana: University of Illinois Press, 1995)

Hindus, Michael Stephen, *Prison and Plantation: Crime, Justice, and Authority in Massachusetts and South Carolina, 1767–1878* (Chapel Hill: University of North Carolina Press, 1980)

Hinkle, Stacy C., *Wings Over the Border: The Army Air Service Armed Patrol of the United States-Mexico Border, 1919–1921* (El Paso: Texas Western Press, 1970)

Hobbes, Thomas, *Leviathan* (New York: Oxford University Press, 1996)

Holden, Henry M., *Aerial Drug Wars: The Story of U.S. Customs Aviation* (Niceville, FL: Wind Canyon Books, 2000)

Howard, Warren S., *American Slavers and the Federal Law, 1832–1862* (Berkeley: University of California Press, 1963)

Hunt, C. W., *Booze, Boats and Billions: Smuggling Liquid Gold!* (Toronto: McClelland and Stewart, 1988)

——*Whisky and Ice: The Saga of Ben Kerr, Canada's Most Daring Rumrunner* (Toronto: Dundurn, 1995)

Ingrisano, Michael N. Jr., *The First Officers of the United States Customs Service: Appointed by President George Washington in 1789* (Washington, D.C.: U.S. Customs Service, 1987)

——*A History of Enforcement in the United States Customs Service, 1789–1875* (Washington, D.C.: U.S. Customs Service, 1988)

Jaher, Frederic, *The Urban Establishment: Upper Strata in Boston, New York, Charleston, Chicago and Los Angeles* (Urbana: University of Illinois Press, 1982)

Johnson, Robert Erwin, *Guardians of the Sea: History of the United States Coast Guard, 1915 to the Present* (Annapolis, MD: Naval Institute Press, 1987)

Jonnes, Jill, *Hep-cats, Narcs, and Pipe Dreams: A History of America's Romance with Illegal Drugs* (New York: Scribner, 1996)

Karras, Alan L., *Smuggling: Contraband and Corruption in World History* (Lanham, MD: Rowman and Littlefield, 2010)

Katcher, Leo, *The Big Bankroll: The Life and Times of Arnold Rothstein* (New York: Harper and Brothers, 1958)

Kavieff, Paul R., *The Purple Gang: Organized Crime in Detroit, 1910–1945* (Ft. Lee, NJ: Barricade Books, 2000)

King, Irving, *George Washington's Coast Guard: Origins of the U.S. Revenue Cutter Service, 1789–1801* (Annapolis, MD: Naval Institute Press, 1978)

——*The Coast Guard Under Sail: The U.S. Revenue Cutter Service, 1789–1865* (Annapolis, MD: Naval Institute Press, 1989)

——*The Coast Guard Expands, 1865–1915: New Roles, New Frontiers* (Annapolis, MD: Naval Institute Press, 1996)

Lane, Roger, *Policing the City: Boston, 1822–1885* (Cambridge, MA: Harvard University Press, 1967)

Langley, Lester D., *America and the Americas: United States in the Western Hemisphere* (Athens: University of Georgia Press, 1983)

Lee, Erika, *At America's Gates: Chinese Immigration During the Exclusion Era, 1882–1943* (Chapel Hill: University of North Carolina Press, 2003)

Lender, Mark Edward and James Kirby Martin, *Drinking in America: A History* (New York: The Free Press, 1982)

Liddick, Donald R., *An Empirical, Theoretical, and Historical Overview of Organized Crime* (Lewiston, NY: Edwin Mellon Press, 1999)

Liss, Peggy K., *Atlantic Empires: The Network of Trade and Revolution, 1712–1826* (Baltimore, MD: Johns Hopkins, 1983)

Lloyd, Thomas, *The Trials of William S. Smith and Samuel G. Ogden, for Misdemeanours, Had in the Circuit Court of the United States for the New York District, in July 1806* (New York: Riley, 1807)

Lonn, Ella, *Salt as a Factor in the Confederacy* (Tuscaloosa: University of Alabama Press, 1965)

Marrus, Michael R., *Mr. Sam: The Life and Times of Samuel Bronfman* (Toronto: Viking, 1991)

Martinez, Oscar J., *Troublesome Border* (Tucson: University of Arizona Press, 1988)

Marx, Leo, *The Machine in the Garden: Technology and the Pastoral Ideal in America* (New York: Oxford University Press, 1964)

Mason, Philip P., *Rumrunning and the Roaring Twenties: Prohibition on the Michigan-Ontario Waterway* (Detroit, MI: Wayne State University, 1995)

May, Robert E., *Manifest Destiny's Underworld: Filibustering in Antebellum America* (Chapel Hill: University of North Carolina Press, 2002)

McGrath, Roger D., *Gunfighters, Highwaymen and Vigilantes: Violence on the Frontier* (Berkeley: University of California Press, 1984)

McIntosh, Dave, *The Collectors: A History of Canadian Customs and Excise* (Toronto: New Canada Publications, 1984)

McLean, Bethany and Peter Elkind, *The Smartest Guys in the Room: The Amazing Rise and Scandalous Fall of Enron* (New York: Penguin, 2004).

Meinig, D. W., *The Shaping of America: A Geographical Perspective on 500 Years of History, Volume 1, Atlantic America, 1492–1800* (New Haven, CT: Yale University Press, 1986)

Merton, Robert K., *Social Theory and Social Structure* (New York: The Free Press, 1968)

Messner, Steven F. and Richard Rosenfeld, *Crime and the American Dream*, 4th edn (Belmont, CA: Thomson Wadsworth, 2007)

Metz, Leon C., *Border: The U.S.-Mexico Line* (El Paso, TX: Mangan, 1989)

Meyer, Kathryn and Terry Parssinen, *Web of Smoke: Smugglers, Warlords, Spies, and the History of the International Drug Trade* (Lanham, MD: Rowman and Littlefield, 1998)

Middleton, Arthur Pierce, *Tobacco Coast: A Maritime History of Chesapeake Bay in the Colonial Era* (Baltimore, MD: Johns Hopkins University Press, 1984)

Miller, Wilbur R., *Cops and Bobbies: Police Authority in New York and London, 1830–1870* (Columbus: Ohio State University Press, 1973; repr. 1997)

Mills, Eric, *Chesapeake Bay in the Civil War* (Centreville, MD: Tidewater, 1996)

——*Chesapeake Rumrunners of the Roaring Twenties* (Centreville, MD: Tidewater, 2000)

Mintz, Steven and Randy Roberts, *Hollywood's America: United States History through Its Films* (St. James, NY: Brandywine Press, 1993)

Monkkonen, Eric H., *Police in Urban America, 1860–1920* (New York: Cambridge University Press, 1981)

Morgan, H. Wayne, *Drugs in America: A Social History, 1800–1980* (Syracuse, NY: Syracuse University Press, 1981)

Morison, Samuel E., *The Maritime History of Massachusetts, 1783–1860* (Boston, MA: Houghton Mifflin, 1921)

Munby, Jonathan, *Public Enemies, Public Heroes: Screening the Gangster from Little Caesar to Touch of Evil* (Chicago: University of Chicago Press, 1999)

Murchison, Kenneth M., *Federal Criminal Law Doctrines: The Forgotten Influence of National Prohibition* (Durham, NC: Duke University, 1994)

Myers, John Myers, *The Border Wardens* (Englewood Cliff, NJ: Prentice-Hall, 1971)

Nadelmann, Ethan A., *Cops across Borders: The Internationalization of U.S. Criminal Law Enforcement* (University Park: Pennsylvania State University Press, 1993)

The New Oxford Annotated Bible with the Apocrypha, RSV (New York: Oxford University Press, 1977)

North, Douglass C., *The Economic Growth of the United States, 1790–1860* (New York: W. W. Norton, 1966)

Okrent, Daniel, *Last Call: The Rise and Fall of Prohibition* (New York: Scribner, 2010)

Papenfuse, Edward C., *In Pursuit of Profit: The Annapolis Merchants in the Era of the American Revolution, 1763–1805* (Baltimore, MD: Johns Hopkins Press, 1975)

Parker, Marion and Robert Tyrrell, *Rumrunner: The Life and Times of Johnny Schnarr* (Victoria, B.C., Canada: Orca Book Publishers, 1988)

Prassel, Frank Richard, *The Western Peace Officer: A Legacy of Law and Order* (Norman: University of Oklahoma Press, 1972)

Prince, Carl E., *The Federalists and the Origins of the U.S. Civil Service* (New York: New York University Press, 1977)

——and Mollie Keller, *The U.S. Customs Service: A Bicentennial History* (Washington, D.C.: U.S. Customs Service, 1989)

Reich, Jerome R., *British Friends of the American Revolution* (Armonk, NY: M.E. Sharpe, 1998)

Reiss, Oscar, *Medicine in Colonial America* (Lanham, MA: University Press of America, 2000)

Richardson, James F., *The New York Police: Colonial Times to 1901* (New York: Oxford University Press, 1970)

Rink, Oliver, *Holland on the Hudson: An Economic and Social History of Dutch New York* (Ithaca, NY: Cornell University Press, 1986)

Roark, Garland, *The Coin of Contraband: The True Story of United States Customs Investigator Al Scharff* (Garden City, NY: Doubleday, 1964)

Robb, George, *White-collar Crime in Modern England: Financial Fraud and Business Morality, 1845–1929* (Cambridge: Cambridge University Press, 1992)

Robinson, Geoff and Dorothy Robinson, *It Came by the Boat Load* (Self-published, 1983)

Roger, N.A.M., *The Command of the Ocean: A Naval History of Britain, 1619–1815* (New York: W. W. Norton, 2004)

Rogozinski, Jan, *A Brief History of the Caribbean* (New York: Plume, 2000)

Rorabaugh, W. J., *Alcoholic Republic: An American Tradition* (New York: Oxford University Press, 1979)

Rosenblum, J. D., *Copper Crucible: How the Arizona Miner's Strike of 1983 Recast Labor-Management Relations in America*, 2nd edn (Ithaca, NY: Cornell University Press, 1988)

Rosoff, Stephen M., Henry N. Pontell, and Robert H. Tillman, *Looting America: Greed, Corruption, Villains, and Victims* (Upper Saddle River, NJ: Prentice Education, 2003)

Royner, Eduardo Saenz, *The Cuban Connection: Drug Trafficking, Smuggling, and Gambling in Cuba from the 1920s to the Revolution* (Chapel Hill: University of North Carolina Press, 2008)

Ruth, David E., *Inventing the Public Enemy: The Gangster in American Culture, 1918–1934* (Chicago: University of Chicago Press, 1996)

Salyer, Lucy E., *Laws Harsh as Tigers: Chinese Immigrants and the Shaping of Modern Immigration Law* (Chapel Hill: University of North Carolina Press, 1995)

Schlesinger, Arthur M., *The Colonial Merchants and the American Revolution* (New York: Columbia University, 1918)

Schmeckebier, Laurence F., *The Customs Service: Its History, Activities, and Organization* (Baltimore, MD: Johns Hopkins Press, 1924)

Schneider, Stephen, *Iced: The Story of Organized Crime in Canada* (Mississauga, Ontario, Canada: John Wiley and Sons, 2009)

Schreiner, Chas., III, Audrey Schreiner, Robert Berryman, and Hal F. Matheny, *A Pictorial History of the Texas Rangers* (Mountain Home, TX: Y-O Press, 1969)

Sellers, Charles, *The Market Revolution: Jacksonian America, 1815–1846* (New York: Oxford University Press, 1991)

Shackelford, George, *Jefferson's Adoptive Son: The Life of William Short, 1759–1848* (Lexington: University of Kentucky Press, 2006)

Shore, Henry N., *Smuggling Days and Smuggling Ways or, the Story of a Lost Art* (London: Cassell & Company, 1892)

Simpson, Jeffrey, *Star-Spangled Canadians: Canadians Living the American Dream* (Toronto: HarperCollins, 2000)

Sinclair, Upton, *The Jungle* (New York: Doubleday, Page, 1906)

Smith, Graham, *King's Cutters: The Revenue Service and the War against Smuggling* (London: Conway Maritime Press, 1983)

Smith, Joshua M., *Borderland Smuggling: Patriots, Loyalists, and Illicit Trade in the Northeast, 1783–1820* (Gainesville: University Press of Florida, 2006)

Spann, Edward K., *Gotham at War: New York City, 1860–1865* (Wilmington, DE: Scholarly Resources, 2002)

Spinelli, Lawrence, *Dry Diplomacy: The United States, Great Britain, and Prohibition* (Wilmington, DE: Scholarly Resources, 1989)

Spivak, Burton, *Jefferson's English Crisis: Commerce, Embargo, and the Republican Revolution* (Charlottesville: University of Virginia Press, 1979)

Strout, Neil R., *The Royal Navy in America, 1760–1775: A Study of Enforcement of British Colonial Policy in the Era of the American Revolution* (Annapolis, MD: Naval Institute Press, 1973)

Sutherland, Edwin H., *Principles of Criminality*, 4th edn (Chicago, IL: J.B. Lippincott, 1947)

——*White Collar Crime: The Uncut Version* (New Haven, CT: Yale University Press, 1983)

Tarbell, Ida M., *The History of the Standard Oil Company* (New York: McClure Phillips, 1904)

Taylor, Alan, *American Colonies: The Settling of North America*, ed. by Eric Foner, The Penguin History of the United States, I (New York: Penguin, 2001)

Thomas, Hugh, *The Slave Trade: The Story of the Atlantic Slave Trade, 1440–1870* (New York: Simon and Schuster, 1997)

Truxes, Thomas M., *Irish-American Trade: 1660–1783* (Cambridge: Cambridge University Press, 1988)

Tyler, John W., *Smugglers and Patriots: Boston Merchants and the Advent of the American Revolution* (Boston, MA: Northeastern University Press, 1986)

U.S. Customs Service, *A Biographical Directory of the U.S. Customs Service, 1771–1989* (Washington, D.C.:U.S. Customs Service, 1985)

——*Neutrality Confidential* (Washington, D.C.: U.S. Customs Service, 1988)

Utley, Robert M., *Lone Star Lawmen: The Second Century of the Texas Lawmen* (New York: Oxford University Press, 2007)

Vahimagi, Tise, *The Untouchables* (London: BFI Publishing, 1998)

Van de Water, Frederic F., *The Real McCoy* (Garden City, NY: Doubleday, Doran & Company, 1931)

——*Lake Champlain and Lake George* (Indianapolis, ID: Bobbs-Merrill, 1946)

Wakeman, Frederic E., *Policing Shanghai, 1927–1937* (Berkeley: University of California, 1995)

Walker, Clifford James, *One Eye Closed, the Other Red: The California Bootlegging Years* (Barstow, CA: Back Door, 1999)

Walker, Samuel, *Popular Justice: A History of American Criminal Justice*, 2nd edn (New York: Oxford University Press, 1998)

Walker, William O., *Drug Control in the Americas*, revised edn (Albuquerque: University of New Mexico Press, 1989)

Waters, Harold, *Smugglers of Spirits: Prohibition and the Coast Guard Patrol* (New York: Hastings House, 1971)

Weber, Max, *The Protestant Ethic and the Spirit of Capitalism*, trans. by Talcott Parsons (New York: Charles Scribner's Sons, 1976)

Williams III, Frank P. and Marilyn D. McShane, *Criminology Theory*, 5th edn (Upper Saddle River, NJ: Prentice Hall, 2010)

Williams, Neville, *Contraband Cargoes: Seven Centuries of Smuggling* (North Haven, CT: Shoe String Press, 1961)

Williamson, Chilton, *Vermont in Quandary* (Montpelier: Vermont Historical Society, 1949)

Willoughby, Malcolm F., *Rum War at Sea* (Washington, D.C.: Government Printing Office, 1964)

Wilson, Gary A., *Honky-Tonk Town: Havre, Montana's Lawless Era* (Guilford, CT: Globe Pequot, 2006)

Wiltse, Charles M., *The New Nation: 1800–1845* (New York: Hill and Wang, 1961)

Wise, Stephen. R., *Lifeline of the Confederacy: Blockade Running during the Civil War* (Columbia: University of South Carolina Press, 1988)

Woodiwiss, Michael, *Organized Crime and American Power: A History* (Toronto: University of Toronto Press, 2001)

Wright, Esmond, *The American Dream: From Reconstruction to Reagan* (Cambridge: Blackwell Publishing, 1996)

Young, Elliott, *Catarino Garza's Revolution on the Texas-Mexico Border* (Durham, NC: Duke University, 2004)

Unpublished Dissertations

Ayer, Robert Copeland, 'Shifty Seafarers, Shifting Winds: Government Policies toward Maritime Smuggling in North America from Colonization to the War of 1812' (unpublished doctoral dissertation, Tufts University, 1993)

Blume, Kenneth J., 'The Mid-Atlantic Arena: The United States, the Confederacy, and the British West Indies, 1861–1865' (unpublished doctoral dissertation, State University of New York at Binghamton, 1984)

Dye, Roy Thomas, 'A Social History of Drug Smuggling in Florida' (unpublished doctoral dissertation, Florida State University, 1998)

Gordinier, Glenn Stine, 'Versatility in Crisis: The Merchants of the New London Customs District Respond to the Embargo of 1807–1809' (unpublished doctoral dissertation, University of Connecticut, 2001)

Margolin, Samuel G., 'Lawlessness on the Maritime Frontier of the Greater Chesapeake, 1650–1750' (unpublished doctoral dissertation, College of William and Mary, 1992)

Rubin, Israel Ira, 'New York State and the Long Embargo' (unpublished doctoral dissertation, New York University, 1961)

Smith, Joshua M., 'The Rogues of 'Quoddy: Smuggling in the Maine-New Brunswick Borderlands, 1783–1820' (unpublished doctoral dissertation, University of Maine, 2003)

Films

The Godfather, dir. by Francis Ford Coppola (Alfran Productions, Paramount Pictures, 1972)

The Godfather, Part II, dir. by Francis Ford Coppola (Paramount Pictures, The Coppola Company, 1974)

The Godfather, Part III, dir. by Francis Ford Coppola (Paramount Pictures, Zoetrope Studio, 1990)

Hell's Angels, dir. by Howard Hughes (The Caddo Company, 1930)
Little Caesar, dir. by Mervyn LeRoy (First National Pictures, 1931)
The Public Enemy, dir. by William A. Wellman (Warner Bros. Pictures, 1931)
Scarface, dir. by Howard Hawks and Richard Rosson (The Caddo Company, 1932)

Legal Cases

Dunbar v. United States, 156 U.S. 185, 15 S.Ct. 325 (1895)
Olmstead v. United States, 277 U.S. 457 (1928)
Ten Cases of Opium, Deady 62, 23 F.Cas. 840 (1864)
Three Thousand Eight Hundred and Eighty Boxes of Opium v. United States, 9 Sawy. 259, 23 F. 367 (1883)
United States v. Dunbar, 60 F. 75 (1894)
United States v. the Haytian Republic, 154 U.S. 118, 14 S.Ct. 992 (1894)
United States v. Phelps-Dodge Mercantile Co. et al., 209 F 910 (1913)
United States v. Steinfeld & Co., et al. 209 Fed. 904 (1913)
United States v. Wilson et al., 60 F. 890 (1894)
United States v. Wilson et al., 69 F. 584 (1895)

Online Databases

National Law Enforcement Officers Memorial Fund, www.nleomf.com/
Officer Down Memorial Page, www.odmp.org/

Index